Annette Salaman

Footsteps in the way of life

A collection of appropriate texts for guidance and comfort from Holy Scripture

Annette Salaman

Footsteps in the way of life
A collection of appropriate texts for guidance and comfort from Holy Scripture

ISBN/EAN: 9783337282875

Printed in Europe, USA, Canada, Australia, Japan

Cover: Foto ©Lupo / pixelio.de

More available books at **www.hansebooks.com**

FOOTSTEPS

IN THE

WAY OF LIFE.

A COLLECTION OF APPROPRIATE TEXTS

FOR GUIDANCE AND COMFORT

FROM

HOLY SCRIPTURE.

BY

ANNETTE A. SALAMAN.

"Thou wilt shew me the path of life: in Thy presence is fulness of joy; at Thy right hand there are pleasures for evermore."—*Psalm* xvi. 2.

London:
TRÜBNER & CO., 57 & 59, LUDGATE HILL.
1873.

TO

THE BARONESS LIONEL DE ROTHSCHILD

THIS COLLECTION OF TEXTS

(BY PERMISSION)

IS RESPECTFULLY INSCRIBED.

PREFACE.

In my early youth, during years of ill-health, when long hours threw me upon religious study for support and guidance, I found deep interest in searching out, comparing and classifying under their respective headings, the following collection of Scripture Texts.

Years have passed away, and I now venture to offer this small volume to the Public, with the earnest desire that the Holy Verses selected may help others, as they have helped me, to find comfort and consolation under every circumstance of earthly trial.

A. A. S.

ERRATA.

Verse on Title Page—*Ps.* xvi.—instead of verse 2 read 11.

Page 175—*Ps.* xxxiv. 6.—after the word him, read *and saved him* out of all his troubles.

CONTENTS.

---o---

		PAGE.
1.	THE WORD OF GOD TO BE OUR ONLY GUIDE. .	1
2.	THE GREATNESS, UNITY, AND GLORY OF GOD .	17
3.	THE OMNISCIENCE AND OMNIPRESENCE OF GOD.	28
4.	GOD OUR FATHER AND PROTECTOR	42
5.	GOD'S GOODNESS, MERCY, AND FAITHFULNESS .	47
6.	STRIVE TO BE PERFECT AND HOLY	58
7.	GOD SEETH THE HEART: HIS POWER TOUCHETH IT.	65
8.	WATCHFULNESS: KEEP THE HEART PURE . . .	72
9.	LOVE TO GOD SHOULD RULE OUR ACTIONS . .	77
10.	THE FEAR OF GOD WILL RESTRAIN US FROM SINNING.	80
11.	ADMIRE, AND MEDITATE ON THE WONDERFUL WORKS OF THE CREATOR	91
12.	WITH THE ALMIGHTY NOTHING IS IMPOSSIBLE . .	100
13.	GOD'S OVERRULING PROVIDENCE AND INTERPOSITION.	106
14.	REJOICE IN THE LORD: SERVE HIM CHEERFULLY.	123
15.	NONE BUT A WILLING SERVICE IS PLEASING TO GOD.	136
16.	HEART WORSHIP AND GOOD ACTS, MORE ACCEPTABLE TO GOD THAN FORMS	139

Contents.

	PAGE.
17. TRIALS ARE FOR OUR GOOD, AND TO PROVE OUR FAITH IN GOD	146
18. THE SIN OF MURMURING: THE VIRTUE OF SUBMISSION	153
19. PRAYER IN TROUBLE	159
20. COMFORT AND SUPPORT IN AFFLICTION	173
21. FAITH IN GOD: BELIEVE AND TRUST IN HIM.	181
22. GOD OUR BEST FRIEND: SEEK COUNSEL AND GUIDANCE OF HIM.	196
23. THE FAVOUR OF GOD A SHIELD AND A BLESSING.	205
24. GRATITUDE TO GOD: PRAISE AND THANKSGIVING.	213
25. THE WICKEDNESS OF INGRATITUDE TO GOD	223
26. THE JUSTICE AND JUDGMENT OF GOD	227
27. CONSCIENCE. SELF-EXAMINATION.	234
28. REPENTANCE: GOD IS WILLING TO PARDON	237
29. PRAYER: GOD HEARETH AND ANSWERETH.	248
30. IT IS GOOD TO BLESS AND PRAY FOR EACH OTHER	259
31. SPIRITUAL LONGINGS. JOYS FOR THE GODLY-MINDED.	263
32. RELIGIOUS ZEAL	272
33. GOD GIVES US STRENGTH	278
34. GOD REQUIRES OF US JUSTICE AND JUDGMENT.	283
35. BE TRUTHFUL AND UPRIGHT, HONEST AND FAITHFUL.	290

		PAGE.
36.	THE SIN OF DECEIT AND HYPOCRISY	295
37.	THE DUTY OF REPROVING SIN	298
38.	GOD PROTECTS THE HELPLESS AND POOR, THE WIDOW AND FATHERLESS.	301
39.	BE CONSIDERATE TO THE POOR, THE SUFFERING AND HELPLESS	307
40.	SYMPATHISE AND BE KIND: RETURN GOOD FOR EVIL.	312
41.	GOD'S CARE FOR ANIMALS: BE KIND TO THEM	318
42.	THE BEAUTY OF HUMILITY AND MEEKNESS.	322
43.	THE SIN OF PRIDE AND HAUGHTINESS	327
44.	THE FOLLY OF CONCEIT	334
45.	WE MUST CONTROL OUR ANGRY PASSIONS	336
46.	GUARD THE TONGUE: AVOID STRIFE AND QUARRELS	340
47.	BE NOT LED AWAY BY THE UNGODLY	346
48.	WORK AND INDUSTRY ENJOINED. IDLENESS AND SLOTH A SHAME	351
49.	A CONTENTED MIND	356
50.	THE VALUE OF A GOOD NAME	359
51.	THE INFLUENCE OF GOOD PERSONS	362
52.	RESPECT OLD AGE.	364
53.	HONOUR AND RESPECT DUE TO PARENTS	366

Contents.

	PAGE.
54. THE SACRED TIE OF MARRIAGE.	371
55. A GOOD MAN.	374
56. A GOOD WOMAN.	378
57. TRAIN UP CHILDREN IN THE WAY OF GOD	380
58. TRUE FRIENDSHIP AND CONSTANCY	386
59. THE RELIGIOUS USE OF MUSIC, AND ITS INFLUENCE.	391
60. THE FRAILTY OF LIFE. PREPARATION FOR DEATH.	398
61. COMFORT AND SUPPORT IN THE HOUR OF DEATH	402
62. LIFE AFTER DEATH. FUTURE HAPPINESS	405
63. CONCLUSION. GOD WILL FULFIL HIS PROMISES.	412

THE WORD OF GOD TO BE OUR ONLY GUIDE.

———o———

...ABRAHAM obeyed my voice, and kept my charge, my commandments, my statutes, and my laws.—*Gen.* xxvi. 5.

And it shall be for a sign unto thee upon thine hand, and for a memorial between thine eyes, that the LORD's law may be in thy mouth.—*Ex.* xiii. 9.

And the Lord said unto Moses, Write this for a memorial in a book, and rehearse it in the ears of Joshua.—*Ex.* xvii. 14.

And thou shalt teach them ordinances and laws, and shalt shew them the way wherein they must walk, and the work that they must do.—*Ex.* xviii. 20.

If thou shalt do this thing, and God command thee so, then thou shalt be able to endure, and all this people shall also go to their place in peace.—23.

Now therefore, if ye will obey my voice indeed, and keep my covenant, then ye shall be a peculiar treasure unto me above all people: for all the earth is mine.—*Ex.* xix. 5.

And all the people answered together, and said, All that the Lord hath spoken we will do. And Moses returned the words of the people unto the Lord.—8.

And he took the book of the covenant, and read in the audience of the people: and they said, All that the Lord hath said will we do, and be obedient.—*Ex.* xxiv. 7.

And the Lord said unto Moses, Come up to me into the mount, and be there: and I will give thee tables of stone, and a law, and commandments which I have written; that thou mayest teach them.—12.

Ye shall do my judgments, and keep mine ordinances, to walk therein: I am the Lord your God.—*Lev.* xviii. 4.

Ye shall therefore keep my statutes, and my judgments: which if a man do, he shall live in them: I am the Lord.—5.

And Balaam said unto Balak, Lo, I am come unto thee: have I now any power at all to say anything? the word that God putteth in my mouth, that shall I speak.—*Num.* xxii. 38.

But Balaam answered and said unto Balak, Told not I thee, saying, all that the Lord speaketh, that I must do?—*Num.* xxiii. 26.

If Balak would give me his house full of silver and gold, I cannot go beyond the commandment of the Lord, to do either good or bad of mine own mind; but what the Lord saith, that will I speak?—*Num.* xxiv. 13.

Now therefore hearken, O Israel, unto the statutes and unto the judgments, which I teach you, for to do them, that ye may live, and go in and possess the land which the Lord God of your fathers giveth you.—*Deut.* iv. 1.

Ye shall not add unto the word which I command you, neither shall ye diminish ought from it, that ye may keep the commandments of the Lord your God which I command you.—2.

Behold, I have taught you statutes and judgments, even as the Lord my God commanded me, that ye should do so in the land whither ye go to possess it.—5.

Keep therefore and do them; for this is your wisdom and your understanding in the sight of the nations, which shall hear all these statutes, and say, Surely this great nation is a wise and understanding people.—6.

And what nation is there so great, that hath statutes and judgments so righteous as all this law, which I set before you this day?—8.

Thou shalt keep therefore his statutes, and his commandments, which I command thee this day, that it may go well with thee, and with thy children after thee.—40.

Go thou near, and hear all that the Lord our God shall say: and speak thou unto us all that the Lord our God shall speak unto thee; and we will hear it, and do it.—*Deut.* v. 27.

O that there were such an heart in them, that they would fear me, and keep all my commandments always, that it might be well with them, and with their children for ever!—29.

Ye shall observe to do therefore as the Lord your God hath commanded you: ye shall not turn aside to the right hand or to the left.—32.

Ye shall walk in all the ways which the Lord your God hath commanded you, that ye may live, and that it may be well with you.—33.

And these words, which I command thee this day, shall be in thine heart:—*Deut.* vi. 6.

And thou shalt teach them diligently unto thy children, and shalt talk of them when thou sittest in thine house, and when thou walkest by the way, and when thou liest down, and when thou risest up.—7.

Ye shall diligently keep the commandments of the Lord your God, and his testimonies, and his statutes, which he hath commanded thee.—17.

And it shall be our righteousness, if we observe to do all these commandments before the Lord our God, as he hath commanded us.—25.

And now, Israel, what doth the Lord thy God require of thee, but to fear the Lord thy God, to walk in all his ways.—*Deut.* x. 12.

To keep the commandments of the Lord, and his statutes, which I command thee this day for thy good?—13.

These are the statutes and judgments, which ye shall observe to do in the land, which the Lord God of thy fathers giveth thee to possess it, all the days that ye live upon the earth.—*Deut.* xii. 1.

What thing soever I command you, observe to do it: thou shalt not add thereto, nor diminish from it.—32.

Ye shall walk after the Lord your God, and fear him, and keep his commandments, and obey his voice, and ye shall serve him, and cleave unto him.—*Deut.* xiii. 4.

This day the Lord thy God hath commanded thee to do these statutes and judgments: thou shalt therefore keep and do them with all thine heart, and with all thy soul.—*Deut.* xxvi. 16.

Thou hast avouched the Lord this day to be thy God, and to walk in his ways, and keep his statutes, and his commandments, and his judgments, and to hearken unto his voice:—17.

...Thou shalt not go aside from any of the words which I command thee this day, to the right hand, or to the left, to go after other gods to serve them.—*Deut.* xxviii. 14.

The secret things belong unto the Lord our God: but those things which are revealed belong unto us and to our children for ever, that we may do all the words of this law.—*Deut.* xxix. 29.

For this commandment which I command thee this day, it is not hidden from thee, neither is it far off. —*Deut.* xxx. 11.

It is not in heaven, that thou shouldst say, Who shall go up for us to heaven, and bring it unto us, that we may hear it, and do it?—12.

Neither is it beyond the sea, that thou shouldst say, Who shall go over the sea for us, and bring it unto us, that we may hear it, and do it? But the word is very nigh unto thee, in thy mouth, and in thy heart, that thou mayest do it.—14.

See, I have set before thee this day life and good, and death and evil;—15.

In that I command thee this day to love the Lord thy God, to walk in his ways, and to keep his commandments and his statutes and his judgments, that that thou mayest live and multiply.—16.

Give ear, O ye heavens, and I will speak: and hear, O earth, the words of my mouth.—*Deut.* xxxii. 1.

My doctrine shall drop as the rain, my speech shall distil as the dew, as the small rain upon the tender herb, and as the showers upon the grass.—2.

Only be thou strong and very courageous, that thou mayest observe to do according to all the law, which Moses my servant commanded thee: turn not from it to the right hand or to the left, that thou mayest prosper whithersoever thou goest —*Josh.* i. 7.

This book of the law shall not depart out of thy mouth; but thou shalt meditate therein day and night, that thou mayest observe to do according to all that is written therein: for then thou shalt make thy way prosperous, and then thou shalt have good success.—8.

Remember the word which Moses the servant of the Lord commanded you, saying, The Lord your God hath given you rest, and hath given you this land.—13.

But take diligent heed to do the commandment and the law, which Moses the servant of the Lord charged you, to love the Lord your God, and to walk in all his ways, and to keep his commandments, and to cleave unto him, and to serve him with all your heart and with all your soul.—*Josh.* xxii. 5.

And the word of the Lord was precious in those days.—1 *Sam.* iii. 1.

Samuel said to Saul,...Stand thou still awhile, that I may shew thee the word of God.—1 *Sam.* ix. 27.

And Samuel said to Saul, Thou hast done foolishly: thou hast not kept the commandment of the Lord thy God, which he commanded thee: for now would the Lord have established thy kingdom upon Israel for ever.—1 *Sam.* xiii. 13.

...Blessed be thou of the Lord: I have performed the commandment of the Lord.—1 *Sam.* xv. 13.

And Saul said unto Samuel, Yea, I have obeyed the voice of the Lord, and have gone the way which the Lord sent me.—20.

And Saul said unto Samuel, I have sinned: for I have transgressed the commandment of the Lord, and thy words: because I feared the people, and obeyed their voice.—24.

And David did so, as the Lord had commanded him.—2 *Sam.* v. 25.

And Nathan said to David...Wherefore hast thou despised the commandment of the Lord, to do evil in his sight?—2 *Sam.* xii. 9.

I have kept the ways of the Lord.—2 *Sam.* xxii. 22.

For all his judgments were before me: and as for his statutes, I did not depart from them.—23.

...And he (David) charged Solomon his son, saying,—1 *Kings* ii. 1.

...Keep the charge of the Lord thy God, to walk in his ways, to keep his statutes, and his commandments, and his judgments, and his testimonies, as it is written in the law of Moses, that thou mayest prosper in all that thou doest, and whithersoever thou turnest thyself:—3.

That the Lord may continue his word which he spake concerning me.—4.

And the king (Josiah) stood by a pillar, and made a covenant before the Lord, to walk after the Lord, and to keep his commandments and his testimonies and his statutes with all their heart and all their soul, to perform the words of this covenant that were written in this book. And all the people stood to the covenant.—2 *Kin.* xxiii. 3.

And the king stood in his place, and made a covenant before the Lord, to walk after the Lord, and to keep his commandments, and his testimonies, and his statutes, with all his heart, and with all his soul, to perform the words of the covenant which are written in this book.—2 *Ch.* xxxiv. 31.

For Ezra had prepared his heart to seek the law of the Lord, and to do it, and to teach in Israel statutes and judgments.—*Ezr.* vii. 10.

And Ezra the priest brought the law before the congregation both of men and women, and all that could hear with understanding.—*Neh.* viii. 2.

And he read therein…and the ears of all the people were attentive unto the book of the law.—3.

And Ezra opened the book in the sight of all the people; and when he opened it, all the people stood up.—5.

And Ezra blessed the Lord, the great God. And all the people answered, Amen, Amen, with lifting up their hands: and they bowed their heads, and worshipped the Lord with their faces to the ground.—6.

And they stood up in their place, and read in the book of the law of the Lord their God one fourth part of the day; and another fourth part they confessed, and worshipped the Lord their God.—*Neh.* ix. 3.

My foot hath held his steps, his way have I kept, and not declined.—*Job.* xxiii. 11.

Neither have I gone back from the commandment of his lips; I have esteemed the words of his mouth more than my necessary food.—12.

Blessed is the man that walketh not in the counsel of the ungodly,—*Ps.* i. 1.

But his delight is in the law of the Lord; and in his law doth he meditate day and night.—2.

The words of the Lord are pure words: as silver tried in a furnace of earth, purified seven times.—*Ps.* xii. 6.

The law of the Lord is perfect, converting the soul: the testimony of the Lord is sure, making wise the simple.—*Ps.* xix. 7.

The statutes of the Lord are right, rejoicing the heart: the commandment of the Lord is pure, enlightening the eyes.—8.

...The judgments of the Lord are true and righteous altogether.—9.

More to be desired are they than gold, yea, than much fine gold: sweeter also than honey and the honeycomb.—10.

Morever by them is thy servant warned: and in keeping of them there is great reward.—11.

The Lord gave the word: great was the company of those that published it.—*Ps.* lxviii. 11.

Give ear, O my people, to my law: incline your ears to the words of my mouth.—*Ps.* lxxviii. 1.

For he established a testimony in Jacob, and appointed a law in Israel, which he commanded our fathers, that they should make them known to their children.—5.

...A good understanding have all they that do his commandments.—*Ps.* cxi. 10.

Blessed are the undefiled in the way, who walk in the way of the Lord.—*Ps.* cxix. 1.

Blessed are they that keep his testimonies.—2.

Thou hast commanded us to keep thy precepts diligently.—4.

O that my ways were directed to keep thy statutes!—5.

Then shall I not be ashamed, when I have respect unto all thy commandments.—6.

I will keep thy statutes.—8.

Wherewithal shall a young man cleanse his ways? by taking heed thereto according to thy word.—9.

...O let me not wander from thy commandments.—10.

Thy word have I hid in mine heart, that I might not sin against thee.—11.

Blessed art thou, O Lord, teach me thy statutes.—12.

I have rejoiced in the way of thy testimonies, as much as in all riches.—14.

I will delight myself in thy statutes: I will not forget thy word.—16.

Open thou mine eyes, that I may behold wondrous things out of thy law.—18.

Thy testimonies are my delight, and my counsellors.—24.

...Quicken thou me according to thy word.—25.

Make me to understand the way of thy precepts.—27.

Teach me, O Lord, the way of thy statutes; and I shall keep it unto the end.—33.

Make me to go in the path of thy commandments; for therein do I delight.—*Ps*. cxix. 35.

...I trust in thy word.—42.

So shall I keep thy law continually for ever and ever.—44.

And I will walk at liberty: for I seek thy precepts.—45.

And I will delight myself in thy commandments, which I have loved.—47.

Remember the word unto thy servant, upon which thou hast caused me to hope.—49.

Thy statutes have been my songs in the house of my pilgrimage.—54.

I have remembered thy name, O Lord, in the night, and have kept thy law.—55.

I made haste, and delayed not to keep thy commandments.—60.

...Thy law is my delight.—77.

All thy commandments are faithful.—86.

I will never forget thy precepts: for with them hast thou quickened me.—93.

I have seen an end of all perfection: but thy commandment is exceeding broad —96.

O how I love thy law! it is my meditation all the day.—97.

Thou through thy commandments hast made me wiser than mine enemies.—98.

I understand more than the ancients, because I keep thy precepts.—100.

How sweet are thy words unto my taste! yea, sweeter than honey to my mouth!—*Ps.* cxix. 103.

Thy word is a lamp unto my feet, and a light unto my path.—105.

I have sworn and I will perform it, that I will keep thy righteous judgments.—106.

Thy testimonies have I taken as an heritage for ever: for they are the rejoicing of my heart.—111.

I hate vain thoughts: but thy law do I love.—113.

Uphold me according to thy word, that I may live.—116.

Therefore I love thy commandments above gold; yea, above fine gold.—127.

Therefore I esteem all thy precepts concerning all things to be right.—128.

Thy testimonies are wonderful: therefore doth my soul keep them.—129.

The entrance of thy words giveth light; it giveth understanding unto the simple.—130.

Thy testimonies that thou hast commanded are righteous and very faithful.—138.

Thy word is very pure: therefore thy servant loveth it.—140.

Order my steps in thy word.—133.

...Thy law is the truth.—142.

I rejoice at thy word, as one that findeth great spoil.—162.

Great peace have they which love thy law: and nothing shall offend them.—165.

Lord, I have hoped for thy salvation, and done thy commandments.—*Ps.* cxix. 166.

My soul hath kept thy testimonies: and I love them exceedingly.—167.

My tongue shall speak of thy word: for all thy commandments are righteous.—172.

Let thine hand help me; for I have chosen thy precepts.—173.

He sheweth his word unto Jacob, his statutes and his judgments unto Israel.—*Ps.*cxlvii. 19.

My son forget not my law; but let thine heart keep my commandments.—*Prov.* iii. 1.

For the commandment is a lamp; and the law is light.—*Prov.* vi. 23.

Keep my commandments, and live; and my law as the apple of thine eye.—*Prov.* vii. 2.

He that keepeth the commandment keepeth his own soul.—*Prov.* xix. 16.

Whoso keepeth the law is a wise son.—*Prov.*xxviii.7

...He that keepeth the law, happy is he.—*Prov.* xxix. 18.

Every word of God is pure :...*Prov.* xxx. 5.

Add thou not unto his words.—6.

Whoso keepeth the commandment shall feel no evil thing.—*Eccl.* viii. 5.

Let us hear the conclusion of the whole matter: Fear God, and keep his commandments: for this is the whole duty of man.—*Eccl.* xii. 13.

And many people shall go and say, Come ye, and let us go up to the mountain of the Lord...and he will teach us of his ways, and we will walk in his paths: for out of Zion shall go forth the law, and the word of the Lord from Jerusalem.—*Isa.* ii, 3.

Wherefore hear the word of the Lord, ye scornful men, that rule this people which is in Jerusalem. —*Isa.* xxviii. 14.

Now go, write it before them in a table, and note it in a book, that it may be for a time to come for ever and ever.—*Isa.* xxx. 8.

Seek ye out of the book of the Lord, and read. —*Isa.* xxxiv. 16.

The grass withereth, the flower fadeth: but the word of our God shall stand for ever.—*Isa.* xl. 8.

O that thou hadst hearkened to my commandments! then had thy peace been as a river, and thy righteousness as the waves of the sea.—*Isa.* xlviii. 18.

Hearken unto me, my people; and give ear unto me,...and I will make my judgment to rest for a light of the people.—*Isa.* li. 4.

Thus speaketh the Lord God of Israel, saying, Write thee all the words that I have spoken unto thee in a book.—*Jer.* xxx. 2.

Therefore, go thou, and read in the roll, which thou hast written from my mouth, the words of the Lord in the ears of the people in the Lord's house upon the fasting day.—*Jer.* xxxvi. 6.

...And I will take the stony heart out of their flesh, and will give them a heart of flesh.—*Eze.* xi. 19.

That they may walk in my statutes, and keep mine ordinances, and do them; and they shall be my people, and I will be their God.—20.

He that...—*Eze.* xviii. 8.

Hath walked in my statutes, and hath kept my judgments, to deal truly; he is just, he shall surely live, saith the Lord God.—9.

And I gave them my statutes, and shewed them my judgments, which if a man do, he shall even live in them.—*Eze.* xx. 11.

I am the Lord your God ; walk in my statutes, and keep my judgments, and do them.—19.

Remember ye the law of Moses my servant, which I commanded unto him in Horeb for all Israel, with the statutes and judgments.—*Mal.* iv. 4.

THE GREATNESS, UNITY, AND GLORY OF GOD.

...There is none like me in all the earth—*Ex.* ix 14.

The Lord shall reign for ever and ever.—*Ex.* xv. 18.

And mount Sinai was altogether on a smoke, because the Lord descended upon it in fire: and the smoke thereof ascended as the smoke of a furnace, and the whole mount quaked greatly.—*Ex.* xix. 18.

Thou shalt have no other gods before me.—*Ex.* xx. 3.

And the sight of the glory of the Lord was like devouring fire on the top of the mount in the eyes of the children of Israel.—xxiv. 17.

...Thou canst not see my face: for there shall no man see me, and live.—*Ex.* xxxiii. 20.

And the Lord said, Behold, there is a place by me, and thou shalt stand upon a rock:—21.

And it shall come to pass, while my glory passeth by, that I will put thee in a cleft of the rock, and will cover thee with my hand while I pass by.—22.

And the Lord descended in the cloud, and stood with him there, and proclaimed the name of the Lord.—*Ex.* xxxiv. 5.

The Lord he is God, in heaven above, and upon the earth beneath: there is none else.—*Deut.* iv. 39.

Hear, O Israel: the Lord our God is one Lord.—*Deut.* vi. 4.

For the Lord your God is God of gods, and Lord of lords, a great God...*Deut.* x. 17.

The Lord alone did lead him, and there was no strange God with him.—*Deut.* xxxii. 12.

See now that I, even I, am he, and there is no god with me: I kill, and I make alive; I wound, and I heal: neither is there any that can deliver out of my hand.—39.

...He shined forth from mount Paran, and he came with ten thousands of saints....*Deut.* xxxiii. 2.

The eternal God is thy refuge...27.

Lord, when thou wentest out of Seir, when thou marchedst out of the field of Edom, the earth trembled, and the heavens dropped, the clouds also dropped water.—*Jud.* v. 4.

The mountains melted from before the Lord, even that Sinai from before the Lord God of Israel.—5.

There is none holy as the Lord: for there is none beside thee: neither is there any rock like our God. 1 *Sam.* ii. 2.

...Prepare your hearts unto the Lord, and serve him only....1 *Sam.* vii. 3.

...Thou art great, O Lord God: for there is none like thee, neither is there any God beside thee.... 2 *Sam*. vii. 22.

For who is God, save the Lord? and who is a rock, save our God?—2 *Sam*. xxii. 32.

...There is no God like thee, in heaven above, or on earth beneath....1 *Kings* viii. 23.

But will God indeed dwell on the earth? behold, the heaven and heaven of heavens cannot contain thee; how much less this house that I have builded?—27.

That all the people of the earth may know that the Lord is God, and that there is none else.—60.

...Him shall ye worship, and to him shall ye do sacrifice.—2 *Kin*. xvii. 36.

...Thou art the God, even thou alone, of all the kingdoms of the earth; thou hast made heaven and earth.—2 *Kin*. xix. 15.

Give unto the Lord, ye kindreds of the people, give unto the Lord glory and strength.—1 *Chron*. xvi. 28.

Give unto the Lord the glory due unto his name...29.

...The Lord God of Israel, (he is the God)...*Ezra* i. 3.

...Stand up and bless the Lord your God for ever and ever: and blessed be thy glorious name, which is exalted above all blessing and praise.—*Neh*. ix. 5.

Thou, even thou, art Lord alone,...and the host of heaven worshippeth thee.—6.

He is not a man, as I am, that I should answer

him, and we should come together in judgment.—*Job* ix. 32.

Is not God in the height of heaven? and behold the height of the stars, how high they are!—*Job* xxii. 12.

Is there any number of his armies? and upon whom doth not his light arise?—*Job* xxv. 3.

Look unto the heavens, and see; and behold the clouds which are higher than thou.—*Job* xxxv. 5.

Behold, God is great, and we know him not... *Job* xxxvi. 26.

...With God is terrible majesty.—*Job* xxxvii. 22.

Touching the Almighty, we cannot find him out...23.

O Lord our Lord, how excellent is thy name in all the earth! who hast set thy glory above the heavens.—*Ps.* viii. 1.

The Lord is in his holy temple, the Lord's throne is in heaven....*Ps.* xi. 4.

The heavens declare the glory of God; and the firmament sheweth his handiwork.—*Ps.* xix. 1.

The earth is the Lord's, and the fulness thereof; the world, and they that dwell therein.—*Ps.* xxiv. 1.

Lift up your heads, O ye gates; even lift them up, ye everlasting doors; and the King of Glory shall come in.—9.

Who is this King of Glory? The Lord of hosts, he is the King of Glory.—10.

Give unto the Lord the glory due unto his name; worship the Lord in the beauty of holiness.—*Ps.* xxix. 2.

Be still, and know that I am God :...I will be exalted in the earth.—*Ps.* xlvi. 10.

The mighty God, even the Lord, hath spoken, and called the earth from the rising of the sun unto the going down thereof.—*Ps.* l. 1.

Out of Zion, the perfection of beauty, God hath shined.—2.

Our God shall come, and shall not keep silence: a fire shall devour before him, and it shall be very tempestuous round about him.—3.

Be thou exalted, O God, above the heavens: let thy glory be above all the earth.—*Ps.* lvii. 11.

Ascribe ye strength unto God: his excellency is over Israel, and his strength is in the clouds.—*Ps.* lxviii. 34.

...The God of Israel is he that giveth strength and power unto his people. Blessed be God.—35.

Thy righteousness also, O God, is very high, who hast done great things: O God, who is like unto thee!—*Ps.* lxxi. 19.

Blessed be the Lord God, the God of Israel, who only doeth wondrous things.—*Ps.* lxxii. 18.

And blessed be his glorious name for ever: and let the whole earth be filled with his glory; Amen, and Amen.—19.

Among the gods there is none like unto thee, O Lord; neither are there any works like unto thy works.—*Ps.* lxxxvi. 8.

For thou art great, and doest wondrous things: thou art God alone.—10.

...Who in heaven can be compared unto the Lord? Who among the sons of the mighty can be likened unto the Lord?—*Ps.* lxxxix. 6.

God is greatly to be feared in the assembly of the saints, and to be had in reverence of all them that are about him.—7.

O Lord, how great are thy works! and thy thoughts are very deep.--*Ps.* xcii. 5.

The Lord reigneth, he is clothed with majesty; the Lord is clothed with strength, wherewith he hath girded himself: the world also is established, that it cannot be moved.—*Ps.* xciii. 1.

Declare his glory among the heathen, his wonders among all people.—*Ps.* xcvi. 3.

For all the gods of the nations are idols: but the Lord made the heavens.—5.

Honour and majesty are before him: strength and beauty are in his sanctuary.—6.

Give unto the Lord, O ye kindreds of the people, give unto the Lord glory and strength.—7.

Give unto the Lord the glory due unto his name...8.

The heavens declare his righteousness, and all the people see his glory.—*Ps.* xcvii. 6.

For thou, Lord, art high above all the earth: thou art exalted far above all gods.—9.

The Lord reigneth; let the people tremble: he

sitteth between the cherubims; let the earth be moved.
—*Ps.* xcix. 1.

The Lord is great in Zion; and he is high above all people.—2.

Let them praise thy great and terrible name; for it is holy.—3.

...O Lord my God, thou art very great; thou art clothed with honour and majesty.—*Ps.* civ. 1.

Who coverest thyself with light as with a garment: who stretchest out the heavens like a curtain :—2.

Who layeth the beams of his chambers in the waters: who maketh the clouds his chariot: who walketh upon the wings of the wind.—3.

The glory of the Lord shall endure for ever: the Lord shall rejoice in his works.—31.

Who can utter the mighty acts of the Lord? who can show forth all his praise?—*Ps.* cvi. 2.

The Lord is high above all nations, and his glory above the heavens.—*Ps.* cxiii. 4.

Who is like unto the Lord our God, who dwelleth on high,—5.

Who humbleth himself to behold the things that are in heaven, and in the earth!—6.

Great is the Lord, and greatly to be praised; and his greatness is unsearchable.—*Ps.* cxlv. 3.

I will speak of the glorious honour of thy majesty, and of thy wondrous works.—5.

Thy kingdom is an everlasting kingdom, and thy dominion endureth throughout all generations.—13.

The Lord is righteous in all his ways, and holy in all his works.—17.

Therefore saith the Lord, the Lord of hosts, the mighty One of Israel.—*Isa.* i. 24.

...I saw also the Lord sitting upon a throne, high and lifted up, and his train filled the temple.— *Isa.* vi. 1.

Above it stood the seraphims :...2.

And one cried unto another, and said, Holy, holy, holy, is the Lord of hosts: the whole earth is full of his glory.—3.

Cry out and shout, thou inhabitant of Zion: for great is the Holy One of Israel in the midst of thee. —*Isa.* xii. 6.

And the Lord shall cause his glorious voice to be heard, and shall shew the lighting down of his arm.... *Isa.* xxx. 30.

The Lord is exalted; for he dwelleth on high.... *Isa.* xxxiii. 5.

Now will I rise, saith the Lord, now will I be exalted ; now will I lift up myself.—10.

All nations before him are as nothing ; and they are counted to him less than nothing, and vanity. —*Isa.* xl. 17.

To whom then will ye liken me, or shall I be equal? saith the Holy One.—25.

I am the Lord: that is my name: and my glory will I not give to another, neither my praise to graven images.—*Isa.* xlii. 8.

...That ye may know and believe me, and understand that I am he: before me there was no God formed, neither shall there be after me.—*Isa.* xliii. 10.

I, even I, am the Lord; and beside me there is no saviour.—11.

...I am the first, and I am the last; and besides me there is no God.—*Isa.* xliv. 6.

...There is no God else beside me; a just God and a Saviour; there is none beside me.—*Isa.* xlv. 21.

Look unto me, and be ye saved, all the ends of the earth: for I am God, and there is none else.—22.

So shall they fear the name of the Lord from the west, and his glory from the rising of the sun....*Isa.* lix. 19.

...The Lord shall arise upon thee, and his glory shall be seen upon thee.—*Isa.* lx. 2.

...Let the Lord be glorified....5.

Forasmuch as there is none like unto thee, O Lord; thou art great, and thy name is great in might.—*Jer.* x. 6.

Who would not fear thee, O King of nations? for to thee doth it appertain: forasmuch as among all the wise men of the nations, and in all their kingdoms, there is none like unto thee.—7.

But the Lord is the true God, he is the living God, and an everlasting king....10.

A glorious high throne from the beginning is the place of our sanctuary.—*Jer.* xvii. 12.

...The Great, the Mighty God, the Lord of hosts, is his name,—*Jer.* xxxii. 18,
Great in counsel, and mighty in work....19.
Thou, O Lord, remainest for ever ; thy throne from generation to generation.—*Lam.* v. 19.
...Above the firmament that was over their heads was the likeness of a throne.—*Eze.* i. 26.
As the appearance of the bow that is in the cloud in the day of rain, so was the appearance of the brightness round about. This was the appearance of the likeness of the glory of the Lord....28.
...Blessed be the glory of the Lord from his place.—*Eze.* iii. 12.
...I will be glorified in the midst of thee : and they shall know that I am the Lord,...xxviii. 22.
And I will sanctify my great name,......and the heathen shall know that I am the Lord, saith the Lord God....*Eze.* xxxvi. 23.
And, behold, the glory of the God of Israel came from the way of the east: and his voice was like a noise of many waters : and the earth shined with his glory.—*Eze.* xliii. 2.
...This gate shall be shut, it shall not be opened, and no man shall enter in by it ; because the Lord, the God of Israel, hath entered in by it....*Eze.* xliv. 2.
...I blessed the most High, and I praised and honoured him that liveth for ever, whose dominion is an everlasting dominion, and his kingdom is from generation to generation.—*Dan.* iv. 34.

...For he is the living God, and steadfast for-ever, and his kingdom that which shall not be destroyed, and his dominion shall be even unto the end.—*Dan.* vi. 26.

And ye shall know that I am in the midst of Israel, and that I am the Lord your God, and none else. ...*Joel* ii. 27.

...His glory covered the heavens, and the earth was full of his praise.—*Hab.* iii. 3.

And the Lord shall be king over all the earth : in that day shall there be one Lord, and his name one. —*Zech.* xiv. 9.

Have we not all one Father ? hath not one God created us ?...*Mal.* ii. 10.

THE OMNISCIENCE AND OMNIPRESENCE OF GOD.

And God saw everything that he had made, and, behold, it was very good.—*Gen.* i. 31.

And they heard the voice of the Lord God walking in the garden in the cool of the day: and Adam and his wife hid themselves from the presence of the Lord God amongst the trees of the garden.—*Gen.* iii. 8.

And God saw that the wickedness of man was great in the earth....*Gen.* vi. 5.

And God looked upon the earth, and, behold, it was corrupt....12.

And God remembered Noah, and every living thing,—*Gen.* viii. 1.

And I will remember my covenant, which is between me and you and every living creature of all flesh. ...*Gen.* ix. 15.

...The Lord came down to see the city and the tower, which the children of men builded.—*Gen.* xi. 5.

And she (Hagar) called the name of the Lord that spake unto her, Thou God seest me: for she said, Have I also here looked after him that seeth me?—*Gen.* xvi. 13.

And Jacob awaked out of his sleep, and he said, Surely the Lord is in this place; and I knew it not. *Gen.* xxviii. 16.

And God remembered Rachel, and God hearkened to her...*Gen.* xxx. 22.

And God came to Laban the Syrian in a dream by night....*Gen.* xxxi. 24.

Except the God of my father, the God of Abraham ...had been with me, surely thou hadst sent me away now empty. God hath seen mine affliction and the labour of my hands, and rebuked thee yesternight.—42.

...Make there an altar unto God, that appeared unto thee when thou fleddest from the face of Esau thy brother.—*Gen.* xxxv. 1.

And the Lord was with Joseph,...*Gen.* xxxix. 2.

And his master saw that the Lord was with him....3.

And God spake unto Israel in the visions of the night....*Gen.* xlvi. 2.

I will go down with thee into Egypt; and I will also surely bring thee up again....4.

And Jacob said unto Joseph, God Almighty appeared unto me at Luz in the land of Canaan, and blessed me....*Gen.* xlviii. 3.

And God looked upon the children of Israel, and God had respect unto them.—*Ex.* ii. 25.

Then the Lord said unto Moses, Now shalt thou see what I will do to Pharoah....*Ex.* vi. 1.

And I have also heard the groaning of the children of Israel,...and I have remembered my covenant.—5.

...To the end thou mayest know that I am the Lord in the midst of the earth.—*Ex.* viii. 22.

For I will pass through the land of Egypt this night, and will smite all the firstborn...and against all the gods of Egypt I will execute judgment: I am the Lord.—*Ex.* xii. 12.

And it came to pass, that in the morning watch the Lord looked unto the host of the Egyptians.... *Ex.* xiv. 24.

...Come near before the Lord: for he hath heard your murmurings.—*Ex.* xvi. 9.

And he called the name of the place Massah, and Meribah, because of the chiding of the children of Israel, and because they tempted the Lord, saying, is the Lord among us, or not?—*Ex.* xvii. 7.

...In all places where I record my name I will come unto thee, and I will bless thee.—*Ex.* xx. 24.

And they shall know that I am the Lord their God, that brought them forth out of the land of Egypt, that I may dwell among them: I am the Lord their God—*Ex.* xxix. 46.

...He knoweth thy walking through this great wilderness: these forty years the Lord thy God hath been with thee....*Deut.* ii. 7.

Know therefore this day, and consider it in thine heart, that the Lord he is God in heaven above, and upon the earth beneath: there is none else.—*Deut.* iv. 39.

These words the Lord spake unto all your assembly in the mount out of the midst of the fire....*Deut.* v. 22.

And ye said, Behold, the Lord our God hath shewed us his glory and his greatness, and we have heard his voice out of the midst of the fire....24.

Go thou near, and hear all that the Lord our God shall say: and speak thou unto us all that the Lord our God shall speak unto thee; and we will hear it, and do it.—27.

And thou shalt remember all the way which the Lord thy God led thee these forty years in the wilderness, ...to know what was in thine heart...*Deut.* viii. 2.

Understand therefore this day, that the Lord thy God is he which goeth over before thee....*Deut.* ix. 3.

Furthermore the Lord spake unto me, saying, I have seen this people....13.

And I stayed in the mount,...and the Lord hearkened unto me at that time also....*Deut.* x. 10.

For the Lord your God is he that goeth with you. ...*Deut.* xx. 4.

When the Most High divided to the nations their inheritance, when he separated the sons of Adam, he set the bounds of the people according to the number of the children of Israel.—*Deut.* xxxii. 8.

He found him in a desert land…he led him about, he instructed him, he kept him as the apple of his eye.—*Deut.* xxxii. 10.

So the Lord alone did lead him….12.

And the angel of the Lord appeared unto him, and said unto him, The Lord is with thee…..*Jud.* vi. 12.

And Gideon said unto him, Oh my Lord, if the Lord be with us, why then is all this befallen us ?…13.

And the Lord looked upon him, and said, Go in this thy might,…14.

And the Lord said unto him, Surely I will be with thee…16.

…The Lord is a God of knowledge, and by him actions are weighed.—1 *Sam.* ii. 3.

…The Lord called Samuel : and he answered, Here am I.—1 *Sam.* iii. 4.

And Samuel grew, and the Lord was with him, and did let none of his words fall to the ground.—19.

And the Lord appeared again in Shiloh : for the Lord revealed himself to Samuel in Shiloh….21.

…The Lord hath sought him a man after his own heart….1 *Sam.* xiii. 14.

…The Lord seeth not as man seeth ; for man looketh on the outward appearance, but the Lord looketh on the heart.—1 *Sam.* xvi. 7.

…Thou, Lord God, knowest thy servant.—2 *Sam.* vii. 20.

It may be that the Lord will look on mine affliction, …2 *Sam.* xvi. 12.

OMNIPRESENCE OF GOD. 33

In my distress I called upon the Lord,...and he did hear my voice....2 *Sam.* xxii. 7.

In Gibeon the Lord appeared to Solomon in a dream by night....1 *Kings* iii. 5.

And I will dwell among the children of Israel, and will not forsake my people Israel.—1. *Kings* vi. 13.

Then spake Solomon, The Lord said that he would dwell in the thick darkness.—1 *Kings* viii. 12.

I have surely built thee a house to dwell in, a settled place for thee to abide in for ever.—13.

But will God indeed dwell on the earth? behold, the heaven and heaven of heavens cannot contain thee; how much less this house that I have builded? —27.

Yet have thou respect unto the prayer of thy servant,...—28.

That thine eyes may be open towards this house night and day, even toward the place of which thou hast said, thy name shall be there.—29.

And hearken thou to the supplication of thy servant, ...and hear thou in heaven thy dwelling place:...30.

...[For thou, even thou only, knowest the hearts of all the children of men.]—39.

...The Lord appeared to Solomon the second time, as he had appeared unto him at Gibeon.—1 *Kings* ix. 2.

And the Lord said unto him, I have heard thy prayer and thy supplication, that thou hast made before me:...and mine eyes and mine heart shall be there perpetually.—3.

...The Lord saw the affliction of Israel, that it was very bitter....2 *Kings* xiv. 26.

It may be the Lord thy God will hear all the words of Rab-shakeh, whom the King of Assyria his master hath sent to reproach the living God; and will reprove the words which the Lord thy God hath heard. ...2 *Kings* xix. 4.

Lord, bow down thine ear, and hear: open, Lord, thine eyes, and see....16.

...I know thy abode, and thy going out, and thy coming in, and thy rage against me.—27.

...The Lord searcheth all hearts, and understandeth all the imaginations of the thoughts...1 *Ch.* xxviii. 9.

For the eyes of the Lord run to and fro throughout the whole earth, to show himself strong in the behalf of them whose heart is perfect towards him.... 2 *Ch.* xvi. 9.

...Deal courageously, and the Lord shall be with the good.—2 *Ch.* xix. 11.

...O Lord God of our fathers, art not thou God in heaven? and rulest not thou over all the kingdoms of the heathen?...2 *Ch.* xx. 6.

For God commanded me to make haste: forbear thee from meddling with God, who is with me.... 2 *Ch.* xxxv. 21.

...For thou knowest that they dealt proudly against them.....*Neh.* ix. 10.

With him is wisdom and strength, he hath counsel and understanding.—*Job* xii. 13.

OMNIPRESENCE OF GOD.

He discovereth deep things out of darkness, and bringeth out to light the shadow of death.—*Job* xii. 22.

...Thou numberest my steps: dost thou not watch over my sin?—*Job* xiv. 16.

Shall any teach God knowledge? seeing he judgeth those that are high.—*Job* xxi. 22.

But he knoweth the way that I take....*Job* xxiii. 10.

...Times are not hidden from the Almighty,...*Job* xxiv. 1.

...His eyes are upon their ways.—23.

...His eye seeth every precious thing.—*Job* xxviii. 10.

God understandeth the way thereof, and he knoweth the place thereof.—23.

For he looketh to the ends of the earth, and seeth under the whole heaven.—24.

Doth not he see my ways, and count all my steps?—*Job* xxxi. 4.

For God speaketh once, yea twice, yet man perceiveth it not.—*Job* xxxiii. 14.

...His eyes are upon the ways of man, and he seeth all his goings.—*Job* xxxiv. 21.

There is no darkness, nor shadow of death, where the workers of iniquity may hide themselves.—22.

Behold, God is mighty, and despiseth not any:...*Job* xxxvi. 5.

He withdraweth not his eyes from the righteous: but with kings are they on the throne; yea, he doth establish them for ever....7.

Then he sheweth them their work, and their transgressions that they have exceeded.—9.

He openeth also their ear to discipline, and commandeth that they return from iniquity.—*Job* xxxvi. 10.

Dost thou know...the wondrous works of him which is perfect in knowledge?—*Job* xxxvii. 16.

I know that thou canst do everything, and that no thought can be withholden from thee.—*Job*, xlii. 2.

For the Lord knoweth the way of the righteous... *Ps.* 1-6.

...The Lord will hear when I call unto him.—*Ps.* iv. 3.

What is man, that thou art mindful of him? and the son of man, that thou visitest him?—*Ps.* viii. 4.

Lord, thou hast heard the desire of the humble....17.

For the righteous Lord loveth righteousness; his countenance doth behold the upright.—*Ps.* xi. 7.

The Lord looked down from heaven upon the children of men, to see if there were any that did understand, and seek God.—*Ps.* xiv. 2.

Let my sentence come forth from thy presence; let thine eyes behold the things that are equal.—*Ps.* xvii. 2.

Yea, though I walk through the valley of the shadow of death, I will fear no evil, for thou art with me....*Ps.* xxiii. 4.

The Lord looketh from heaven; he beholdeth all the sons of men.—*Ps.* xxxiii. 13.

From the place of his habitation he looketh upon all the inhabitants of the earth.—14.

Behold, the eye of the Lord is upon them that fear him, upon them that hope in his mercy.—18.

OMNIPRESENCE OF GOD.   37

This thou hast seen, O Lord: keep not silence: O Lord, be not far from me.—*Ps.* xxxv. 22.

The Lord knoweth the days of the upright....*Ps.* xxxvii. 18.

The steps of a good man are ordered by the Lord....23.

Shall not God search this out? for he knoweth the secrets of the heart.—*Ps.* xliv. 21.

O God, thou knowest my foolishness; and my sins are not hid from thee.—lxix. 5.

Thou hast known my reproach,...mine adversaries are all before thee.—19.

For the Lord heareth the poor, and despiseth not his prisoners.—33.

...Thy thoughts are very deep.—*Ps.* xcii. 5.

He that planted the ear, shall he not hear? he that formed the eye, shall he not see?—*Ps.* xciv. 9.

...He that teacheth man knowledge, shall not he know?—10.

The Lord knoweth the thoughts of man, that they are vanity.—11.

For he knoweth our frame; he remembereth that we are dust.—*Ps.* ciii. 14.

Who is like unto the Lord our God, who dwelleth on high.—*Ps.* cxiii. 5.

Who humbleth himself to behold the things that are in heaven, and in the earth!—6.

He will not suffer thy foot to be moved: he that keepeth thee will not slumber.—*Ps.* cxxi. 3.

Behold, he that keepeth Israel shall neither slumber nor sleep.—*Ps.* cxxi. 4.

If thou, Lord, shouldest mark iniquities, O Lord, who shall stand?—*Ps.* cxxx. 3.

O Lord, thou has searched me, and known me.—*Ps.* cxxxix. 1.

Thou knowest my down sitting and mine uprising, thou understandest my thought afar off.—2.

Thou compassest my path and my lying down, and art acquainted with all my ways.—3.

For there is not a word in my tongue, but lo, O Lord, thou knowest it altogether.—4.

Whither shall I go from thy spirit? or whither shall I flee from thy presence?—7.

If I ascend up to heaven, thou art there: if I make my bed in hell, behold, thou art there.—8.

Even there shall thy hand lead me, and thy right hand shall hold me.—10.

Yea, the darkness hideth not from thee; but the night shineth as the day: the darkness and the light are both alike to thee.—12.

My substance was not hid from thee, when I was made in secret,...15.

Thine eyes did see my substance, yet being imperfect; and in thy book all my members were written, which in continuance were fashioned, when as yet there was none of them.—16.

How precious also are thy thoughts unto me, O God! how great is the sum of them!—17.

OMNIPRESENCE OF GOD.

When my spirit was overwhelmed within me, then thou knewest my path.—*Ps.* cxlii. 3.

The Lord is nigh unto all them that call upon him, to all that call upon him in truth.—*Ps.* cxlv. 18.

He telleth the number of the stars; he calleth them all by their names.—*Ps.* cxlvii. 4.

The Lord by wisdom hath founded the earth; by understanding hath he established the heavens.—*Prov.* iii. 19.

By his knowledge the depths are broken up, and the clouds drop down the dew.—20.

For the ways of man are before the eyes of the Lord, and he pondereth all his goings.—*Prov.* v. 21.

The eyes of the Lord are in every place, beholding the evil and the good.—*Prov.* xv. 3.

...Doth not he that pondereth the heart consider it? and he that keepeth thy soul, doth not he know it? ...*Prov.* xxiv. 12.

Who hath wrougth and done it, calling the generations from the beginning? I the Lord....*Isa.* xli. 4.

When thou passest through the waters, I will be with thee...*Isa.* xliii. 2.

And who, as I, shall call, and shall declare it, and set it in order for me, since I appointed the ancient people? and the things that are coming, and shall come,...*Isa.* xliv. 7.

I will go before thee, and make the crooked places straight.—*Isa.* xlv. 2.

I have even from the beginning declared it to thee; before it came to pass I showed it thee:...*Isa.* xlviii. 5.

...I have shewed thee new things from this time, even hidden things, and thou didst not know them.—6.

Behold, I have graven thee upon the palms of my hands; thy walls are continually before me.—*Isa.* xlix. 16.

For thus saith the high and lofty One that inhabiteth eternity, whose name is Holy; I dwell in the high and holy place, with him also that is of a contrite and humble spirit....*Isa.* lvii. 15.

Behold, the Lord's hand is not shortened, that it cannot save: neither his ear heavy, that it cannot hear.—*Isa.* lix. 1.

Thus saith the Lord, the heaven is my throne, and the earth is my footstool: where is the house that ye build unto me? and where is the place of my rest? *Isa.* lxvi. 1.

...I know their works and their thoughts....18.

Am I a God at hand, saith the Lord, and not a God afar off?—*Jer.* xxiii. 23.

Can any hide himself in secret places that I shall not see him? saith the Lord. Do not I fill heaven and earth? saith the Lord.—24.

Great in counsel, and mighty in work: for thine eyes are open upon all the ways of the sons of men; ....*Jer.* xxxii. 19.

...I know the things that come into your mind, every one of them.—*Ez.* xi. 5.

...The name of the city from that day shall be, the Lord is there.—*Ez.* xlviii. 35.

He revealeth the deep and secret things: he knoweth what is in the darkness, and the light dwelleth with him.—*Dan.* ii. 22.

...And I blessed the most High...whose dominion is an everlasting dominion, and his kingdom is from generation to generation.—*Dan.* iv. 34.

O my God, incline thine ear, and hear; open thine eyes, and behold our desolations, and the city which is called by thy name....*Dan.* ix. 18.

...Jonah rose up to flee unto Tarshish from the presence of the Lord....*Jon.* i. 3.

And God saw their works, that they turned from their evil way.....*Jon.* iii. 10.

The Lord is good,...and he knoweth them that trust in him.—*Nah.* i. 7.

Thus saith the Lord; I am returned unto Zion, and will dwell in the midst of Jerusalem....*Zec.* viii. 3.

...I will open mine eyes upon the house of Judah....*Zec.* xii. 4.

And the Lord shall be king over all the earth. ...*Zec.* xiv. 9.

GOD OUR FATHER AND PROTECTOR.

---o---

...Thus saith the Lord, Israel is my son, even my first-born:—*Ex.* iv. 22.

And I say unto thee, let my son go, that he may serve me.—23.

Ye have seen what I did unto the Egyptians, and how I bare you on eagles' wings, and brought you unto myself.—*Ex.* xix. 4.

And in the wilderness, where thou hast seen how that the Lord thy God bare thee, as a man doth bear his son, in all the way that ye went, until ye came into this place.—*Deut.* i. 31.

Thou shalt also consider in thine heart, that, as a man chasteneth his son, so the Lord thy God chasteneth thee.—*Deut.* viii. 5.

Ye are the children of the Lord your God....*Deut.* xiv. 1.

They have corrupted themselves, their spot is not the spot of his children....*Deut.* xxxii. 5.

Do ye thus requite the Lord, O foolish people and unwise? is not he thy father that hath bought thee? hath he not made thee, and established thee?—6.

GOD OUR FATHER, &c.

As an eagle stirreth up her nest, fluttereth over her young, spreadeth abroad her wings, taketh them, beareth them on her wings:—*Deut.* xxxii. 11.

So the Lord alone did lead him....12.

I will be his father, and he shall be my son. If he commit iniquity, I will chasten him with the rod of men....2 *Sam.* vii. 14.

...I have chosen him to be my son, and I will be his father.—1 *Ch.* xxviii. 6.

...Blessed be thou, Lord God of Israel our father, for ever and ever.—1 *Ch.* xxix. 10.

...The Lord hath said unto me, Thou art my Son; this day have I begotten thee.—*Ps.* ii. 7.

The Lord is my shepherd; I shall not want.—*Ps.* xxiii. 1.

When my father and mother forsake me, then the Lord will take me up.—*Ps.* xxvii. 10.

Thou leddest thy people like a flock by the hand of Moses and Aaron.—*Ps.* lxxvii. 20.

He chose David also his servant, and took him from the sheep-folds.—*Ps.* lxxviii. 70.

He shall cry unto me, Thou art my father, my God, and the rock of my salvation.—*Ps.* lxxxix. 26.

Also I will make him my first-born, higher than the kings of the earth.—27.

Know ye that the Lord he is God: it is he that hath made us, and not we ourselves; we are his people, and the sheep of his pasture.—*Ps.* c. 3.

Like as a father pitieth his children, so the Lord pitieth them that fear him.—ciii. 13.

For the Lord hath chosen Jacob unto himself, and Israel for his peculiar treasure.—*Ps.* cxxxv. 4.

...Whom the Lord loveth he correcteth; even as a father the son in whom he delighteth.—*Prov.* iii. 12.

Now therefore hearken unto me, O ye children: for blessed are they that keep my ways.—*Prov.* viii. 32.

In the fear of the Lord is strong confidence: and his children shall have a place of refuge.—*Prov.* xiv. 26.

But thou, Israel, art my servant, Jacob whom I have chosen, the seed of Abraham my friend.—*Isa.* xli. 8.

Thou whom I have taken from the ends of the earth, and called thee from the chief men thereof, and said unto thee, Thou art my servant; I have chosen thee, and not cast thee away.—9.

Behold my servant, whom I uphold; mine elect, in whom my soul delighteth....*Isa.* xlii. 1.

...Thus saith the Lord that created thee, O Jacob, and he that formed thee, O Israel, Fear not: for I have redeemed thee, I have called thee by thy name; thou art mine.—*Isa.* xliii. 1.

I will say to the north, Give up; and to the south, Keep not back: bring my sons from far, and my daughters from the ends of the earth;—6.

Even every one that is called by my name: for I have created him for my glory, I have formed him; yea, I have made him.—7.

This people have I formed for myself....21.

Can a woman forget her sucking child, that she should not have compassion on the son of her womb? yea, they may forget, yet will I not forget thee.—*Isa.* xlix. 15.

For thy Maker is thine husband; the Lord of hosts is his name....*Isa.* liv. 5.

Thou shalt no more be termed Forsaken;...for the Lord delighteth in thee, and thy land shall be married.—*Isa.* lxii. 4.

...As the bridegroom rejoiceth over the bride, so shall thy God rejoice over thee.—5.

For he said, Surely they are my people, children that will not lie: so he was their Saviour.—*Isa.* lxiii. 8.

Doubtless thou art our Father, though Abraham be ignorant of us, and Israel acknowledge us not: thou, O Lord, art our Father, our redeemer.—16.

But now, O Lord, thou art our Father; we are the clay, and thou our potter; and we all are the work of thy hand.—*Isa.* lxiv. 8.

Wilt thou not from this time cry unto me, My father, thou art the guide of my youth?—*Jer.* iii. 4.

...Thou shalt call me, my father; and shalt not turn away from me.—19.

And ye shall be my people, and I will be your God.—*Jer.* xxx. 22.

...For I am a father to Israel, and Ephraim is my firstborn.—*Jer.* xxxi. 9.

Is Ephraim my dear Son? is he a pleasant child? for since I spake against him, I do earnestly remember him still....20.

...Yea, I sware unto thee, and entered into a covenant with thee, saith the Lord God, and thou becamest mine.—*Ez.* xvi. 8.

For thus saith the Lord God; Behold, I, even I, will both search my sheep, and seek them out.—*Ez.* xxxiv. 11.

...And ye my flock, the flock of my pasture, are men, and I am your God,...31.

...And it shall come to pass, that in the place where it was said unto them, Ye are not my people, there it shall be said unto them, Ye are the sons of the living God.—*Hos.* i. 10.

And I will betroth thee unto me for ever; yea, I will betroth thee unto me in righteousness,... *Hos.* ii. 19.

...I will say to them which were not my people, Thou art my people; and they shall say, Thou art my God.—23.

When Israel was a child, then I loved him, and called my son out of Egypt.—*Hos.* xi. 1.

A son honoureth his father, and a servant his master: if then I be a father, where is mine honour? ...saith the Lord of hosts.—*Mal.* i. 6.

Have we not all one father? hath not one God created us?...*Mal.* ii. 10.

And they shall be mine, saith the Lord of hosts, ...and I will spare them, as a man spareth his own son that serveth him.—*Mal.* iii. 17.

GOD'S GOODNESS, MERCY, AND FAITHFULNESS.

———o———

...And the Lord said in his heart, I will not again curse the ground any more for man's sake,...neither will I again smite any more every thing living... *Gen.* viii. 21.

While the earth remaineth, seed time and harvest, and cold and heat, and summer and winter, and day and night shall not cease.—22.

Behold 'now, thy servant hath found grace in thy sight, and thou hast magnified thy mercy, which thou hast shewed unto me in saving my life...*Gen.* xix. 19.

And Jethro rejoiced for all the goodness which the Lord had done to Israel...*Eze.* xviii. 9.

...Blessed be the Lord who hath delivered you out of the hand of the Egyptians...10.

...I will make all my goodness pass before thee, and I will proclaim the name of the Lord before thee; and I will be gracious to whom I will be gracious, and will shew mercy on whom I will shew mercy. *Eze.* xxxiii. 19.

...The Lord, the Lord God, merciful and gracious, longsuffering, and abundant in goodness and truth. *Exe.* xxxiv. 6.

Keeping mercy for thousands...7.

[For the Lord thy God is a merciful God;] he will not forsake thee, neither destroy thee...*Deut.* iv. 31.

...Shewing mercy unto thousands of them that love me and keep my commandments.—*Deut.* v. 10.

Know therefore that the Lord thy God, he is God, the faithful God, which keepeth covenant and mercy with them that love him...to a thousand generations. *Deut.* vii. 9.

...The Lord will again rejoice over thee for good, as he rejoiced over thy fathers...*Deut.* xxx. 9.

With the merciful thou wilt show thyself merciful.—2 *Sam.* xxii. 26.

And David said unto God, I am in a great strait: let us fall now into the hand of the Lord; for his mercies are great...2 *Sam.* xxiv. 14.

...There is no God like thee in heaven above, or on earth beneath, who keepest covenant and mercy with thy servants that walk before thee with all their heart.—1 *Kings* viii. 23.

...And they blessed the king and went unto their tents joyful and glad of heart for all the goodness that the Lord had done for David his servant, and for Israel his people.—66.

O give thanks unto the Lord: for he is good; for his mercy endureth for ever.—1 *Ch.* xvi. 34.

...The Lord your God is gracious and merciful, and will not turn away his face from you, if ye return unto him.—2 *Ch.* xxx. 9.

For we were bondmen; yet our God hath not forsaken us in our bondage, but hath extended mercy unto us in the sight of the kings of Persia...*Ezra* ix. 9.

...Thou art a God ready to pardon, gracious and merciful, slow to anger, and of great kindness, and forsookest them not.—*Neh.* ix. 17.

Thou gavest also thy good spirit to instruct them, and withheldest not thy manna from their mouth, and gavest them water for their thirst.—20.

Their children also multipliedst thou as the stars of heaven, and broughtest them into the land; concerning which thou hadst promised to their fathers, that they should go in to possess it.—23.

...So they did eat, and were filled,...and delighted themselves in thy great goodness.—25.

...Remember me, O my God, concerning this also, and spare me according to the greatness of thy mercy.—*Neh.* xiii. 22.

For the king trusteth in the Lord, and through the mercy of the most High he shall not be moved. *Ps.* xxi. 7.

Surely goodness and mercy shall follow me all the days of my life...*Ps.* xxiii. 6.

Remember, O Lord, thy tender mercies and thy lovingkindnesses; for they have been ever of old. *Ps.* xxv. 6.

...According to thy mercy remember thou me for thy goodness' sake, O Lord.—*Ps.* xxv. 7.

Good and upright is the Lord: therefore will he teach sinners in the way.—8.

For thy lovingkindness is before mine eyes...*Ps.* xxvi. 3.

I had fainted, unless I had believed to see the goodness of the Lord in the land of the living.—*Ps.* xxvii. 13.

For his anger endureth but a moment; in his favour is life...*Ps.* xxx. 5.

I will be glad and rejoice in thy mercy: for thou hast considered my trouble; thou hast known my soul in adversities.—*Ps.* xxxi. 7.

Oh how great is thy goodness, which thou hast laid up for them that fear thee; which thou hast wrought for them that trust in thee before the sons of men!—19.

O taste and see that the Lord is good...*Ps.* xxxiv. 8.

O continue thy lovingkindness unto them that know thee; and thy righteousness to the upright in heart.—*Ps.* xxxvi. 10.

Withhold not thou thy tender mercies from me, O Lord: let thy lovingkindness and thy truth continually preserve me.—*Ps.* xl. 11.

Arise for our help, and redeem us for thy mercies' sake—*Ps.* xliv. 26.

Have mercy upon me, O God, according to thy

lovingkindness : according unto the multitude of thy tender mercies blot out my transgressions.—*Ps.* li. 1.

...I will sing aloud of thy mercy in the morning... *Ps.* lix. 16.

...Unto thee, O Lord, belongeth mercy.—*Ps.* lxii. 12.

Because thy lovingkindness is better than life, my lips shall praise thee.—*Ps.* lxiii. 3.

...Thou makest the outgoings of the morning and evening to rejoice.—*Ps.* lxv. 8.

Thou visitest the earth, and waterest it : thou greatly enrichest it :...thou preparest them corn, when thou hast so provided for it.—9.

Thou waterest the ridges thereof abundantly :... thou makest it soft with showers : thou blessest the springing thereof.—10.

Thou crownest the year with thy goodness; and thy paths drop fatness.—11.

The pastures are clothed with flocks; the valleys also are covered over with corn; they shout for joy, they also sing.—13.

Blessed be God, which hath not turned away my prayer, nor his mercy from me.—*Ps.* lxvi. 20.

A father of the fatherless, and a judge of the widows, is God in his holy habitation.—*Ps.* lxviii. 5.

...Thou, O God, hast prepared of thy goodness for the poor.—10.

Hear me, O Lord; for thy lovingkindness is good : turn unto me according to the multitude of thy tender mercies.—*Ps.* lxix. 16.

Truly God is good to Israel, even to such as are of a clean heart.—*Ps.* lxxiii. 1.

For thou, Lord, art good, and ready to forgive: and plenteous in mercy unto all them that call upon thee.—*Ps.* lxxxvi. 5.

For great is thy mercy toward me...13.

...Thou, O Lord, art a God full of compassion, and gracious, longsuffering, and plenteous in mercy and truth.—15.

I will sing of the mercies of the Lord for ever: with my mouth will I make known thy faithfulness to all generations.—*Ps.* lxxxix. 1.

For I have said, Mercy shall be built up for ever: thy faithfulness shalt thou establish in the very heavens.—2.

Justice and judgment are the habitation of thy throne: mercy and truth shall go before thy face.—14.

My Mercy will I keep for him for evermore, and my covenant shall stand fast with him.—28.

To show forth thy lovingkindness in the morning, and thy faithfulness every night.—*Ps.* xcii. 2.

The Lord hath made known his salvation: his righteousness hath he openly shewed in the sight of the heathen.—*Ps.* xcviii. 2.

He hath remembered his mercy and his truth toward the house of Israel: all the ends of the earth have seen the salvation of our God.—3.

For the Lord is good; his mercy is everlasting; and his truth endureth to all generations.—*Ps.* c. v.

The Lord is merciful and gracious, slow to anger, and plenteous in mercy.—*Ps.* ciii. 8.

He will not always chide: neither will he keep his anger for ever.—9.

He hath not dealt with us after our sins; nor rewarded us according to our iniquities.—10.

For as the heaven is high above the earth, so great is his mercy toward them that fear him.—13.

For he knoweth our frame; he remembereth that we are dust.—14.

But the mercy of the Lord is from everlasting to everlasting upon them that fear him, and his righteousness unto children's children.—17.

Whoso is wise, and will observe these things, even they shall understand the lovingkindness of the Lord.—*Ps.* cvii. 43.

For thy Mercy is great above the heavens: and thy truth reacheth unto the clouds.—*Ps.* cviii. 4.

Not unto us, O Lord, not unto us, but unto thy name give glory, for thy mercy, and for thy truth's sake.—*Ps.* cxv. 1.

The Lord hath been mindful of us: he will bless us…12.

…Return unto thy rest, O my soul; for the Lord hath dealt bountifully with thee.—*Ps.* cxvi. 7.

For his merciful kindness is great toward us: and the truth of the Lord endureth for ever.—*Ps.* cxvii. 2.

Let them now that fear the Lord say, that his mercy endureth for ever.—*Ps.* cxviii. 4.

I know, O Lord, that thy judgments are right, and that thou in faithfulness hast afflicted me.—*Ps.* cxix. 75.

Let, I pray thee, thy merciful kindness be for my comfort, according to thy word unto thy servant.—76.

Let thy tender mercies come unto me, that I may live…77.

Quicken me after thy lovingkindness; so shall I keep the testimony of thy mouth.—88.

Let Israel hope in the Lord: for with the Lord there is mercy, and with him is plenteous redemption.—*Ps.* cxxx. 7.

O give thanks unto the Lord; for he is good: for his mercy endureth for ever.—*Ps.* cxxxvi. 1.

Who remembered us in our low estate: for his mercy endureth for ever:—23.

And hath redeemed us from our enemies: for his mercy endureth for ever.—24.

Who giveth food to all flesh: for his mercy endureth for ever.—25.

I will worship toward thy holy temple, and praise thy name for thy lovingkindness and thy truth… *Ps.* cxxxviii. 2.

…In thy faithfulness answer me, and in thy righteousness.—*Ps.* cxliii. 1.

Cause me to hear thy lovingkindness in the morning.—8.

It is he that giveth salvation…*Ps.* cxliv. 10.

They shall abundantly utter the memory of thy

great goodness, and shall sing of thy righteousness. —*Ps.* cxlv. 7.

The Lord is gracious, and full of compassion, slow to anger, and of great mercy.—8.

The Lord is good to all: and his tender mercies are over all his works.—9.

The eyes of all wait upon thee; and thou givest them their meat in due season.—15.

Thou openest thine hand, and satisfiest the desire of every living thing.—16.

The Lord is righteous in all his ways.—17.

And therefore will the Lord wait, that he may be gracious unto you, and therefore will he be exalted, that he may have mercy upon you:...blessed are all they that wait for him.—*Isa.* xxx. 18.

For a small moment have I forsaken thee ; but with great mercies will I gather thee.—*Isa.* liv. 7.

In a little wrath I hid my face from thee for a moment; but with everlasting kindness will I have mercy on thee, saith the Lord thy Redeemer.—8.

For the mountains shall depart, and the hills be removed ; but my kindness shall not depart from thee, neither shall the covenant of my peace be removed, saith the Lord that hath mercy on thee.—10.

...Let him that glorieth glory in this, that he understandeth and knoweth me, that I am the Lord which exercise lovingkindness, judgment, and righteousness, in the earth : for in these things I delight, saith the Lord.—*Jer.* ix. 24.

The Lord hath appeared of old unto me, saying, Yea, I have loved thee with an everlasting love: therefore with lovingkindness have I drawn thee.—*Jer.* xxxi. 3.

Is Ephraim my dear son?...I will surely have mercy upon him, saith the Lord.—20.

But fear not thou...and be not dismayed, O Israel: for, behold, I will save thee from afar off;...and Jacob shall return, and be in rest and at ease, and none shall make him afraid.—*Jer.* xlvi. 27.

It is of the Lord's mercies that we are not consumed, because his compassions fail not.—*Lam.* iii. 22.

They are new every morning: great is thy faithfulness.—23.

For the Lord will not cast off for ever:—31.

But though he cause grief, yet will he have compassion according to the multitude of his mercies.—32.

For he doth not afflict willingly nor grieve the children of men.—33.

To the Lord our God belong mercies and forgivenesses, though we have rebelled against him.—*Dan.* ix. 9.

And I will betroth thee unto me for ever; yea, I will betroth thee unto me in righteousness, and in judgment, and in lovingkindness, and in mercies.—*Hos.* ii. 19.

I will even betroth thee unto me in faithfulness.—20.

...Turn unto the Lord your God: for he is gracious

and merciful, slow to anger, and of great kindness... Joel ii. 13.

...He retaineth not his anger for ever, because he delighteth in mercy.—*Micah* vii. 18.

He will turn again, he will have compassion upon us...19.

The Lord is good, a strong hold in the day of trouble.—*Nahum* i. 7.

The Lord thy God in the midst of thee is mighty; he will save, he will rejoice over thee with joy; he will rest in his love...*Zeph.* iii. 17.

For how great is his goodness, and how great is his beauty! corn shall make the young men cheerful...*Zech.* ix. 17.

...And I will bring them again to place them; for I have mercy upon them...*Zech.* x. 6.

For I am the Lord, I change not; therefore ye sons of Jacob are not consumed.—*Mal.* iii. 6.

STRIVE TO BE PERFECT AND HOLY.

And Enoch walked with God: and he was not; for God took him.—*Gen.* v. 24.

...Noah was a just man and perfect in his generations, and Noah walked with God.—*Gen.* vi. 9.

...The Lord appeared to Abram, and said unto him, I am the Almighty God; walk before me, and be thou perfect.—*Gen.* xvii. 1.

...Ye shall be unto me a kingdom of priests, and an holy nation....*Ex.* xix. 6.

And Moses went down from the mount unto the people, and sanctified the people; and they washed their clothes.—14.

And let the priests also, which come near to the Lord, sanctify themselves...22.

And ye shall be holy men unto me...*Ex.* xxii. 31.

...This is it that the Lord spake, saying, I will be sanctified in them that come nigh me...*Lev.* x. 3.

For I am the Lord your God: ye shall therefore sanctify yourselves, and ye shall be holy; for I am holy...*Lev.* xi. 44.

Speak unto all the congregation of the children of Israel, and say unto them, Ye shall be holy: for I the Lord your God am holy.—*Lev.* xix. 2.

And ye shall keep my statutes, and do them: I am the Lord which sanctify you.—*Lev.* xx. 8.

And ye shall be holy unto me: for I the Lord am holy, and have severed you from other people, that ye should be mine.—26.

They shall be holy unto their God, and not profane the name of their God...*Lev.* xxi. 6.

...But I will be hallowed among the children of Israel: I am the Lord which hallow you.—*Lev.* xxii. 32.

Ye shall keep my sabbaths, and reverence my sanctuary: I am the Lord.—*Lev.* xxvi. 2.

...That ye seek not after your own heart and your own eyes...*Num.* xv. 39.

That ye may remember, and do all my commandments, and be holy unto your God.—40.

...The Lord will shew who are his, and who is holy...*Num.* xvi. 5.

For thou art an holy people unto the Lord thy God, and the Lord hath chosen thee to be a peculiar people unto himself, above all the nations that are upon the earth.—*Deut.* xiv. 2.

Thou shalt be perfect with the Lord thy God.—*Deut.* xviii. 13.

...That thou mayest be an holy people unto the Lord thy God, as he hath spoken.—*Deut.* xxvi. 19.

...The Lord came from Sinai...he came with ten thousands of saints...*Deut.* xxxiii. 2.

Yea, he loved the people; all his saints are in thy hand: and they sat down at thy feet; every one shall receive of thy words.—3.

Up, sanctify the people, and say, Sanctify yourselves against to-morrow...*Jos.* vii. 13.

...Then said the priest, Let us draw near hither unto God.—1 *Sam.* xiv. 36.

Let your heart therefore be perfect with the Lord our God, to walk in his statutes, and to keep his commandments, as at this day.—1 *Kings* viii. 61.

I beseech thee, O Lord, remember now how I have walked before thee in truth and with a perfect heart. 2 *Kings.* xx. 3.

...Ye are the chief of the fathers of the Levites: sanctify yourselves, both ye and your brethren, that ye may bring up the ark of the Lord God of Israel unto the place that I have prepared for it.—1 *Ch.* xv. 12.

Give unto the Lord the glory due unto his name... worship the Lord in the beauty of holiness.—1 *Ch.* xvi. 29.

And thou, Solomon my son, know thou the God of thy father, and serve him with a perfect heart and with a willing mind...1 *Ch.* xxviii. 9.

Then the people rejoiced, for that they offered willingly, because with perfect heart they offered willingly to the Lord.—1 *Ch.* xxix. 9.

...The heart of Asa was perfect all his days.—2 *Ch.* xv. 17.

And he brought into the house of God the things that his father had dedicated, and that he himself had dedicated...18.

For the eyes of the Lord run to and fro throughout the whole earth, to show himself strong in the behalf of them whose heart is perfect toward him...2 *Ch.* xvi. 9.

And the Lord was with Jehoshaphat, because he walked in the first ways of his father David... 2 *Ch.* xvii. 3.

And his heart was lifted up in the ways of the Lord...6.

...And he went out again through the people...and brought them back unto the Lord God of their fathers.—2 *Ch.* xix. 4.

And he charged them, saying, Thus shall ye do in the fear of the Lord, faithfully, and with a perfect heart.—9.

So Jotham became mighty, because he prepared his ways before the Lord his God.—2 *Ch.* xxvii. 6.

He (Hezekiah) in the first year of his reign, in the first month, opened the doors of the house of the Lord, and repaired them.—2 *Ch.* xxix. 3.

And he brought in the priests and the Levites...4.

And said unto them, Hear me, ye Levites, sanctify now yourselves, and sanctify the house of the Lord God of your fathers...5.

Now it is in mine heart to make a covenant with the Lord God of Israel...2 *Ch.* xxix. 10.

My sons, be not now negligent: for the Lord hath chosen you to stand before him, to serve him, and that ye should minister unto him...11.

...Yield yourselves unto the Lord, and enter into his sanctuary, which he hath sanctified for ever: and serve the Lord your God...2 *Ch.* xxx. 8.

...And a great number of priests sanctified themselves.—24.

...For in their set office they sanctified themselves in holiness.—2 *Ch.* xxxi. 18.

And thus did Hezekiah throughout all Judah, and wrought that which was good and right and truth before the Lord his God.—20.

And in every work that he began in the service of the house of God, and in the law, and in the commandments, to seek his God, he did it with all his heart, and prospered.—21.

There was a man in the land of Uz, whose name was Job; and that man was perfect and upright, and one that feared God, and eschewed evil.—*Job* i. 1.

Behold, God will not cast away a perfect man,... *Job* viii. 20.

But know that the Lord hath set apart him that is godly for himself...*Ps.* iv. 3.

Stand in awe, and sin not: commune with your own heart upon your bed, and be still.—4.

But as for me, I will come into thine house...and

in thy fear will I worship toward thy holy temple. —*Ps.* v. 7.

With the pure thou wilt shew thyself pure... *Ps.* xviii. 26.

It is God that girdeth me with strength, and maketh my way perfect.—32.

Who shall ascend unto the hill of the Lord? or who shall stand in his holy place?—*Ps.* xxiv. 3.

He that hath clean hands, and a pure heart;...4.

He shall receive the blessing from the Lord, and righteousness from the God of his salvation.—5.

I will wash mine hands in innocency: so will I compass thine altar, O Lord.—*Ps.* xxvi. 6.

Mark the perfect man, and behold the upright: for the end of that man is peace.—*Ps.* xxxvii. 37.

Truly God is good to Israel, even to such as are of a clean heart.—*Ps.* lxxiii. 1.

But it is good for me to draw near to God...28.

Preserve my soul; for I am holy...*Ps.* lxxxvi. 2.

...For unto thee, O Lord, do I lift up my soul.—4.

I will behave myself wisely in a perfect way. O when wilt thou come unto me? I will walk within my house with a perfect heart.—*Ps.* ci. 2.

I will set no wicked thing before mine eyes...it shall not cleave to me.—3.

Blessed are the undefiled in the way, who walk in the law of the Lord.—*Ps.* cxix. 1.

The Lord will perfect that which concerneth me... *Ps.* cxxxviii. 8.

For the upright shall dwell in the land, and the perfect shall remain in it.—*Prov.* ii. 21.

In the way of righteousness is life; and in the pathway thereof there is no death.—*Prov.* xii. 28.

...The words of the pure are pleasant words.—*Prov.* xv. 26.

And it shall come to pass, that he that is left in Zion, and he that remaineth in Jerusalem, shall be called holy, even every one that is written among the living in Jerusalem.—*Isa.* iv. 3.

And an highway shall be there, and a way, and it shall be called The way of holiness; the unclean shall not pass over it...*Isa.* xxxv. 8.

But ye shall be named the Priests of the Lord: men shall call you the Ministers of our God... *Isa.* lxi. 6.

And they shall call them, The holy people, The redeemed of the Lord...*Isa.* lxii. 12.

Let us lift up our heart with our hands unto God in the heavens.—*Lam.* iii. 41.

But the priests the Levites, the sons of Zadok, that kept the charge of my sanctuary when the Children of Israel went astray from me, they shall come near to me to minister unto me,...*Eze.* xliv. 15.

And they shall teach my people the difference between the holy and profane, and cause them to discern between the unclean and the clean.—23.

GOD SEETH THE HEART, HIS POWER TOUCHETH IT.

—o—

And the Lord said unto Noah,...thee have I seen righteous before me in this generation.—*Gen.* vii. 1.

And God said unto him in a dream, Yea, I know that thou didst this in the integrity of thy heart; for I also withheld thee from sinning against me... *Gen.* xx. 6.

...See, the Lord hath called by name Bezaleel... *Ex.* xxxv. 30.

And he hath filled him with the spirit of God, in wisdom, in understanding, and in knowledge...31.

And he hath put in his heart that he may teach, both he, and Aholiab...34.

Them hath he filled with wisdom of heart, to work all manner of work...35.

And Moses called Bezaleel and Aholiab, and every wise hearted man, in whose heart the Lord had put wisdom, even every one whose heart stirred him up to come unto the work to do it.—*Ex.* xxxvi. 2.

And the Spirit of the Lord will come upon thee,

and thou shalt prophesy with them, and shalt be turned into another man.—1 *Sam.* x. 6.

And it was so, that when he had turned his back to go from Samuel, God gave him another heart…9.

And Saul also went home to Gibeah; and there went with him a band of men, whose hearts God had touched.—26.

But the Lord said unto Samuel, Look not on his countenance, or on the height of his stature; because I have refused him: for the Lord seeth not as man seeth; for man looketh on the outward appearance, but the Lord looketh on the heart.—1 *Sam.* xvi. 7.

…And the Spirit of the Lord came upon David from that day forward…13.

And now, O Lord my God, thou hast made thy servant king instead of David my father: and I am but a little child: I know not how to go out or come in.—1 *Kings* iii. 7.

Give therefore thy servant an understanding heart to judge thy people, that I may discern between good and bad: for who is able to judge this thy so great a people?—9.

And God said unto him, Because thou hast asked this thing, and hast not asked for thyself long life; neither hast asked riches for thyself, nor hast asked the life of thine enemies; but hast asked for thyself understanding to discern judgment;—11.

Behold, I have done according to thy words: lo,

I have given thee a wise and an understanding heart...1 *Kings* iii. 12.

And God gave Solomon wisdom and understanding exceeding much, and largeness of heart, even as the sand that is on the sea shore.—1 *Kings* iv. 29.

The Lord our God be with us, as he was with our fathers : let him not leave us, nor forsake us :— 1 *Kings* viii. 57.

That he may incline our hearts unto him...58.

And all the earth sought to Solomon, to hear his wisdom, which God had put in his heart.—1 *Kings* x. 24.

Hear me, O Lord, hear me, that this people may know that thou art the Lord God, and that thou hast turned their heart back again.—1 *Kings* xviii. 37.

...For the Lord searcheth all hearts, and understandeth all the imaginations of the thoughts... 1 *Ch.* xxviii. 9.

I know also, my God, that thou triest the heart, and hast pleasure in uprightness...1 *Ch.* xxix. 17.

O Lord God of Abraham, Isaac, and of Israel, our fathers, keep this for ever in the imagination of the thoughts of the heart of thy people, and prepare their heart unto thee :—18.

And give unto Solomon my son a perfect heart, to keep thy commandments...19.

Then hear thou from heaven thy dwelling place, and forgive, and render unto every man according unto all his ways, whose heart thou knowest; (for thou only knowest the hearts of the children of men :)—2 *Ch.* vi. 30.

Also in Judah the hand of God was to give them one heart to do the commandment of the king and of the princes, by the word of the Lord.—2 *Ch.* xxx. 12.

...For the Lord had made them joyful, and turned the heart of the King of Assyria unto them, to strengthen their hands in the work of the house of God, the God of Israel.—*Ezra* vi. 22.

Blessed be the Lord God of our fathers, which hath put such a thing as this in the king's heart, to beautify the house of the Lord which is in Jerusalem.—*Ezra* vii. 27.

And I (Nehemiah) arose in the night,...neither told I any man what my God had put in my heart to do at Jerusalem...*Neh.* ii. 12.

And my God put into mine heart to gather together the nobles, and the rulers, and the people, that they might be reckoned by genealogy...*Neh.* vii. 5.

Thou art the Lord the God, who didst choose Abram,...*Neh.* ix. 7.

And foundest his heart faithful before thee...8.

Thou hast put gladness in my heart.—*Ps.* iv. 7.

Lord, thou hast heard the desire of the humble: thou wilt prepare their heart, thou wilt cause thine ear to hear.—*Ps.* x. 17.

Wait on the Lord: be of good courage, and he shall strengthen thine heart...*Ps.* xxvii. 14.

The Lord looketh from heaven; he beholdeth all the sons of men.—*Ps.* xxxiii. 13.

He fashioneth their hearts alike...15.

If we have forgotten the name of our God,...*Ps.* xliv. 20.

Shall not God search this out? for he knoweth the secrets of the heart.—21.

Behold, thou desirest truth in the inward parts: and in the hidden part thou shalt make me to know wisdom.—*Ps.* li. 6.

Create in me a clean heart, O God; and renew a right spirit within me.—10.

Teach me thy way, O Lord; I will walk in thy truth: unite my heart to fear thy name.—*Ps.* lxxxvi. 11.

The Lord knoweth the thoughts of man, that they are vanity.—*Ps.* xciv. 11.

I will run the way of thy commandments, when thou shalt enlarge my heart.—*Ps.* cxix. 32.

Incline my heart unto thy testimonies, and not to covetousness.—36.

O Lord, thou hast searched me, and known me.—*Ps.* cxxxix. 1.

...Thou understandest my thoughts afar off.—2.

For there is not a word in my tongue, but, lo, O Lord, thou knowest it altogether.—4.

Search me, O God, and know my heart: try me, and know my thoughts.—23.

The preparations of the heart in man, and the answer of the tongue, is from the Lord.—*Prov.* xvi. 1.

The king's heart is in the hand of the Lord, as the rivers of water: he turneth it withersoever he will.—*Prov.* xxi. 1.

Every way of a man is right in his own eyes: but the Lord pondereth the hearts.—2.

If thou sayest, Behold, we knew it not; doth not he that pondereth the heart consider it? and he that keepeth thy soul, doth not he know it?...*Prov.* xxiv. 12.

But thou, O Lord, knowest me: thou hast seen me, and tried mine heart toward thee....*Jer.* xii. 3.

But, O Lord of hosts, that triest the righteous, and seest the reins and the heart....*Jer.* xx. 12.

Thus saith the Lord, the God of Israel,...I acknowledge them that are carried away captive of Judah,...*Jer.* xxiv. 5.

And I will give them an heart to know me, that I am the Lord:...for they shall return unto me with their whole heart.—7.

...After those days, saith the Lord, I will put my law in their inward parts, and write it in their hearts...*Jer.* xxxi. 33.

And I will give them one heart, and one way, that they may fear me for ever, for the good of them, and of their children after them.—*Jer.* xxxii. 39.

...I will put my fear in their hearts, that they shall not depart from me.—40.

A new heart also will I give you, and a new spirit

will I put within you : and I will take away the stony heart out of your flesh, and I will give you an heart of flesh.—*Eze.* xxxvi. 26.

And I will put my spirit within you, and cause you to walk in my statutes, and ye shall keep my judgments, and do them.—27.

WATCHFULNESS.
KEEP THE HEART PURE.

——o——

And in all things that I have said unto you be circumspect...*Ex.* xxiii. 13.

Take heed to thyself, lest thou make a covenant with the inhabitants of the land whither thou goest. ...*Ex.* xxxiv. 12.

...Seek not after your own heart and your own eyes. ...*Num.* xv. 39.

Only take heed to thyself, and keep thy soul diligently, lest thou forget the things which thine eyes have seen, and lest they depart from thy heart all the days of thy life...*Deut.* iv. 9.

...Love the Lord thy God with all thine heart, and and with all thy soul...*Deut.* vi. 5.

Take heed to yourselves, that your heart be not deceived, and ye turn aside, and serve other gods, and worship them.—*Deut.* xi. 16.

Therefore shall ye lay up these my words in your heart and in your soul...18.

Beware that there be not a thought in thy wicked heart, saying, The seventh year, the year of release, is at hand; and thine eye be evil against thy poor brother...*Deut.* xv. 9.

Thou shalt surely give him, and thine heart shall not be grieved when thou givest unto him...10.

...Take diligent heed to do the commandment and the law...*Josh.* xxii. 5.

Take good heed therefore unto yourselves, that ye love the Lord your God.—*Josh.* xxiii. 11.

...Incline your heart unto the Lord God of Israel. —*Josh.* xxiv. 23.

...If ye do return unto the Lord with all your hearts, then put away the strange gods from among you, and prepare your hearts unto the Lord, and serve him only...1 *Sam.* vii. 3.

Now set your heart and your soul to seek the Lord your God...1 *Ch.* xxii. 19.

And his (Jehoshaphat's) heart was lifted up in the ways of the Lord...2 *Ch.* xvii. 6.

...As yet the people had not prepared their hearts unto the God of their fathers.—2 *Ch.* xx. 33.

For Ezra had prepared his heart to seek the law of the Lord and to do it...*Ezra* vii. 10.

If thou prepare thine heart, and stretch out thine hands toward him;—*Job* xi. 13.

...Then shalt thou lift up thy face without spot; yea, thou shalt be stedfast, and shalt not fear.—15.

Acquaint now thyself with him, and be at peace: thereby good shall come unto thee....*Job* xxii. 21.

...And lay up his words in thine heart.—22.

…My heart shall not reproach me so long as I live.
—Job xxvii. 6.

Take heed, regard not iniquity.—Job xxxvi. 21.

Commune with your own heart upon your bed, and be still.—Ps. iv. 4.

Who shall ascend unto the hill of the Lord?... Ps. xxiv. 3.

He that hath clean hands, and a pure heart…4.

The law of his God is in his heart; none of his steps shall slide.—Ps xxxvii. 31.

I said, I will take heed to my ways, that I sin not with my tongue…Ps. xxxix. 1.

If I regard iniquity in my heart, the Lord will not hear me.—Ps. lxvi. 18.

Truly God is good to Israel, even to such as are of a clean heart.—Ps. lxxiii. 1.

…I commune with mine own heart: and my spirit made diligent search.—Ps. lxxvii. 6.

…I will walk within my house with a perfect heart.—Ps. ci. 2.

Wherewithal shall a young man cleanse his way? by taking heed thereto according to thy word.—Ps. cxix. 9.

Thy word have I hid in mine heart, that I might not sin against thee.—11.

Let my heart be sound in thy statutes; that I be not ashamed.—80.

I have inclined mine heart to perform thy statutes alway, even unto the end.—112.

...My heart standeth in awe of thy word.—*Ps.* cxix. 161.

My soul hath kept thy testimonies; and I love them exceedingly.—167.

Lord, my heart is not haughty, nor mine eyes lofty...*Ps.* cxxxi. 1.

My son, attend to my words;—*Prov.* iv. 20.

Let them not depart from thine eyes; keep them in the midst of thine heart.—21.

Keep thy heart with all diligence; for out of it are the issues of life.—23.

...He that keepeth his way preserveth his soul.—*Prov.* xvi. 17.

The heart of the wise teacheth his mouth, and addeth learning to his lips.—23.

The heart of the prudent getteth knowledge.—*Prov.* xviii. 15.

He that loveth pureness of heart, for the grace of his lips the king shall be his friend.—*Prov.* xxii. 11.

...Apply thine heart unto my knowledge.—17.

Apply thine heart unto instruction, and thine ears to the words of knowledge.—*Prov.* xxiii. 12.

Let not thine heart envy sinners...17.

...Let not thine heart be glad when he (thine enemy) stumbleth.—*Prov.* xxiv. 17.

He that trusteth in his own heart is a fool: but whoso walketh wisely, he shall be delivered.—xxviii. 26.

Be not rash with thy mouth, and let not thine heart be hasty to utter anything before God.... *Eccl.* v. 2.

I applied mine heart to know, and to search, and to seek out wisdom, and the reason of things... *Eccl.* vii. 25.

...A wise man's heart discerneth both time and judgment.—*Eccl.* viii. 5.

Let none of you imagine evil in your hearts against your neighbour...*Zech.* viii. 17.

Take heed to your spirit, that ye deal not treacherously.—*Mal.* ii. 16.

LOVE TO GOD SHOULD RULE OUR ACTIONS.

———o———

I am the Lord your God which have brought thee out of the land of Egypt...*Ex.* xx. 2.
...Shewing mercy unto thousands of them that love me, and keep my commandments.—6.

And thou shalt love the Lord thy God with all thine heart, and with all thy soul, and with all thy might.—*Deut.* vi. 5.

Know therefore that the Lord thy God, he is God, the faithful God, which keepeth covenant and mercy with them that love him and keep his commandments to a thousand generations.—*Deut.* vii. 9.

And now, Israel, what doth the Lord thy God require of thee, but to fear the Lord thy God, to walk in all his ways, and to love him and to serve the Lord thy God with all thy heart and with all thy soul.—*Deut.* x. 12.

Therefore thou shalt love the Lord thy God, and keep his charge...*Deut.* xi. 1.

See, I have set before thee this day life and good, and death and evil;—*Deut.* xxx. 15.

In that I command thee this day to love the Lord thy God, to walk in his ways...*Deut.* xxx. 16.

That thou mayest love the Lord thy God, and that thou mayest obey his voice, and that thou mayest cleave unto him...20.

But take diligent heed to do the commandment and the law, which Moses the servant of the Lord charged you, to love the Lord your God, and to walk in all his ways, and to keep his commandments, and to cleave unto him, and to serve him with all your heart and with all your soul.—*Josh.* xxii. 5.

Take good heed therefore unto yourselves, that ye love the Lord your God.—*Josh.* xxiii. 11.

And Solomon loved the Lord, walking in the statutes of David his father.—1 *Kings* iii. 3.

...Let them that love thy name be joyful in thee. —*Ps.* v. 11.

I will love thee, O Lord, my strength.—*Ps.* xviii. 1.

O love the Lord, all ye his saints: for the Lord preserveth the faithful.—*Ps.* xxxi. 23.

Delight thyself also in the Lord...*Ps.* xxxvii. 4.

...He is thy Lord; and worship thou him.—*Ps.* xlv. 11.

For God will save Zion...that they may dwell there, and have it in possession.—*Ps.* lxix. 35.

...And they that love his name shall dwell therein. —36.

Whom have I in heaven but thee? and there is none upon earth that I desire beside thee.— *Ps.* lxxiii. 25.

Because he hath set his love upon me, therefore will I deliver him: I will set him on high, because he hath known my name.—*Ps*. xci. 14.

Ye that love the Lord, hate evil.—*Ps*. xcvii. 10.

I love the Lord, because he hath heard my voice and my supplications.—*Ps*. cxvi. 1.

...They Shall prosper that love thee.—*Ps*. cxxii. 6.

The Lord preserveth all them that love him.—*Ps*. cxlv. 20.

I love them that love me; and they that seek me early shall find me.—*Prov*. xviii. 17.

My Son, give me thine heart, and let thine eyes observe my ways.—*Prov*. xxiii. 26.

Also the sons of the stranger, that join themselves to the Lord, to serve him, and to love the name of the Lord, to be his servants,...*Isa*. lvi. 6.

Even them will I bring to my holy mountain, and make them joyful in my house of prayer...7.

THE FEAR OF GOD WILL RESTRAIN US FROM SINNING.

...Now I know that thou fearest God, seeing thou hast not withheld thy son, thine only son from me. —*Gen.* xxii. 12.

...How then can I do this great wickedness, and sin against God?—*Gen.* xxxix. 9.

And Joseph said unto them the third day, This do, and live; for I fear God.—*Gen.* xlii. 18.

But the midwives feared God, and did not as the king of Egypt commanded them, but saved the men children alive.—*Ex.* i. 17.

And Israel saw that great work which the Lord did upon the Egyptians: and the people feared the Lord, and believed the Lord, and his servant Moses. —*Ex.* xiv. 31.

...Thou shalt provide out of all the people able men, such as fear God, men of truth, hating covetousness. —*Ex.* xviii. 21.

And Moses said unto the people, Fear not: for God is come to prove you, and that his fear may be before your faces, that ye sin not.—*Ex.* xx. 20.

...Honour the face of the old man, and fear thy God: I am the Lord.—*Lev.* xix. 32.

Ye shall not therefore oppress one another; but thou shalt fear thy God: for I am the Lord your God.—*Lev.* xxv. 17.

Thou shalt not rule over him with rigour; but shalt fear thy God.—43.

...I will make them hear my words, that they may learn to fear me all the days that they shall live upon the earth, and that they may teach their children.—*Deut.* iv. 10.

O that there were such an heart in them, that they would fear me, and keep all my commandments always, that it might be well with them, and with their children for ever!—*Deut.* v. 29.

That thou mightest fear the Lord thy God, to keep all his statutes and his commandments, which I command thee...*Deut.* vi. 2.

And now, Israel, what doth the Lord thy God require of thee, but to fear the Lord thy God, to walk in all his ways, and to love him...*Deut.* x. 12.

Ye shall walk after the Lord your God, and fear him, and keep his commandments...*Deut.* xiii. 4.

And all Israel shall hear, and fear, and shall do no more any such wickedness as this is among you.—11.

...That thou mayest learn to fear the Lord thy God always.—*Deut.* xiv. 23.

That all the people of the earth might know the

hand of the Lord, that it is mighty: that ye might fear the Lord your God for ever.—*Josh.* iv. 24.

Now therefore fear the Lord, and serve him in sincerity and in truth....*Josh.* xxiv. 14.

If ye will fear the Lord, and serve him, and obey his voice,...then shall both ye and also the king that reigneth over you continue following the Lord your God.—1 *Sam.* xii. 14.

So Samuel called unto the Lord; and the Lord sent thunder and rain that day: and all the people greatly feared the Lord and Samuel.—18.

Only fear the Lord, and serve him in truth with all your heart...24.

...He that ruleth over men must be just, ruling in the fear of God.—2 *Sam.* xxiii. 3.

That they may fear thee all the days that they live in the land which thou gavest unto our fathers.—1 *Kings* viii. 40.

...Now Obadiah feared the Lord greatly.—1 *Kings* xviii. 3.

I thy servant fear the Lord from my youth—12.

Then one of the priests...came and dwelt in Bethel, and taught them how they should fear the Lord.—2 *Kings* xvii. 28.

So they feared the Lord...32.

But the Lord, who brought you up out of the land of Egypt with great power and a stretched out arm, him shall ye fear, and him shall ye worship...36.

And the covenant that I have made with you ye shall not forget; neither shall ye fear other gods. —2 *Kings* xvii. 38.

But the Lord your God ye shall fear...39.

Wherefore now let the fear of the Lord be upon you; take heed and do it: for there is no iniquity with the Lord our God.—2 *Ch.* xix. 7.

...Thus shall ye do in the fear of the Lord, faithfully, and with a perfect heart.—9.

And Jehoshaphat feared, and set himself to seek the Lord...2 *Ch.* xx. 3.

And the fear of God was on all the kingdoms of those countries, when they heard that the Lord fought against the enemies of Israel.—29.

...Ought ye not to walk in the fear of our God because of the reproach of the heathen our enemies? —*Neh.* v. 9.

...He (Hanani) was a faithful man, and feared God above many.—*Neh.* vii. 2.

And the Lord said unto Satan, Hast thou considered my servant Job, that there is none like him in the earth, a perfect and an upright man, one that feareth God, and escheweth evil?—*Job* i. 8.

...Behold, the fear of the Lord, that is wisdom; and to depart from evil is understanding.—*Job* xxviii. 28.

Men do therefore fear him: he respecteth not any that are wise of heart.—*Job* xxxvii. 24.

Serve the Lord with fear, and rejoice with trembling.—*Ps.* ii. 11.

Stand in awe, and sin not...*Ps.* iv. 4.

...He honoureth them that fear the Lord.—*Ps.* xv. 4.

The fear of the Lord is clean, enduring for ever.—*Ps.* xix. 9.

Ye that fear the Lord, praise him; all ye the seed of Jacob, glorify him; and fear him, all ye the seed of Israel.—*Ps.* xxii. 23.

What man is he that feareth the Lord? him shall he teach in the way that he shall choose.—*Ps.* xxv. 12.

The secret of the Lord is with them that fear him; and he will shew them his covenant.—14.

Oh how great is thy goodness, which thou hast laid up for them that fear thee!...*Ps.* xxxi. 19.

Let all the earth fear the Lord: let all the inhabitants of the world stand in awe of him.—*Ps.* xxxiii. 8.

Behold, the eye of the Lord is upon them that fear him...18.

The angel of the Lord encampeth round about them that fear him, and delivereth them.—*Ps.* xxxiv. 7.

O fear the Lord, ye his saints: for there is no want to them that fear him.—9.

Come, ye children, hearken unto me: I will teach you the fear of the Lord.—11.

Thou hast given a banner to them that fear thee, that it may be displayed because of the truth.—*Ps.* lx. 4.

And all men shall fear, and shall declare the work of God...*Ps.* lxiv. 9.

God shall bless us; and all the ends of the earth shall fear him.—*Ps.* lxvii. 7.

They shall fear thee as long as the sun and moon endure, throughout all generations.—*Ps.* lxxii. 5.

Thou, even thou, art to be feared: and who may stand in thy sight when once thou art angry?—*Ps.* lxxvi. 7.

Surely his salvation is nigh them that fear him; that glory may dwell in our land.—*Ps.* lxxxv. 9.

...Unite my heart to fear thy name.—*Ps.* lxxxvi. 11.

God is greatly to be feared in the assembly of the saints, and to be had in reverence of all them that are about him.—*Ps.* lxxxix. 7.

For the Lord is great, and greatly to be praised: he is to be feared above all gods.—*Ps.* xcvi. 4.

...Fear before him, all the earth.—9.

So the heathen shall fear the name of the Lord, and all the kings of the earth thy glory.—*Ps.* cii. 15.

For as the heaven is high above the earth, so great is his mercy toward them that fear him.—*Ps.* ciii. 11.

Like as a father pitieth his children, so the Lord pitieth them that fear him.—13.

The mercy of the Lord is from everlasting to everlasting upon them that fear him...17.

He hath given meat unto them that fear him.—*Ps.* cxi. 5.

The fear of the Lord is the beginning of wisdom ...10.

Blessed is the man that feareth the Lord... *Ps.* cxii. 1.

Ye that fear the Lord, trust in the Lord.... *Ps.* cxv. 11.

He will bless them that fear the Lord, both small and great.—13.

Let them now that fear the Lord say, that his mercy endureth for ever.—*Ps.* cxviii. 4.

I am a companion of all them that fear thee, and of them that keep they precepts.—*Ps.* cxix. 63.

They that fear thee will be glad when they see me; because I have hoped in thy word.—74.

Let those that fear thee turn unto me, and those that have known thy testimonies.—79.

Blessed is every one that feareth the Lord; that walketh in his ways.—*Ps.* cxxviii. 1.

For thou shalt eat the labour of thine hands: happy shalt thou be, and it shall be well with thee.—2.

...Thus shall the man be blessed that feareth the Lord.—4.

But there is forgiveness with thee, that thou mayest be feared.—*Ps.* cxxx. 4.

...Ye that fear the Lord, bless the Lord.—*Ps.* cxxxv. 20.

He will fulfil the desire of them that fear him: he also will hear their cry, and will save them.—*Ps.* cxlv. 19.

The Lord taketh pleasure in them that fear him... *Ps.* cxlvii. 11.

For that they hated knowledge, and did not choose the fear of the Lord.—*Prov.* i. 29.

Yea, if thou criest after knowledge, and liftest up thy voice for understanding;—*Prov.* ii. 3.

Then shalt thou understand the fear of the Lord, and find the knowledge of God.—5.

Fear the Lord, and depart from evil.—*Prov.* iii. 7.

The fear of the Lord is to hate evil.—*Prov.* viii. 13.

The fear of the Lord prolongeth days...*Prov.* x. 27.

Whoso despiseth the word shall be destroyed: but he that feareth the commandment shall be rewarded. —*Prov.* xiii. 13.

He that walketh in his uprightness feareth the Lord: but he that is perverse in his ways despiseth him.—*Prov.* xiv. 2.

A wise man feareth, and departeth from evil.—16.

In the fear of the Lord is strong confidence: and his children shall have a place of refuge.—26.

The fear of the Lord is a fountain of life, to depart from the snares of death.—27.

Better is little with the fear of the Lord than great treasure and trouble therewith.—*Prov.* xv. 16.

The fear of the Lord is the instruction of wisdom. —33.

...By the fear of the Lord men depart from evil.— *Prov.* xvi. 6.

The fear of the Lord tendeth to life: and he that hath it shall abide satisfied; he shall not be visited with evil.—*Prov.* xix. 23.

By humility and the fear of the Lord are riches, and honour, and life.—*Prov.* xxii. 4.

Let not thine heart envy sinners: but be thou in the fear of the Lord all the day long.—*Prov.* xxiii. 17.

Happy is the man that feareth alway: but he that hardeneth his heart shall fall into mischief.—*Prov.* xxviii. 14.

Favour is deceitful, and beauty is vain: but a woman that feareth the Lord, she shall be praised.—*Prov.* xxxi. 30.

I know that, whatsoever God doeth, it shall be for ever: nothing can be put to it, nor anything taken from it: and God doeth it, that men should fear before him.—*Eccl.* iii. 14.

...Surely I know that it shall be well with them that fear God, which fear before him.—*Eccl.* viii. 12.

...Fear God, and keep his commandments: for this is the whole duty of man.—*Eccl.* xii. 13.

Sanctify the Lord of hosts himself; and let him be your fear...*Isa.* viii. 13.

But when he seeth his children, the work of mine hands, in the midst of him, they shall sanctify my name, and sanctify the Holy One of Jacob, and shall fear the God of Israel.—*Isa.* xxix. 23.

...The fear of the Lord is his treasure.—*Isa.* xxxiii. 6.

Who is among you that feareth the Lord?...let him trust in the name of the Lord, and stay upon his God.—*Isa.* l. 10.

So shall they fear the name of the Lord from the

west, and his glory from the rising of the sun... *Isa.* lix. 19.

Fear ye not me? saith the Lord: will ye not tremble at my presence, which have placed the sand for the bound of the sea by a perpetual decree, that it cannot pass it?....*Jer.* v. 22.

Who would not fear thee, O King of nations? for to thee doth it appertain: forasmuch as among all the wise men of the nations, and in all their kingdoms, there is none like unto thee.—*Jer.* x. 7.

And I will give them one heart, and one way, that they may fear me for ever, for the good of them, and of their children after them.—*Jer.* xxxii. 39.

...I will put my fear in their hearts, that they shall not depart from me.—40.

Afterward shall the children of Israel return, and seek the Lord their God, and David their king; and shall fear the Lord and his goodness in the latter days.—*Hos.* iii. 5.

I said, Surely thou wilt fear me, thou wilt receive instruction; so their dwelling should not be cut off.—*Zeph.* iii. 7.

A son honoureth his father, and a servant his master: if then I be a father, where is mine honour? and if I be a master, where is my fear? saith the Lord of hosts unto you, O priests, that despise my name.—*Mal.* i. 6.

Then they that feared the Lord spake often one to another: and the Lord hearkened, and heard it, and a book of remembrance was written before him for them that feared the Lord, and that thought upon his name.—*Mal.* iii. 16.

And they shall be mine, saith the Lord of hosts, in that day when I make up my jewels; and I will spare them as a man spareth his own son that serveth him.—17.

But unto you that fear my name shall the Sun of righteousness arise with healing in his wings... *Mal.* iv. 2.

ADMIRE, AND MEDITATE ON THE WONDERFUL WORKS OF THE CREATOR.

———o———

And Isaac went out to meditate in the field at the eventide...*Gen.* xxiv. 63.

And Moses said, I will now turn aside, and see this great sight, why the bush is not burnt.—*Ex.* iii. 3.

And when the Lord saw that he turned aside to see, God called unto him out of the midst of the bush...4.

Who is like unto thee, O Lord, among the Gods? Who is like thee, glorious in holiness, fearful in praises, doing wonders?—*Ex.* xv. 11.

Know therefore this day, and consider it in thine heart, that the Lord he is God in heaven above, and upon the earth beneath: there is none else.—*Deut.* iv. 39.

Thou shalt also consider in thine heart, that, as a man chasteneth his son, so the Lord thy God chasteneth thee.—*Deut.* viii. 5.

Therefore shall ye lay up these my words in your heart and in your soul...*Deut.* xi. 18.

Remember the days of old, consider the years of many generations: ask thy father, and he will shew thee; thy elders, and they will tell thee.—*Deut.* xxxii. 7.

This book of the law shall not depart out of thy mouth; but thou shalt meditate therein day and night, that thou mayest observe to do according to all that is written therein....*Josh.* i. 8.

I would seek unto God, and unto God would I commit my cause:—*Job* v. 8.

Which doeth great things and unsearchable; marvellous things without number.—9.

He divideth the sea with his power....*Job* xxvi. 12.

By his spirit he hath garnished the heavens...13.

Lo, these are parts of his ways: but how little a portion is heard of him? but the thunder of his power who can understand?—14.

Hear attentively the noise of his voice, and the sound that goeth out of his mouth.—*Job* xxxvii. 2.

God thundereth marvellously with his voice; great things doeth he, which we cannot comprehend.—5.

Hearken unto this;...stand still and consider the wondrous works of God.—14.

Dost thou know the balancings of the clouds, the wondrous works of him which is perfect in knowledge?—16.

Blessed is the man that walketh not in the counsel of the ungodly,...*Ps.* i. 1.

But his delight is in the law of the Lord; and in his law doth he meditate day and night.—2.

WONDERFUL WORKS of the CREATOR.

O Lord our Lord, how excellent is thy name in all the earth! who hast set thy glory above the heavens.—*Ps.* viii. 1.

When I consider thy heavens, the work of thy fingers, the moon and the stars, which thou hast ordained;—*3*.

What is man, that thou art mindful of him? and the son of man, that thou visitest him?—*4*.

Thou madest him to have dominion over the works of thy hands; thou hast put all things under his feet:—*6*.

All sheep and oxen, yea, and the beasts of the field:—*7*.

O Lord our Lord, how excellent is thy name in all the earth!—*9*.

I will praise thee, O Lord, with my whole heart; I will shew forth all thy marvellous works.—*Ps.* ix. 1.

The heavens declare the glory of God; and the firmament sheweth his handiwork.—*Ps.* xix. 1.

Day unto day uttereth speech, and night unto night sheweth knowledge.—*2*.

There is no speech nor language, where their voice is not heard.—*3*.

Let the words of my mouth, and the meditation of my heart, be acceptable in thy sight, O Lord, my strength, and my redeemer.—*14*.

They (the wicked) regard not the works of the Lord, nor the operation of his hands...*Ps.* xxviii. 5.

For the word of the Lord is right; and all his works are done in truth.—*Ps.* xxxiii. 4.

By the word of the Lord were the heavens made; and all the host of them by the breath of his mouth.—6.

He gathereth the waters of the sea together as an heap: he layeth up the depth in storehouses.—7.

For he spake, and it was done; he commanded, and it stood fast.—9.

Many, O Lord my God, are thy wonderful works which thou hast done, and thy thoughts which are to us-ward: they cannot be reckoned up in order unto thee: if I would declare and speak of them, they are more than can be numbered.—*Ps.* xl. 5.

Come, behold the works of the Lord...*Ps.* xlvi. 8.

The mighty God, even the Lord, hath spoken, and called the earth from the rising of the sun unto the going down thereof.—*Ps.* l. 1.

Out of Zion, the perfection of beauty, God hath shined.—2.

And all men shall fear, and shall declare the work of God; for they shall wisely consider of his doing. —*Ps.* lxiv. 9.

Thou visitest the earth, and waterest it: thou greatly enrichest it with the river of God, which is full of water: thou preparest them corn, when thou hast so provided for it.—*Ps.* lxv. 9.

Thou waterest the ridges thereof abundantly: thou settlest the furrows thereof: thou makest it soft with showers: thou blessest the springing thereof.—10.

Thou crownest the year with thy goodness; and thy paths drop fatness.—*Ps*. lxv. 11.

They drop upon the pastures of the wilderness: and the little hills rejoice on every side.—12.

The pastures are clothed with flocks; the valleys also are covered over with corn; they shout for joy, they also sing.—13.

Come and see the works of God...*Ps*. lxvi. 5.

Unto thee, O God, do we give thanks, unto thee do we give thanks: for that thy name is near thy wondrous works declare.—*Ps*. lxxv. 1.

I have considered the days of old, the years of ancient times.—*Ps*. lxxvii. 5.

I call to remembrance my song in the night: I commune with mine own heart: and my spirit made diligent search.—6.

I will remember the works of the Lord: surely I will remember thy wonders of old.—11.

I will meditate also of all thy work, and talk of thy doings.—12.

Thou art the God that doest wonders: thou hast declared thy strength among the people.—14.

We will not hide them from their children, showing to the generation to come the praises of the Lord, and his strength, and his wonderful works that he hath done.—*Ps*. lxxviii. 4.

Marvellous things did he in the sight of their fathers...12.

He divided the sea, and caused them to pass through; and he made the waters to stand as an heap.—*Ps*. lxxviii. 13.

In the daytime also he led them with a cloud, and all the night with a light of fire.—14.

He clave the rocks in the wilderness, and gave them drink as out of the great depths.—15.

He brought streams also out of the rock, and caused waters to run down like rivers.—16.

...He had commanded the clouds from above, and opened the doors of heaven.—23.

And had rained down manna upon them to eat, and had given them of the corn of heaven.—24.

Let thy work appear unto thy servants, and thy glory unto their children.—*Ps*. xc. 16.

For thou, Lord, hast made me glad through thy work : I will triumph in the works of thy hands. —*Ps*. xcii. 4.

O Lord, how great are thy works! and thy thoughts are very deep.—5.

In the multitude of my thoughts within me thy comforts delight my soul.—*Ps*. xciv. 19.

In his hand are the deep places of the earth: the strength of the hills is his also.—*Ps*. xcv. 4.

The sea is his, and he made it: and his hands formed the dry land.—5.

Declare his glory among the heathen, his wonders among all people.—*Ps*. xcvi. 3.

...The Lord made the heavens.—5.

O Lord, how manifold are thy works! in wisdom hast thou made them all: the earth is full of thy riches.—*Ps.* civ. 24.

My meditation of him shall be sweet: I will be glad in the Lord.—34.

Remember his marvellous works that he hath done; his wonders, and the judgments of his mouth. *Ps.* cv. 5.

Oh that men would praise the Lord for his goodness, and for his wonderful works to the children of men!—*Ps.* cvii. 8.

They that go down to the sea in ships, that do business in great waters;—23.

These see the works of the Lord, and his wonders in the deep.—24.

The works of the Lord are great, sought out of all them that have pleasure therein.—*Ps.* cxi. 2.

His work is honourable and glorious...3.

He hath made his wonderful works to be remembered...4.

He hath shewed his people the power of his works...6.

The works of his hands are verity and judgment...7.

I will meditate in thy precepts, and have respect unto thy ways.—*Ps.* cxix. 15.

Mine eyes prevent the night watches, that I might meditate in thy word.—148.

I will praise thee; for I am fearfully and wonderfully made: marvellous are thy works: and that my soul knoweth right well.—*Ps.* cxxxix. 14.

How precious also are thy thoughts unto me, O God! how great is the sum of them!—17.

If I should count them, they are more in number than the sand: when I awake, I am still with thee.—18.

I remember the days of old; I meditate on all thy works; I muse on the work of thy hands.—*Ps.* cxliii. 5.

I will speak of the glorious honour of thy majesty, and of thy wondrous works.—*Ps.* cxlv. 5.

All thy works shall praise thee, O Lord...10.

He hath made everything beautiful in his time: also he hath set the world in their heart, so that no man can find out the work that God maketh from the beginning to the end.—*Eccl.* iii. 11.

Consider the work of God.—*Eccl.* vii. 13.

...Even so thou knowest not the works of God who maketh all.—*Eccl.* xi. 5.

Mine hand also hath laid the foundation of the earth, and my right hand hath spanned the heavens. ...*Isa.* xlviii. 13.

He hath made the earth by his power, he hath established the world by his wisdom, and hath stretched out the heavens by his discretion.—*Jer.* x. 12.

When he uttereth his voice, there is a multitude of waters in the heavens, and he causes the vapours to ascend from the ends of the earth; he maketh lightenings with rain, and bringeth forth the wind out of his treasures.—*Jer.* x. 13.

How great are his signs! and how mighty are his wonders!...*Dan.* iv. 3.

...Extol and honour the King of heaven, all whose works are truth, and his ways judgment...37.

WITH THE ALMIGHTY NOTHING IS IMPOSSIBLE.

———o———

Is anything too hard for the Lord ? At the time appointed I will return unto thee...*Gen.* xviii. 14.

And Moses said unto the Lord, O my Lord, I am not eloquent, neither heretofore, nor since thou hast spoken unto thy servant: but I am slow of speech, and of a slow tongue.—*Ex.* iv. 10.

And the Lord said unto him, Who hath made man's mouth ? or who maketh the dumb, or deaf, or the seeing, or the blind ? have not I the Lord ?—11.

Now therefore go, and I will be with thy mouth, and teach thee what thou shalt say.—12.

Then the Lord said unto Moses, Now shalt thou see what I will do to Pharaoh: for with a strong hand shall he let them go, and with a strong hand shall he drive them out of his land.—*Ex.* vi. 1.

Wherefore say unto the children of Israel, I am the Lord, and I will bring you out from under the burdens of the Egyptians, and I will rid you out of their bondage, and I will redeem you with a stretched out arm, and with great judgments.—6.

And the Egyptians shall know that I am the Lord, when I stretch forth mine hand upon Egypt, and bring out the children of Israel from among them. *Ex*. vii. 5.

And it came to pass, that at midnight the Lord smote all the firstborn in the land of Egypt, from the firstborn of Pharaoh that sat on his throne unto the firstborn of the captive that was in the dungeon; and all the firstborn of cattle.—*Ex*. xii. 29.

And Moses said unto the people, Fear ye not, stand still, and see the salvation of the Lord, which he will shew to you to day: for the Egyptians whom ye have seen to day, ye shall see them again no more for ever.—*Ex*. xiv. 13.

The Lord shall fight for you, and ye shall hold your peace.—14.

And Moses stretched out his hand over the sea; and the Lord caused the sea to go back by a strong east wind all that night, and made the sea dry land, and the waters were divided.—21.

...And the Lord overthrew the Egyptians in the midst of the sea.—27.

But the children of Israel walked upon dry land in the midst of the sea; and the waters were a wall unto them on their right hand, and on their left.—29.

And Israel saw that great work which the Lord did upon the Egyptians: and the people feared the the Lord, and believed the Lord, and his servant Moses.—31.

Thy right hand, O Lord, is become glorious in power...*Ex.* xv. 6.

And the Lord said unto Moses, Is the Lord's hand waxed short ? thou shalt see now whether my word shall come to pass unto thee or not.—*Num.* xi. 23.

God is not a man, that he should lie;...hath he said, and shall he not do it ? or hath he spoken, and shall he not make it good ?—*Num.* xxiii. 19.

O Lord God, thou hast begun to shew thy servant thy greatness, and thy mighty hand: for what God is there in heaven or in earth, that can do according to thy works, and according to thy might ?—*Deut.* iii. 24.

...It may be that the Lord will work for us: for there is no restraint to the Lord to save by many or by few.—1 *Sam.* xiv. 6.

David said moreover, The Lord that delivered me out of the paw of the lion, and out of the paw of the bear, he will deliver me out of the hand of this Philistine. And Saul said unto David, Go, and the Lord be with thee.—1 *Sam.* xvii. 37.

And all this assembly shall know that the Lord saveth not with sword and spear: for the battle is the Lord's, and he will give you into our hands.—47.

And Asa cried unto the Lord his God, and said, Lord, it is nothing with thee to help, whether with many, or with them that have no power: help us, O Lord our God; for we rest on thee, and in thy name

NOTHING IS IMPOSSIBLE. 103

we go against this multitude. O Lord, thou art our God; let not man prevail against thee.—2 *Ch.* xiv. 11.

...Art not thou God in heaven? and rulest not thou over all the kingdoms of the heathen? and in thine hand is there not power and might, so that none is able to withstand thee?—2 *Ch.* xx. 6.

...God shall make thee fall before the enemy: for God hath power to help, and to cast down.—2 *Ch.* xxv. 8.

And Amaziah said to the man of God, But what shall we do for the hundred talents which I have given to the army of Israel? And the man of God answered, The Lord is able to give thee much more than this.—9.

...Be not afraid nor dismayed for the king of Assyria, nor for all the multitude that is with him: for there be more with us than with him:—2 *Ch.* xxxii. 7.

With him is an arm of flesh; but with us is the Lord our God to help us, and to fight our battles. And the people rested themselves upon the words of Hezekiah.—8.

...Great things doeth he, which we cannot comprehend.—*Job* xxxvii. 5.

I know that thou canst do everything.—*Job* xlii. 1.

And they tempted God in their heart by asking meat.—*Ps.* lxxviii. 18.

Yea, they spake against God; they said, Can God furnish a table in the wilderness?—19.

Behold, he smote the rock, that the waters gushed

out, and the streams overflowed; can he give bread also? can he provide flesh for his people?—*Ps.* lxxviii. 20.

Though he had commanded the clouds from above, and opened the doors of heaven.—23.

And had rained down manna upon them to eat, and had given them of the corn of heaven.—24.

Man did eat angels' food: he sent them meat to the full.—25.

Whatsoever the Lord pleased, that did he in heaven, and in earth, in the seas, and all deep places.—*Ps.* cxxxv. 6.

Behold,...he taketh up the isles as a very little thing.—*Isa.* xl. 15.

I will bring the blind by a way that they knew not; I will lead them in paths that they have not known: I will make darkness light before them, and crooked things straight....*Isa.* xlii. 16.

Yea, before the day was I am he; and there is none that can deliver out of my hand: I will work, and who shall let it?—*Isa.* xliii. 13.

...Is my hand shortened at all, that it cannot redeem? or have I no power to deliver? Behold, at my rebuke I dry up the sea, I make the rivers a wilderness.—*Isa.* l. 2.

Behold, the Lord's hand is not shortened, that it cannot save; neither his ear heavy, that it cannot hear.—*Isa.* lix. 1.

Ah Lord God! behold, thou hast made the heaven

NOTHING IS IMPOSSIBLE.

and the earth by thy great power and stretched out arm, and there is nothing too hard for thee.—*Jer.* xxxii. 17.

Behold, I am the Lord, the God of all flesh: is there anything too hard for me?—27.

Who is he that saith, and it cometh to pass, when the Lord commandeth it not?—*Lam.* iii. 37.

If it be so, our God whom we serve is able to deliver us from the burning fiery furnace, and he will deliver us out of thine hand, O king.—*Dan.* iii. 17.

...There is no other God that can deliver after this sort.—29.

He delivereth and rescueth, and he worketh signs and wonders in heaven and in earth, who hath delivered Daniel from the power of the lions.—*Dan.* vi. 27.

GOD'S OVERRULING PROVIDENCE AND INTERPOSITION.

---o---

...And the Lord had blessed Abraham in all things.
—*Gen.* xxiv. 1.

And Abraham said unto his eldest servant of his house,...2.

...Thou shalt go unto my country, and to my kindred, and take a wife unto my son Isaac.—4.

And Abraham said unto him,...6.

The Lord God of heaven, which took me from my father's house,...he shall send his angel before thee, and thou shalt take a wife unto my son from thence.—7.

And he (the servant) said, O Lord God of my master Abraham, I pray thee, send me good speed this day, and shew kindness unto my master Abraham.—12.

And let it come to pass, that the damsel to whom I shall say, Let down thy pitcher, I pray thee, that I may drink; and she shall say, Drink, and I will give thy camels drink also: let the same be she that thou hast appointed for thy servant Isaac; and thereby shall I know that thou hast shewed kindness unto my master.—*Gen.* xxiv. 14.

And it came to pass, before he had done speaking, that, behold, Rebekah came out, who was born to Bethuel, son of Milcah, the wife of Nahor, Abraham's brother, with her pitcher upon her shoulder.—15.

And she said, Drink, my lord: and she hasted, and let down her pitcher upon her hand, and gave him drink.—18.

And when she had done giving him drink, she said, I will draw water for thy camels also, until they have done drinking.—19.

And the man wondering at her held his peace, to wit whether the Lord had made his journey prosperous or not.—21.

And said, Whose daughter art thou?...23.

And she said unto him, I am the daughter of Bethuel...24.

And the man bowed down his head, and worshipped the Lord.—26.

And he said, Blessed be the Lord God of my master Abraham, who hath not left destitute my master of his mercy and his truth: I being in the way, the Lord led me to the house of my master's brethren.—27.

Now Israel loved Joseph more than all his children, because he was the son of his old age: and he made him a coat of many colours.—*Gen.* xxxvii. 3.

And his brethren envied him...*Gen.* xxxvii. 11.

And Israel said unto Joseph, Do not thy brethren feed the flock in Shechem? come, and I will send thee unto them. And he said to him, Here am I.—13.

...And Joseph went after his brethren, and found them in Dothan.—17.

And when they saw him afar off,...they conspired against him to slay him.—18.

And Reuben heard it, and he delivered him out of their hands; and said, Let us not kill him.—21.

And they took him, and cast him into a pit: and the pit was empty, there was no water in it.—24.

And Judah said unto his brethren, What profit is it if we slay our brother, and conceal his blood?—26.

Then there passed by Midianites merchantmen; and they drew and lifted up Joseph out of the pit, and sold Joseph to the Ishmeelites:...and they brought Joseph into Egypt.—28.

And the Lord was with Joseph, and he was a prosperous man;—*Gen.* xxxix. 2.

And his master saw that the Lord was with him, and that the Lord made all that he did to prosper in his hand.—3.

And when all the land of Egypt was famished, the people cried to Pharaoh for bread: and Pharaoh said unto all the Egyptians, Go unto Joseph; what he saith to you, do.—*Gen.* xli. 55.

Now when Jacob saw that there was corn in

Egypt, Jacob said unto his sons, Why do ye look one upon another?—*Gen.* xlii. 1.

And he said, Behold, I have heard that there is corn in Egypt: get you down thither, and buy for us from thence; that we may live and not die.—2.

And Joseph's ten brethren went down to buy corn in Egypt.—3.

And Joseph was the governor over the land, and he it was that sold to all the people of the land: and Joseph's brethren came, and bowed down themselves before him with their faces to the earth.—6.

And Joseph knew his brethren, but they knew not him.—8.

And Joseph said unto his brethren, Come near to me, I pray you. And they came near. And he said, I am Joseph your brother, whom ye sold into Egypt. —*Gen.* xlv. 4.

Now therefore be not grieved, nor angry with yourselves, that ye sold me hither: for God did send me before you to preserve life.—5.

And God sent me before you to preserve you a posterity in the earth, and to save your lives by a great deliverance.—7.

So now it was not you that sent me hither, but God: and he hath made me a father to Pharaoh, and lord of all his house, and a ruler throughout all the land of Egypt.—8.

But as for you, ye thought evil against me; but

God meant it unto good, to bring to pass, as it is this day, to save much people alive.—*Gen.* 1. 20.

And there went a man of the house of Levi, and took to wife a daughter of Levi.—*Ex.* ii. 1.

And the woman conceived, and bare a son: and when she saw him that he was a goodly child, she hid him three months.—2.

And when she could not longer hide him, she took for him an ark of bulrushes,...and she laid it in the flags by the river's brink.—3.

And the daughter of Pharaoh came down to wash herself at the river...and when she saw the ark among the flags, she sent her maid to fetch it.—5.

And when she had opened it, she saw the child: and, behold, the babe wept. And she had compassion on him, and said, This is one of the Hebrews' children.—6.

Then said his sister to Pharaoh's daughter, Shall I go and call to thee a nurse of the Hebrew women, that she may nurse the child for thee?—7.

And Pharaoh's daughter said to her, Go. And the maid went and called the child's mother.—8.

And Pharaoh's daughter said unto her, Take this child away, and nurse it for me, and I will give thee thy wages. And the woman took the child, and nursed it.—9.

And the child grew, and she brought him unto

Pharaoh's daughter, and he became her son. And she called his name Moses: and she said, Because I drew him out of the water.—*Ex.* ii. 10.

And the Lord said, I have surely seen the affliction of my people which are in Egypt....*Ex.* iii. 7.

And I am come down to deliver them out of the hand of the Egyptians, and to bring them up out of that land unto a good land and a large, unto a land flowing with milk and honey...8.

Come now therefore, and I will send thee unto Pharaoh,...10.

And Moses said unto God, Who am I, that I should go unto Pharaoh, and that I should bring forth the children of Israel out of Egypt?—11.

And he said, Certainly I will be with thee...12.

Wherefore say unto the children of Israel, I am the Lord, and I will bring you out from under the burdens of the Egyptians, and I will rid you out of their bondage, and I will redeem you with a stretched out arm, and with great judgments:—*Ex.* vi. 6.

And I will take you to me for a people, and I will be to you a God: and ye shall know that I am the Lord your God, which bringeth you out from under the burdens of the Egyptians.—7.

And the Egyptians shall know that I am the Lord, when I stretch forth mine hand upon Egypt, and bring out the children of Israel from among them.—*Ex.* vii. 5.

When Pharaoh shall speak unto you, saying, Shew

a miracle for you: then thou shalt say unto Aaron, Take thy rod, and cast it before Pharaoh, and it shall become a serpent.—Ex. vii. 9.

Then Pharaoh also called the wise men and the sorcerers: now the magicians of Egypt, they also did in like manner with their enchantments.—11.

And the Lord spake unto Moses, Say unto Aaron, Take thy rod, and stretch out thine hand upon the waters of Egypt, upon their streams, upon their rivers, and upon their ponds, and upon all their pools of water, that they may become blood; and that there may be blood throughout all the land of Egypt, both in vessels of wood, and in vessels of stone.—19.

Then the magicians said unto Pharaoh, This is the finger of God...Ex. viii. 19.

Behold, I send an angel before thee, to keep thee in the way, and to bring thee into the place which I have prepared.—Ex. xxiii. 20.

The Lord your God which goeth before you, he shall fight for you, according to all that he did for you in Egypt before your eyes;—Deut. i. 30.

And in the wilderness, where thou hast seen how that the Lord thy God bare thee, as a man doth bare his son, in all the way that ye went, until ye came into this place.—31.

...The Lord thy God is with thee whithersoever thou goest.—Josh. i. 9.

...Thus saith the Lord of hosts, I took thee from the sheepcote, from following the sheep, to be ruler over my people, over Israel:—2 *Sam.* vii. 8.

And I was with thee whithersoever thou wentest...9.

And the word of the Lord came unto him, (Elijah) saying,—1 *Kings* xvii. 2.

Get thee hence, and turn thee eastward, and hide thyself by the brook Cherith, that is before Jordan.—3.

And it shall be, that thou shalt drink of the brook; and I have commanded the ravens to feed thee there.—4.

So he went and did according unto the word of the Lord...5.

And the ravens brought him bread and flesh in the morning, and bread and flesh in the evening; and he drank of the brook.—6.

And it came to pass after a while, that the brook dried up, because there had been no rain in the land.—7.

And the word of the Lord came unto him, saying.—8.

Arise, get thee to Zarephath,...behold, I have commanded a widow woman there to sustain thee.—9.

So he arose and went to Zarephath. And when he came to the gate of the city, behold, the widow woman was there...and he called to her, and said...10.

...Bring me, I pray thee, a morsel of bread in thine hand.—11.

And she said, As the Lord thy God liveth, I have

not a cake, but an handful of meal in a barrel, and a little oil in a cruse: and, behold, I am gathering two sticks, that I may go in and dress it for me and my son, that we may eat it, and die.—1 *Kings* xvii. 12.

And Elijah said unto her, Fear not; go and do as thou hast said: but make me thereof a little cake first,...13.

For thus saith the Lord God of Israel, The barrel of meal shall not waste, neither shall the cruse of oil fail, until the day that the Lord sendeth rain upon the earth.—14.

And the barrel of meal wasted not, neither did the cruse of oil fail, according to the word of the Lord, which he spake by Elijah.—16.

And it came to pass, that when all our enemies heard thereof, and all the heathen that were about us saw these things, they were much cast down in their own eyes: for they perceived that this work was wrought of our God.—*Neh.* vi. 16.

Now in Shushan the palace there was a certain Jew, whose name was Mordecai,...*Est.* ii. 5.

Who had been carried away from Jerusalem...6.

And he brought up Esther, his uncle's daughter: for she had neither father nor mother, and the maid was fair and beautiful;...7.

So it came to pass, when the king's commandment and his decree was heard, and when many maidens were gathered together unto Shushan,...that Esther was brought also unto the king's house...*Est.* ii. 8.

And the maiden pleased him, and she obtained kindness of him...9.

Esther had not shewed her people nor her kindred: for Mordecai had charged her that she should not shew it.—10.

...And Esther had obtained favour in the sight of all them that looked upon her.—15.

And the king loved Esther above all the women, and she obtained grace and favour in his sight more than all the virgins; so that he set the royal crown upon her head, and made her queen instead of Vashti.—17.

In those days, while Mordecai sat in the king's gate, two of the king's chamberlains, of those which kept the door, were wroth, and sought to lay hand on the king Ahasuerus.—21.

And the thing was known to Mordecai, who told it unto Esther the queen; and Esther certified the king thereof in Mordecai's name.—22.

And when inquisition was made of the matter, it was found out; therefore they were both hanged on a tree: and it was written in the book of the chronicles before the king.—23.

After these things did king Ahasuerus promote Haman and advanced him, and set his seat above all the princes that were with him.—*Est.* iii. 1.

And all the king's servants, that were in the king's

gate, bowed, and reverenced Haman :...But Mordecai bowed not...*Est.* iii. 2.

And when Haman saw that Mordecai bowed not, ...then was Haman full of wroth.—5.

And he thought scorn to lay hands on Mordecai alone; for they had shewed him the people of Mordecai: wherefore Haman sought to destroy all the Jews that were throughout the whole kingdom of Ahasuerus, even the people of Mordecai.—6.

...And the king and Haman sat down to drink; but the city Shushan was perplexed.—15.

When Mordecai perceived all that was done, Mordecai rent his clothes, and put on sackcloth with ashes, and went out into the midst of the city, and cried with a loud and a bitter cry.—*Est.* iv. 1.

So Esther's maids...came and told it her. Then was the queen exceedingly grieved; and she sent raiment to clothe Mordecai, and to take away his sackcloth from him : but he received it not.—4.

Then called Esther for Hatach,...to know what it was, and why it was.—5.

And Mordecai told him of all that had happened unto him, and of the sum of the money that Haman had promised to pay to the king's treasuries for the Jews, to destroy them.—7.

Then Mordecai commanded to answer Esther, Think not with thyself that thou shalt escape in the king's house, more than all the Jews.—13.

AND INTERPOSITION. 117

...And who knoweth whether thou art come to the kingdom for such a time as this?—*Est.* iv. 14.

On that night could not the king sleep, and he commanded to bring the book of records of the chronicles; and they were read before the king.—*Est.* vi. 1.

And it was found written, that Mordecai had told of two of the king's chamberlains,...who sought to lay hand on the king Ahasuerus.—2.

And the king said, what honour and dignity hath been done to Mordecai for this? Then said the king's servants,...There is nothing done for him.—3.

...Haman came in. And the king said unto him, What shall be done unto the man whom the king delighteth to honour?...6.

And Haman answered the king, For the man whom the king delighteth to honour,—7.

Let the royal apparel be brought which the king useth to wear, and the horse that the king rideth upon, and the crown royal which is set upon his head.—8.

Then the king said to Haman, Make haste, and take the apparel and the horse, as thou hast said, and do even so to Mordecai the Jew, that sitteth at the king's gate: let nothing fail of all that thou hast spoken.—10.

And Mordecai came again to the king's gate. But Haman hasted to his house mourning...12.

...So they hanged Haman on the gallows that he had prepared for Mordecai...*Est.* vii. 10.

And Mordecai went out from the presence of the king in royal apparel...and the city of Shushan rejoiced and was glad.—*Est.* viii. 15.

The Jews had light, and gladness, and joy, and honour.—16.

...In the day that the enemies of the Jews hoped to have power over them, (though it was turned to the contrary, that the Jews had rule over them that hated them.)—*Est.* ix. 1.

He disappointeth the devices of the crafty, so that their hands cannot perform their enterprise.—*Job* v. 12.

He taketh the wise in their own craftiness: and the counsel of the froward is carried headlong.—13.

Who knoweth not in all these that the hand of the Lord hath wrought this?—*Job* xii. 9.

In whose hand is the soul of every living thing, and the breath of all mankind.—10.

He putteth down one, and setteth up another.—*Ps.* lxxv. 7.

There are many devices in a man's heart; nevertheless the counsel of the Lord, that shall stand.—*Prov.* xix. 21.

The lot is cast into the lap; but the whole disposing thereof is of the Lord.—*Prov.* xvi. 33.

As birds flying, so will the Lord of hosts defend Jerusalem; defending also he will deliver it; and passing over he will preserve it.—*Isa.* xxxi. 5.

Therefore thus saith the Lord concerning the king of Assyria, He shall not come into this city, nor shoot an arrow there, nor come before it with shields,...*Isa.* xxxvii. 33.

For I will defend this city to save it for mine own sake, and for my servant David's sake.—35.

Then the angel of the Lord went forth, and smote in the camp of the Assyrians a hundred and fourscore and five thousand: and when they arose early in the morning, behold, they were all dead corpses.—36.

Who raised up the righteous man from the east, called him to his foot, gave the nations before him, and made him rule over kings? he gave them as the dust to his sword, and as driven stubble to his bow. —*Isa.* xli. 2.

Who hath wrought and done it, calling the generations from the beginning? I the Lord, the first, and with the last; I am he.—4.

...For your sake I have sent to Babylon, and have brought down all their nobles, and the Chaldeans, whose cry is in the ships.—*Isa.* xliii. 14.

I have raised him up in righteousness, and I will direct all his ways: he shall build my city, and he shall let go my captives, not for price nor reward, saith the Lord of hosts.—*Isa.* xlv. 13.

...The Lord hath loved him: he will do his pleasure on Babylon, and his arm shall be on the Chaldeans. —*Isa.* xlviii. 14.

I, even I, have spoken; yea, I have called him: I have brought him, and he shall make his way prosperous.—*Isa.* xlviii. 15.

Therefore thus saith the Lord God; Behold, I will give the land of Egypt unto Nebuchadnezzar king of Babylon; and he shall take her multitude, and take her spoil, and take her prey; and it shall be the wages for his army.—*Ezek.* xxix. 19.

I have given him the land of Egypt for his labour wherewith he served against it, because they wrought for me, saith the Lord God.—20.

And He changeth the times and the seasons: he removeth kings, and setteth up kings...*Dan.* ii. 21.

...These three men Shadrach, Meshach, and Abednego, fell down bound into the midst of the burning fiery furnace.—*Dan.* iii. 23.

Then Nebuchadnezzar the king was astonished, and rose up in haste, and spake, and said unto his counsellors, Did not we cast three men bound into the midst of the fire?...24.

...Lo, I see four men loose, walking in the midst of the fire, and they have no hurt...25.

...Blessed be the God of Shadrach, Meshach, and Abednego, who hath sent his angel, and delivered his servants that trusted in him:...28.

...There is no other God that can deliver after this sort.—29.

They drank wine, and praised the gods of gold, and of silver,...*Dan.* v. 4.

In the same hour came forth fingers of a man's hand, and wrote over against the candlestick upon the plaister of the wall of the king's palace: and the king saw the part of the hand that wrote.—*Dan.* v. 5.

Then the king's countenance was changed, and his thoughts troubled him, so that the joints of his loins were loosed, and his knees smote one against another.—6.

Then Daniel answered and said before the king,...17.

O thou king, the most high God gave Nebuchadnezzar thy father a kingdom, and majesty, and glory, and honour :—18.

But when his heart was lifted up...he was deposed from his kingly throne, and they took his glory from him :—20.

And he was driven from the sons of men ;...till he knew that the most high God ruled in the kingdom of men, and that he appointeth over it whomsoever he will.—21.

Then the king (Darius) commanded, and they brought Daniel, and cast him into the den of lions. Now the king spake and said unto Daniel, Thy God whom thou servest continually, he will deliver thee.
—*Dan.* vi. 16.

Then the king arose very early in the morning, and went in haste unto the den of lions.—19.

...And the king spake and said to Daniel, O Daniel, servant of the living God, is thy God, whom thou servest continually, able to deliver thee from the lions?—*Dan.* vi. 20.

Then said Daniel unto the king...21.

My God hath sent his angel, and hath shut the lions' mouths, that they have not hurt me...22.

REJOICE IN THE LORD: SERVE HIM CHEERFULLY.

———o———

And Jethro rejoiced for all the goodness which the Lord had done to Israel...*Ex.* xviii. 9.

...Ye shall rejoice in all that ye put your hand unto, ye and your households, wherein the Lord thy God hath blessed thee.—*Deut.* xii. 7.

And thou shalt rejoice before the Lord thy God, thou, and thy son, and thy daughter, and thy manservant, and thy maidservant, and the Levite that is within thy gates, and the stranger, and the fatherless, and the widow, that are among you, in the place which the Lord thy God hath chosen to place his name there.—*Deut.* xvi. 11.

And thou shalt rejoice in thy feast...14.

...Because the Lord thy God shall bless thee in all thine increase, and in all the works of thine hands, therefore thou shalt surely rejoice.—15.

And thou shalt rejoice in every good thing which the Lord thy God hath given unto thee, and unto thine house, thou, and the Levite, and the stranger that is among you.—*Deut.* xxvi. 11.

And thou shalt offer peace offerings, and shalt eat there, and rejoice before the Lord thy God.—*Deut.* xxvii. 7.

My heart rejoiceth in the Lord, mine horn is exalted in the Lord:...I rejoice in thy salvation.—1 *Sam.* ii. 1.

...And the Lord wrought a great salvation for all Israel: thou sawest it, and didst rejoice.—1 *Sam.* xix. 5.

...They blessed the king, and went unto their tents joyful and glad of heart for all the goodness that the Lord had done for David his servant, and for Israel his people.—1 *Kings* viii. 66.

Glory and honour are in his presence; strength and gladness are in his place.—1 *Ch.* xvi. 27.

Let the heavens be glad, and let the earth rejoice...31.

Then the people rejoiced, for that they offered willingly, because with perfect heart they offered willingly to the Lord: and David the king also rejoiced with great joy.—1 *Ch.* xxix. 9.

...As for me, in the uprightness of mine heart I have willingly offered all these things: and now have I seen with joy thy people, which are present here, to offer willingly unto thee.—17.

...And they sang praises with gladness, and they bowed their heads and worshipped.—2 *Ch.* xxix. 30.

And Hezekiah spake comfortably unto all the

Levites that taught the good knowledge of the Lord :...2 *Ch.* xxx. 22.

And the whole assembly took counsel to keep other seven days: and they kept other seven days with gladness.—23.

...And all the congregation that came out of Israel, and the strangers that came out of the land of Israel, and that dwelt in Judah, rejoiced.—25.

So there was great joy in Jerusalem: for since the time of Solomon...there was not the like in Jerusalem.—26.

...And all the people shouted with a great shout, when they praised the Lord, because the foundation of the house of the Lord was laid.—*Ezra* iii. 11.

But many of the priests and Levites...that had seen the first house, when the foundation of this house was laid before their eyes, wept with a loud voice; and many shouted aloud for joy:—12.

So that the people could not discern the noise of the shout of joy from the noise of the weeping of the people: for the people shouted with a loud shout, and the noise was heard afar off.—13.

...And kept the feast of unleavened bread seven days with joy: for the Lord had made them joyful... *Ezra* vi. 22.

And Nehemiah...said unto all the people, This day is holy unto the Lord your God; mourn not, nor weep. For all the people wept, when they heard the words of the law.—*Neh.* viii. 9.

Then he said unto them, Go your way, eat the fat, and drink the sweet, and send portions unto them for whom nothing is prepared: for this day is holy unto our Lord: neither be ye sorry; for the joy of the Lord is your strength.—*Neh.* viii. 10.

So the Levites stilled all the people, saying, Hold your peace, for the day is holy; neither be ye grieved.—11.

And all the people went their way to eat, and to drink, and to send portions, and to make great mirth, because they had understood the words that were declared unto them.—12.

...And there was very great gladness.—17.

Also that day they offered great sacrifices, and rejoiced: for God had made them rejoice with great joy: the wives also and the children rejoiced: so that the joy of Jerusalem was heard even afar off.—*Neh.* xii. 43.

...And the city of Shushan rejoiced and was glad. —*Est.* viii. 15.

The Jews had light, and gladness, and joy, and honour.—16.

And in every province, and in every city, whithersoever the king's commandment and his decree came, the Jews had joy and gladness...17.

...Then shalt thou have thy delight in the Almighty, and shalt lift up thy face unto God.—*Job* xxii. 26.

He shall pray unto God, and he will be favourable

unto him: and he shall see his face with joy...*Job* xxxiii. 26.

Blessed is the man that walketh not in the counsel of the ungodly...*Ps.* i. 1.

But his delight is in the law of the Lord...2.

Thou hast put gladness in my heart, more than in the time that their corn and their wine increased.—*Ps.* iv. 7.

But let all those that put their trust in thee rejoice: let them ever shout for joy, because thou defendest them: let them also that love thy name be joyful in thee.—*Ps.* v. 11.

I will be glad and rejoice in thee...*Ps.* ix. 2.

...I will rejoice in thy salvation.—14.

But I have trusted in thy mercy; my heart shall rejoice in thy salvation.—*Ps.* xiii. 5.

I will sing unto the Lord, because he hath dealt bountifully with me.—6.

...When the Lord bringeth back the captivity of his people, Jacob shall rejoice, and Israel shall be glad. —*Ps.* xiv. 7.

I have set the Lord always before me: because he is at my right hand, I shall not be moved.—*Ps.* xvi. 8.

Therefore my heart is glad, and my glory rejoiceth:...9.

...In thy presence is fulness of joy; at thy right hand there are pleasures for evermore.—11.

The statutes of the Lord are right, rejoicing the heart...*Ps.* xix. 8.

We will rejoice in thy salvation, and in the name of our God we will set up our banners.—*Ps.* xx. 5.

The king shall joy in thy strength, O Lord; and in thy salvation how greatly shall he rejoice!—*Ps.* xxi. 1.

For thou hast made him most blessed for ever; thou hast made him exceeding glad with thy countenance.—6.

He maketh me to lie down in green pastures: he leadeth me beside the still waters.—*Ps.* xxiii. 2.

...Therefore will I offer in his tabernacle sacrifices of joy; I will sing, yea, I will sing praises unto the Lord.—*Ps.* xxvii. 6.

...My heart trusted in him, and I am helped: therefore my heart greatly rejoiceth; and with my song will I praise him.—*Ps.* xxviii. 7.

...Weeping may endure for a night, but joy cometh in the morning.—*Ps.* xxx. 5.

Thou hast turned for me my morning into dancing: thou hast put off my sackcloth, and girded me with gladness.—11.

I will be glad and rejoice in thy mercy...*Ps.* xxxi. 7.

Be glad in the Lord, and rejoice, ye righteous: and shout for joy all ye that are upright in heart. —*Ps.* xxxii. 11.

Rejoice in the Lord, O ye righteous...*Ps.* xxxiii. 1.

For our heart shall rejoice in him, because we have trusted in his holy name.—21.

My soul shall make her boast in the Lord: the humble shall hear thereof, and be glad.—*Ps.* xxxiv. 2.

And my soul shall be joyful in the Lord: it shall rejoice in his salvation.—*Ps.* xxxv. 9.

Let them shout for joy, and be glad, that favour my righteous cause...27.

Delight thyself also in the Lord; and he shall give thee the desires of thine heart.—*Ps.* xxxvii. 4.

I delight to do thy will, O my God...*Ps.* xl. 8.

Let all those that seek thee rejoice and be glad in thee...16.

...I went with them to the house of God, with the voice of joy and praise, with a multitude that kept holyday.—*Ps.* xlii. 4.

Then will I go unto the altar of God, unto God my exceeding joy:...*Ps.* xliii. 4.

Why art thou cast down, O my soul? and why art thou disquieted within me? hope in God: for I shall yet praise him, who is the health of my countenance, and my God.—5.

Thou lovest righteousness, and hatest wickedness: therefore God, thy God, hath anointed thee with the oil of gladness above thy fellows.—*Ps.* xlv. 7.

With gladness and rejoicing shall they be brought. ...15.

There is a river, the streams whereof shall make glad the city of God.—*Ps.* xlvi. 4.

My soul shall be satisfied as with marrow and fat-

ness; and my mouth shall praise thee with joyful lips.
—*Ps.* lxiii. 5.

Because thou hast been my help, therefore in the shadow of thy wings will I rejoice.—7.

The king shall rejoice in God; every one that sweareth by him shall glory...11.

The righteous shall be glad in the Lord,...and all the upright in heart shall glory.—*Ps.* lxiv. 10.

...Thou makest the outgoings of the morning and evening to rejoice.—*Ps.* lxv. 8.

The pastures are clothed with flocks; the valleys also are covered over with corn; they shout for joy, they also sing.—13.

Make a joyful noise unto God, all ye lands.—*Ps.* lxvi. 1.

O let the nations be glad and sing for joy...*Ps.* lxvii. 4.

But let the righteous be glad; let them rejoice before God: yea, let them exceedingly rejoice.—*Ps.* lxviii. 3.

...Extol him that rideth upon the heavens by his name JAH, and rejoice before him.—4.

Let all those that seek thee rejoice and be glad in thee.—*Ps.* lxx. 4.

My lips shall greatly rejoice when I sing unto thee; and my soul, which thou hast redeemed.—*Ps.* lxxi. 23.

...Make a joyful noise unto the God of Jacob.—*Ps.* lxxxi. 1.

Wilt thou not revive us again: that thy people may rejoice in thee?—*Ps.* lxxxv. 6.

...Tabor and Herman shall rejoice in thy name. —*Ps.* lxxxix. 12.

In thy name shall they rejoice all the day.—16.

In the multitude of my thoughts within me thy comforts delight my soul.—*Ps.* xciv. 19.

O come, let us sing unto the Lord: let us make a joyful noise to the rock of our salvation.—*Ps.* xcv. 1.

Let the heavens rejoice, and let the earth be glad; ...*Ps.* xcvi. 11.

Let the field be joyful, and all that is therein: then shall all the trees of the wood rejoice.—12.

The Lord reigneth; let the earth rejoice; let the multitude of isles be glad thereof.—*Ps.* xcvii. 1.

Zion heard, and was glad; and the daughters of Judah rejoiced because of thy judgments, O Lord.—8.

Light is sown for the righteous, and gladness for the upright in heart.—11.

Rejoice in the Lord, ye righteous...12.

Make a joyful noise unto the Lord, all the earth: make a loud noise, and rejoice, and sing praise.—*Ps.* xcviii. 4.

Let the floods clap their hands: let the hills be joyful together.—8.

Serve the Lord with gladness: come before his presence with singing.—*Ps.* c. 2.

...I will be glad in the Lord.—*Ps.* civ. 34.

Glory ye in his holy name: let the heart of them rejoice that seek the Lord.—*Ps.* cv. 3.

...Declare his works with rejoicing.—*Ps.* cvii. 22.

The voice of rejoicing and salvation is in the tabernacles of the righteous...*Ps.* cxviii. 15.

I have rejoiced in the way of thy testimonies, as much as in all riches.—*Ps.* cxix. 14.

I will delight myself in thy statutes...16.

Thy testimonies also are my delight and my counsellors.—24.

And I will delight myself in thy commandments, which I have loved.—47.

Thy testimonies have I taken as an heritage for ever: for they are the rejoicing of my heart.—111.

I rejoice at thy word, as one that findeth great spoil.—162.

The Lord hath done great things for us; whereof we are glad.—*Ps.* cxxvi. 3.

They that sow in tears shall reap in joy.—5.

He that goeth forth and weepeth, bearing precious seed, shall doubtless come again with rejoicing, bringing his sheaves with him.—6.

I will also clothe her priests with salvation: and her saints shall shout aloud for joy.—*Ps.* cxxxii. 16.

Let Israel rejoice in him that made him: let the children of Zion be joyful in their king.—*Ps.* cxlix. 2.

Let the saints be joyful in glory: let them sing aloud upon their beds.—5.

The hope of the righteous shall be gladness... *Prov.* x. 28.

The light of the righteous rejoiceth...*Prov.* xiii. 9.

For God giveth to a man that is good in his sight wisdom, and knowledge, and joy...*Eccl.* ii. 26.

I know that there is no good in them, but for a man to rejoice, and to do good in his life.—*Eccl.* iii. 12.

...The Lord JEHOVAH is my strength and my song;...*Isa.* xii. 2.

Therefore with joy shall ye draw water out of the wells of salvation.—3.

The whole earth is at rest, and is quiet: they break forth into singing.—*Isa.* xiv. 7.

Yea, the fir trees rejoice at thee...8.

...This is the Lord; we have waited for him, we will be glad and rejoice in his salvation.—*Isa.* xxv. 9.

The meek also shall increase their joy in the Lord, and the poor among men shall rejoice in the Holy One of Israel.—*Isa.* xxix. 19.

Ye shall have a song, as in the night when a holy solemnity is kept; and gladness of heart...*Isa.* xxx. 29.

...And thou shalt rejoice in the Lord, and shalt glory in the Holy One of Israel.—*Isa.* xli. 16.

Therefore the redeemed of the Lord shall return, and come with singing unto Zion; and everlasting joy shall be upon their head: they shall obtain gladness and joy; and sorrow and mourning shall flee away.—*Isa.* li. 11.

Break forth into joy, sing together ... for the Lord hath comforted his people, he hath redeemed Jerusalem.—*Isa.* lii. 9.

Even them will I bring to my holy mountain, and make them joyful in my house of prayer...*Isa.* lvi. 7.

Then shalt thou delight thyself in the Lord...*Isa.* lviii. 14.

I will greatly rejoice in the Lord, my soul shall be joyful in my God...*Isa.* lxi. 10.

Behold, my servants shall sing for joy of heart...*Isa.* lxv. 14.

But be ye glad and rejoice for ever in that which I create: for, behold, I create Jerusalem a rejoicing, and her people a joy.—18.

And when ye see this, your heart shall rejoice,...*Isa.* lxvi. 14.

...Thy word was unto me the joy and rejoicing of mine heart...*Jer.* xv. 16.

For thus saith the Lord; Sing with gladness for Jacob, and shout among the chief of the nations...*Jer.* xxxi. 7.

Then shall the virgin rejoice in the dance, both young men and old together: for I will turn their mourning into joy, and will comfort them, and make them rejoice from their sorrow.—13.

The voice of joy, and the voice of gladness, the voice of the bridegroom, and the voice of the bride, the voice of them that shall say, Praise the Lord of hosts: for the Lord is good; for his mercy endureth for ever...*Jer.* xxxiii. 11.

Be glad then, ye children of Zion, and rejoice in the Lord your God...*Joel* ii. 23.

Although the fig tree shall not blossom, neither shall fruit be in the vines; the labour of the olive shall fail, and the fields shall yield no meat; the flock shall be cut off from the fold, and there shall be no herd in the stalls :—*Habak.* iii. 17.

Yet I will rejoice in the Lord, I will joy in the God of my salvation.—18.

Sing, O daughter of Zion; shout, O Israel; be glad and rejoice with all the heart, O daughter of Jerusa'em.—*Zeph.* iii. 14.

Sing and rejoice, O daughter of Zion: for, lo, I come, and I will dwell in the midst of thee, saith the Lord.—*Zech.* ii. 10.

Thus saith the Lord of hosts; the fast of the fourth month, and the fast of the fifth, and the fast of the seventh, and the fast of the tenth, shall be to the house of Judah joy and gladness, and cheerful feasts; therefore love the truth and peace.—*Zech.* viii. 19.

And they of Ephraim shall be like a mighty man, and their heart shall rejoice as through wine: yea, their children shall see it, and be glad; their heart shall rejoice in the Lord.—*Zech.* x. 7.

And all nations shall call you blessed: for ye shall be a delightsome land, saith the Lord of hosts.—*Mal.* iii. 12.

NONE BUT A WILLING SERVICE IS PLEASING TO GOD.

―――o―――

Take ye from among you an offering unto the Lord whosoever is of a willing heart, let him bring it, an offering of the Lord...*Ex.* xxxv. 5.

And they came, every one whose heart stirred him up, and every one whom his spirit made willing, and they brought the Lord's offering to the work of the tabernacle of the congregation, and for all his service...21.

And they came, both men and women, as many as were willing hearted...22.

The children of Israel brought a willing offering unto the Lord, every man and woman, whose heart made them willing to bring for all manner of work, which the Lord had commanded to be made by the hand of Moses.—29.

And if ye offer a sacrifice of peace offerings unto the Lord, ye shall offer it at your own will.—*Lev.* xix. 5.

And when ye will offer a sacrifice of thanksgiving unto the Lord, offer it at your own will.—*Lev.* xxii. 29.

Every man shall give as he is able, according to the blessing of the Lord thy God which he hath given thee.—*Deut.* xvi. 17.

...Choose you this day whom ye will serve;...but as for me and my house, we will serve the Lord.—*Josh.* xxiv. 15.

My heart is toward the governors of Israel, that offered themselves willingly among the people. Bless ye the Lord.—*Jud.* v. 9.

...Know thou the God of thy father, and serve him with a perfect heart and with a willing mind... 1 *Ch.* xxviii. 9.

...Who then is willing to consecrate his service this day unto the Lord?—1 *Ch.* xxix. 5.

Then the chief of the fathers and princes of the tribes of Israel,...offered willingly.—6.

Then the people rejoiced, for that they offered willingly, because with perfect heart they offered willingly to the Lord...9.

But who am I, and what is my people, that we should be able to offer so willingly after this sort? for all things come of thee, and of thine own have we given thee.—14.

...As for me, in the uprightness of mine heart I have willingly offered all these things: and now have I seen with joy thy people, which are present here, to offer willingly unto thee.—17.

And next him was Amasiah the son of Zichri, who willingly offered himself unto the Lord.—2 *Ch.* xvii. 16.

...And the congregation brought in sacrifices and thank offerings: and as many as were of a free heart burnt offerings.—2 *Ch*. xxix. 31.

And all the silver and gold that thou canst find in all the province of Babylon, with the freewill offering of the people, and of the priests, offering willingly for the house of their God which is in Jerusalem.—*Ezra* vii. 16.

I will freely sacrifice unto thee: I will praise thy name, O Lord.—*Ps*. liv. 6.

Accept, I beseech thee, the freewill offerings of my mouth, O Lord, and teach me thy judgments. —*Ps*. cxix. 108.

THE WORSHIP OF THE HEART AND GOOD ACTS, MORE ACCEPTABLE TO GOD THAN OUTWARD FORMS.

And in process of time it came to pass, that Cain brought of the fruit of the ground an offering unto the Lord.—*Gen.* iv. 3.

And Abel, he also brought of the firstlings of his flock and of the fat thereof. And the Lord had respect unto Abel and to his offering:—4.

But unto Cain and to his offering he had not respect. And Cain was very wroth, and his countenance fell.—5.

And the Lord said unto Cain, Why art thou wroth? and why is thy countenance fallen?—6.

If thou doest well, shalt thou not be accepted? and if thou doest not well, sin lieth at the door...7.

...Hath the Lord as great delight in burnt offerings and sacrifices, as in obeying the voice of the Lord? Behold, to obey is better than sacrifice, and to hearken than the fat of rams.—1 *Sam.* xv. 22.

...Bring an offering, and come before him: worship the Lord in the beauty of holiness.—1 *Ch.* xvi. 29.

To offer burnt offerings unto the Lord,...and to do ac ording to all that is written in the law of the Lord, which he commanded Israel.—1 *Ch*. xvi. 40.

And Josiah took away all the abominations out of all the countries that pertained to the children of Israel, and made all that were present in Israel to serve, even to serve the Lord their God.— 2 *Ch*. xxxiv. 33.

Offer the sacrifices of righteousness, and put your trust in the Lord.—*Ps*. iv. 5.

'...Therefore will I offer in his tabernacle sacrifices of joy; I will sing, yea, I will sing praises unto the Lord.—*Ps*. xxvii. 6.

Sacrifice and offering thou didst not desire; mine ears hast thou opened : burnt offering and sin offering hast thou not required.—*Ps*. xl. 6.

I delight to do thy will, O my God : yea, thy law is within my heart.—8.

Hear, O my people, and I will speak; O Israel, and I will testify against thee : I am God, even thy God.—*Ps*. l. 7.

I will not reprove thee for thy sacrifices or thy burnt offerings, to have been continually before me.—8.

I will take no bullock out of thy house, nor he goats out of thy folds.—9.

For every beast of the forest is mine, and the cattle upon a thousand hills.—10.

I know all the fowls of the mountains: and the wild beasts of the field are mine.—*Ps.* l. 11.

If I were hungry, I would not tell thee: for the world is mine, and the fulness thereof.—12.

Will I eat the flesh of bulls, or drink the blood of goats?—13.

Offer unto God thanksgiving; and pay thy vows unto the most High:—14.

And call upon me in the day of trouble: I will deliver thee, and thou shalt glorify me.—15.

For thou desirest not sacrifice; else would I give it: thou delightest not in burnt offering.—*Ps.* li. 16.

The sacrifices of God are a broken spirit: a broken and a contrite heart, O God, thou wilt not despise.—17.

Then shalt thou be pleased with the sacrifices of righteousness...19.

I will praise the name of God with a song, and will magnify him with thanksgiving.—*Ps.* lxix. 30.

This also shall please the Lord better than an ox or bullock that hath horns and hoofs.—31.

Nevertheless they did flatter him with their mouth, and they lied unto him with their tongues.—*Ps.* lxxviii. 36.

For their heart was not right with him, neither were they stedfast in his covenant.—37.

And let them sacrifice the sacrifices of thanksgiving, and declare his works with rejoicing.—*Ps.* cvii. 22.

I will offer to thee the sacrifice of thanksgiving, and will call upon the name of the Lord.—*Ps.* cxvi. 17.

The sacrifice of the wicked is an abomination to the Lord: but the prayer of the upright is his delight.—*Prov.* xv. 8.

To do justice and judgment is more acceptable to the Lord than sacrifice.—*Prov.* xxi. 3.

Keep thy foot when thou goest to the house of God, and be more ready to hear, than to give the sacrifice of fools: for they consider not that they do evil.—*Eccl.* v. 1.

To what purpose is the multitude of your sacrifices unto me? saith the Lord: I am full of the burnt offerings of rams, and the fat of the fed beasts; and I delight not in the blood of bullocks, or of lambs, or of he goats.—*Isa.* i. 11.

When ye come to appear before me, who hath required this at your hand, to tread my courts?—12.

Bring no more vain oblations; incense is an abomination unto me; the new moons and sabbaths, the calling of assemblies, I cannot away with; it is iniquity, even the solemn meeting.—13.

Your new moons and your appointed feasts my soul hateth: they are a trouble unto me; I am weary to bear them.—14.

And when ye spread forth your hands, I will hide mine eyes from you: yea, when ye make many prayers, I will not hear:—15.

Wash you, make you clean; put away the evil of your doings from before mine eyes; cease to do evil;—16.

Learn to do well; seek judgment, relieve the oppressed, judge the fatherless, plead for the widow.—*Isa*. i. 17.

...This people draw near me with their mouth, and with their lips do honour me, but have removed their heart far from me....*Isa*. xxix. 13.

Cry aloud, spare not, lift up thy voice like a trumpet, and shew my people their transgression, and the house of Jacob their sins.—*Isa*. lviii. 1.

Yet they seek me daily, and delight to know my ways, as a nation that did righteousness, and forsook not the ordinance of their God: they ask of me the ordinances of justice; they take delight in approaching to God.—2.

Wherefore have we fasted, say they, and thou seest not? wherefore have we afflicted our soul, and thou takest no knowledge? Behold, in the day of your fast ye find pleasure, and exact all your labours.—3.

Behold, ye fast for strife and debate, and to smite with the fist of wickedness: ye shall not fast as ye do this day, to make your voice to be heard on high.—4.

Is it such a fast that I have chosen? a day for a man to afflict his soul? is it to bow down his head as a bulrush, and to spread sackcloth and ashes under him? wilt thou call this a fast, and an acceptable day to the Lord?—5.

Is not this the fast that I have chosen? to loose

the bands of wickedness, to undo the heavy burdens, and to let the oppressed go free, and that ye break every yoke?—*Isa*. lviii. 6.

Is it not to deal thy bread to the hungry, and that thou bring the poor that are cast out to thy house? when thou seest the naked, that thou cover him; and that thou hide not thyself from thine own flesh?—7.

For I the Lord love judgment, I hate robbery for burnt offering...*Isa*. lxi. 8.

To what purpose cometh there to me incense from Sheba, and the sweet cane from a far country? your burnt offerings are not acceptable, nor your sacrifices sweet unto me.—*Jer*. vi. 20.

Thus saith the Lord of hosts, the God of Israel, Amend your ways and your doings....*Jer*. vii. 2.

...Put your burnt offerings unto your sacrifices, and eat flesh.—21.

For I spake not unto your fathers, nor commanded them in the day that I brought them out of the land of Egypt, concerning burnt offerings or sacrifices:—22.

But this thing commanded I them, saying, Obey my voice, and I will be your God, and ye shall be my people: and walk ye in all the ways that I have commanded you, that it may be well unto you.—23.

When they fast, I will not hear their cry; and when they offer burnt offering and an oblation, I will not accept them...*Jer*. xiv. 12.

For I desired mercy, and not sacrifice; and the knowledge of God more than burnt offerings.—*Hos*. vi. 6.

And rend your heart, and not your garments, and turn unto the Lord your God....*Joel* ii. 13.

I will sacrifice unto thee with the voice of thanksgiving; I will pay *that* that I have vowed.—*Jonah* ii. 9.

Wherewith shall I come before the Lord, and bow myself before the high God? shall I come before him with burnt offerings, with calves of a year old?—*Micah* vi. 6.

Will the Lord be pleased with thousands of rams, or with ten thousands of rivers of oil? shall I give my firstborn for my transgression, the fruit of my body for the sin of my soul?—7.

He hath shewed thee, O man, what is good; and what doth the Lord require of thee, but to do justly, and to love mercy, and to walk humbly with thy God?—8.

...That they may offer unto the Lord an offering in righteousness.—*Mal.* iii. 3.

TRIALS ARE FOR OUR GOOD, AND TO PROVE OUR FAITH IN GOD.

———o———

And it came to pass,...that God did tempt Abraham, and said unto him, Abraham: and he said, Behold, here I am.—*Gen.* xxii. 1.

And he said, Take now thy son, thine only son Isaac, whom thou lovest, and get thee into the land of Moriah; and offer him there for a burnt offering upon one of the mountains which I will tell thee of.—2.

And Abraham rose up early in the morning, and saddled his ass, and took two of his young men with him, and Isaac his son, and clave the wood for the burnt offering, and rose up, and went unto the place of which God had told him.—3.

And Abraham took the wood of the burnt offering, and laid it upon Isaac his son; and he took the fire in his hand, and a knife; and they went both of them together.—6.

And Isaac spake unto Abraham his father, and said, My father: and he said, Here am I, my son. And he said, Behold the fire and the wood: but where is the lamb for a burnt offering?—7.

And Abraham said, my son, God will provide himself a lamb for a burnt offering: so they went both of them together.—*Gen.* xxii. 8.

And they came to the place which God had told him of; and Abraham built an altar there, and laid the wood in order, and bound Isaac his son, and laid him on the altar upon the wood.—9.

And Abraham stretched forth his hand, and took the knife to slay his son.—10.

And the angel of the Lord called unto him out of heaven, and said, Abraham, Abraham: and he said, Here am I.—11.

And he said, Lay not thine hand upon the lad, neither do thou any thing unto him: for now I know that thou fearest God, seeing thou hast not withheld thy son, thine only son from me.—12.

And when his (Joseph's) brethren saw that their father loved him more than all his brethren, they hated him, and could not speak peaceably unto him.—*Gen.* xxxvii. 4.

And when they saw him afar off, even before he came near unto them, they conspired against him to slay him.—18.

And they said one to another, We are verily guilty concerning our brother, in that we saw the anguish of his soul, when he besought us, and we would not hear; therefore is this distress come upon us. —*Gen.* xlii. 21.

And Joseph said unto them, Fear not: for am I in the place of God?—*Gen.* 1. 19.

But as for you, ye thought evil against me; but God meant it unto good, to bring to pass, as it is this day, to save much people alive.—20.

...Remember all the way which the Lord thy God led thee these forty years in the wilderness, to humble thee, and to prove thee, to know what was in thine heart, whether thou wouldest keep his commandments, or no.—*Deut.* viii. 2.

And he humbled thee, and suffered thee to hunger, and fed thee with manna, which thou knewest not, neither did thy fathers know; that he might make thee know that man doth not live by bread only, but by every word that proceedeth out of the mouth of the Lord doth man live.—3.

Thou shalt also consider in thine heart, that, as a man chasteneth his son, so the Lord thy God chasteneth thee.—5.

...That he might humble thee, and that he might prove thee, to do thee good at thy latter end.—16.

And the Lord said unto Satan, Hast thou considered my servant Job, that there is none like him in the earth?...*Job* i. 8.

Then Satan answered the Lord, and said, Doth Job fear God for nought?—9.

But put forth thine hand now, and touch all that he hath, and he will curse thee to thy face.—*Job* i. 11.

And the Lord said unto Satan, Behold, all that he hath is in thy power...12.

And there was a day when his sons and his daughters were eating and drinking wine in their eldest brother's house:—13.

And there came a messenger unto Job, and said, The oxen were plowing, and the asses feeding beside them:—14.

And the Sabeans fell upon them, and took them away; yea, they have slain the servants with the edge of the sword; and I only am escaped alone to tell thee.—15.

While he was yet speaking, there came also another, and said, The fire of God is fallen from heaven, and hath burned up the sheep, and the servants, and consumed them...16.

...There came also another, and said, The Chaldeans made out three bands, and fell upon the camels, and have carried them away, yea, and slain the servants with the edge of the sword...17.

...There came also another, and said, Thy sons and thy daughters were eating and drinking wine in their eldest brother's house:—18.

And, behold, there came a great wind from the wilderness, and smote the four corners of the house, and it fell upon the young men, and they are dead...19.

Then Job arose, and rent his mantle, and shaved his head, and fell down upon the ground, and worshipped,—Job i. 20.

And said,...The Lord gave, and the Lord hath taken away; blessed be the name of the Lord.—21.

In all this Job sinned not, nor charged God foolishly.—22.

And the Lord said unto Satan, Hast thou considered my servant Job,...a perfect and an upright man, one that feareth God, and escheweth evil? and still he holdeth fast his integrity, although thou movedst me against him, to destroy him without cause.—Job ii. 3.

And Satan answered the Lord, and said, Skin for skin, yea, all that a man hath will he give for his life.—4.

But put forth thine hand now, and touch his bone and his flesh, and he will curse thee to thy face.—5.

And the Lord said unto Satan, Behold, he is in thine hand; but save his life.—6.

So went Satan...and smote Job with sore boils from the sole of his foot unto his crown.—7.

Then said his wife unto him, Dost thou still retain thine integrity?...9.

But he said unto her,...What? shall we receive good at the hand of God, and shall we not receive evil? In all this did not Job sin with his lips.—10.

...Affliction cometh not forth of the dust, neither doth trouble spring out of the ground.—Job v. 6.

TO PROVE OUR FAITH IN GOD.

Behold, happy is the man whom God correcteth: therefore despise not thou the chastening of the Almighty.—*Job* v. 17.

...When he hath tried me, I shall come forth as gold.—*Job* xxiii. 10.

...The righteous God trieth the hearts and reins.—*Ps.* vii. 9.

The Lord trieth the righteous...*Ps.* xi. 5.

Thou hast proved mine heart; thou hast visited me in the night; thou hast tried me, and shall find nothing; I am purposed that my mouth shall not transgress.—*Ps.* xvii. 3.

Examine me, O Lord, and prove me; try my reins and my heart.—*Ps.* xxvi. 2.

For thou, O God, hast proved us: thou hast tried us, as silver is tried.—*Ps.* lxvi. 10.

I believed, therefore have I spoken: I was greatly afflicted.—*Ps.* cxvi. 10.

Before I was afflicted I went astray: but now have I kept thy word.—*Ps.* cxix. 67.

It is good for me that I have been afflicted; that I might learn thy statutes.—71.

The fining pot is for silver, and the furnace for gold: but the Lord trieth the hearts.—*Prov.* xvii. 3.

Sorrow is better than laughter: for by the sadness of the countenance the heart is made better.—*Eccl.* vii. 3.

Behold, I have refined thee, but not with silver;

I have chosen thee in the furnace of affliction.—*Isa.* xlviii. 10.

For a small moment have I forsaken thee; but with great mercies will I gather thee.—*Isa.* liv. 7.

In a little wrath I hid my face from thee for a moment; but with everlasting kindness will I have mercy on thee, saith the Lord thy Redeemer.—8.

...In my wrath I smote thee, but in my favour have I had mercy on thee.—*Isa.* lx. 10.

...O Lord of hosts, that triest the righteous, and seest the reins and the heart.—*Jer.* xx. 12.

It is good for a man that he bear the yoke in his youth.—*Lam.* iii. 27.

And I will cause you to pass under the rod, and I will bring you into the bond of the covenant.—*Ezek.* xx. 37.

The Lord's voice crieth unto the city,...hear ye the rod, and who hath appointed it.—*Micah* vi. 9.

And I will bring the third part through the fire, and will refine them as silver is refined, and will try them as gold is tried: they shall call on my name, and I will hear them.—*Zech.* xiii. 9.

And he shall sit as a refiner and purifier of silver: and he shall purify the sons of Levi, and purge them as gold and silver, that they may offer unto the Lord an offering in righteousness.—*Mal.* iii. 3.

THE SIN OF MURMURING.
THE VIRTUE OF SUBMISSION.

And the angel of the Lord said unto her, (Hagar) Return to thy mistress, and submit thyself under her hands.—*Gen.* xvi. 9.

And they said unto Moses, Because there were no graves in Egypt, hast thou taken us away to die in the wilderness? wherefore hast thou dealt thus with us, to carry us forth out of Egypt?—*Ex.* xiv. 11.

Is not this the word that we did tell thee in Egypt, saying, Let us alone that we may serve the Egyptians? For it had been better for us to serve the Egyptians, than that we should die in the wilderness.—12.

And when they came to Marah, they could not drink of the waters of Marah, for they were bitter... *Ex.* xv. 23.

And the people murmured against Moses, saying, what shall we drink?—24.

And the whole congregation of the children of Israel murmured against Moses and Aaron in the wilderness :—*Ex.* xvi. 2.

And the children of Israel said unto them, Would to God we had died by the hand of the Lord in the land of Egypt:...for ye have brought us forth into this wilderness, to kill this whole assembly with hunger.—*Ex.* xvi. 3.

Then said the Lord unto Moses, Behold, I will rain bread from heaven for you; and the people shall go out and gather a certain rate every day, that I may prove them, whether they will walk in my law, or no.—4.

And in the morning, then ye shall see the glory of the Lord; for that he heareth your murmurings against the Lord: and what are we, that ye murmur against us?—7.

And Moses said, This shall be, when the Lord shall give you in the evening flesh to eat, and in the morning bread to the full; for that the Lord heareth your murmurings which ye murmur against him: and what are we? your murmurings are not against us, but against the Lord.—8.

...Come near before the Lord: for he hath heard your murmurings.—9.

And the Lord spake unto Moses, saying,—11.

I have heard the murmurings of the children of Israel...12.

Wherefore the people did chide with Moses, and said, Give us water that we may drink. And Moses said unto them, Why chide ye with me? wherefore do ye tempt the Lord?—*Ex.* xvii. 2.

And the people thirsted there for water; and the people murmured against Moses, and said, Wherefore is this that thou hast brought us up out of Egypt, to kill us and our children and our cattle with thirst? —*Ex.* xvii. 3.

And Moses cried unto the Lord, saying, What shall I do unto this people? they be almost ready to stone me.—4.

And the Lord said unto Moses, Go on before the people...5.

Behold, I will stand before thee there upon the rock in Horeb; and thou shalt smite the rock, and there shall come water out of it, that the people may drink. And Moses did so in the sight of the elders of Israel.—6.

And he called the name of the place Massah, and Meribah, because of the chiding of the children of Israel, and because they tempted the Lord, saying, Is the Lord among us, or not?—7.

Only rebel not ye against the Lord...*Num.* xiv. 9.

And the Lord spake unto Moses and Aaron, saying, —26.

How long shall I bear with this evil congregation, which murmur against me? I have heard the murmurings of the children of Israel, which they murmur against me.—27.

And the people spake against God, and against Moses, Wherefore have ye brought us up out of Egypt to die in the wilderness? for there is no bread, neither is there any water; and our soul loatheth this light bread.—*Num.* xxi. 5.

And the Lord sent fiery serpents among the people, and they bit the people...6.

Therefore the people came to Moses, and said, We have sinned, for we have spoken against the Lord, and against thee: pray unto the Lord, that he take away the serpents from us. And Moses prayed for the people.—7.

...It is a good land which the Lord our God doth give us.—*Deut.* i. 25.

Notwithstanding ye would not go up, but rebelled against the commandment of the Lord your God:—26.

And ye murmured in your tents, and said, Because the Lord hated us, he hath brought us forth out of the land of Egypt, to deliver us into the hand of the Amorites, to destroy us.—27.

And the children of Israel said unto the Lord, We have sinned: do thou unto us whatsoever seemeth good unto thee.—2 *Judg.* x. 15.

...It is the Lord: let him do what seemeth him good.—1 *Sam.* iii. 18.

But if he thus say, I have no delight in thee; behold, here am I, let him do to me as seemeth good unto him.—2 *Sam.* xv. 26.

...The Lord gave, and the Lord hath taken away; blessed be the name of the Lord.—*Job* i. 21.

In all this Job sinned not, nor charged God foolishly.—22.

THE VIRTUE OF SUBMISSION.

Shall we receive good at the hand of God, and shall we not receive evil?—*Job* ii. 10.

Why doth thine heart carry thee away? and what do thy eyes wink at,—*Job* xv. 12.

That thou turnest thy spirit against God, and lettest such words go out of thy mouth?—13.

For he addeth rebellion unto his sin, he clappeth his hands among us, and multiplieth his words against God.—*Job* xxxiv. 37.

I was dumb, I opened not my mouth; because thou didst it.—*Ps.* xxxix. 9.

I delight to do thy will, O my God: yea, thy law is within my heart.—*Ps.* xl. 8.

...They waited not for his counsel:—*Ps.* cvi. 13.

...And tempted God in the desert.—14.

And he gave them their request; but sent leanness into their soul.—15.

They envied Moses also in the camp, and Aaron the saint of the Lord.—16.

Because they rebelled against the words of God, and contemned the counsel of the most High.—*Ps.* cvii. 11.

Therefore he brought down their heart with labour...12.

I know, O Lord, that thy judgments are right, and that thou in faithfulness hast afflicted me.—*Ps.* cxix. 75.

Deal with thy servant according unto thy mercy, and teach me thy statutes.—124.

My son, despise not the chastening of the Lord; neither be weary of his correction.—*Prov.* iii. 11.

The foolishness of man perverteth his way: and his heart fretteth against the Lord.—*Prov.* xix. 3.

Say not thou, What is the cause that the former days were better than these? for thou dost not enquire wisely concerning this.—*Eccl.* vii. 10.

They also that erred in spirit shall come to understanding, and they that murmured shall learn doctrine.—*Isa.* xxix. 24.

Woe is me for my hurt! my wound is grievous: but I said, Truly this is a grief, and I must bear it.—*Jer.* x. 19.

It is good that a man should both hope and quietly wait for the salvation of the Lord.—*Lam.* iii. 26.

He sitteth alone and keepeth silence, because he hath borne it upon him.—28.

Wherefore doth a living man complain, a man for the punishment of his sins?—39.

...O Lord, take, I beseech thee, my life from me; for it is better for me to die than to live.—*Jonah* iv. 3.

Then said the Lord, Doest thou well to be angry?—4.

I will bear the indignation of the Lord, because I have sinned against him...*Micah* vii. 9.

PRAYER IN TROUBLE.

———o———

And she (Hannah) was in bitterness of soul, and prayed unto the Lord, and wept sore.—1 *Sam.* i. 10.

And said....I am a woman of a sorrowful spirit :... but have poured out my soul before the Lord.—15.

...For out of the abundance of my complaint and grief have I spoken hitherto.—16.

And he (David) said, while the child was yet alive, I fasted and wept : for I said, Who can tell whether God will be gracious to me, that the child may live ?—2 *Sam.* xii. 22.

My soul is weary of my life ; I will leave my complaint upon myself; I will speak in the bitterness of my soul.—*Job* x. 1.

My friends scorn me : but mine eye poureth out tears unto God.—*Job* xvi. 20.

Mine eye also is dim by reason of sorrow, and all my members are as a shadow.—*Job* xvii. 7.

Lord, how are they increased that trouble me! many are they that rise up against me.—*Ps.* iii. 1.

O Lord, rebuke me not in thine anger, neither chasten me in thy hot displeasure.—*Ps.* vi. 1.

Have mercy upon me, O Lord; for I am weak: O Lord, heal me; for my bones are vexed.—*Ps.* vi. 2.

My soul is also sore vexed; but thou, O Lord, how long?—3.

I am weary with my groaning; all the night make I my bed to swim; I water my couch with my tears.—6.

Mine eye is consumed because of grief...7.

Have mercy upon me, O Lord; consider my trouble which I suffer of them that hate me,...*Ps.* ix. 13.

Why standest thou afar off, O Lord? why hidest thou thyself in times of trouble?—*Ps.* x. 1.

How long wilt thou forget me, O Lord? for ever? how long wilt thou hide thy face from me?—*Ps.* xiii. 1.

How long shall I take counsel in my soul, having sorrow in my heart daily?—2.

My God, my God, why hast thou forsaken me? why art thou so far from helping me, and from the words of my roaring?—*Ps.* xxii. 1.

O my God, I cry in the day time, but thou hearest not; and in the night season, and am not silent.—2.

But I am a worm, and no man; a reproach of men, and despised of the people.—6.

All they that see me laugh me to scorn: they shoot out the lip, they shake the head, saying,—7.

He trusted on the Lord that he would deliver him: let him deliver him, seeing he delighted in him.—8.

Be not far from me; for trouble is near; for there is none to help.—11.

PRAYER IN TROUBLE.

I am poured out like water, and all my bones are out of joint: my heart is like wax...*Ps.* xxii. 14.

...Thou art the God of my salvation; on thee do I wait all the day.—*Ps.* xxv. 5.

Turn thee unto me, and have mercy upon me; for I am desolate and afflicted.—16.

The troubles of my heart are enlarged: O bring thou me out of my distresses.—17.

Look upon mine affliction and my pain...18.

Redeem Israel, O God, out of all his troubles.—22.

Hide not thy face far from me; put not thy servant away in anger: thou hast been my help; leave me not, neither forsake me, O God of my salvation.—*Ps.* xxvii. 9.

Bow down thine ear to me; deliver me speedily: be thou my strong rock, for an house of defence to save me.—*Ps.* xxxi. 2.

Have mercy upon me, O Lord, for I am in trouble: mine eye is consumed with grief.—9.

For my life is spent with grief, and my years with sighing:...10.

I was a reproach among all mine enemies, but especially among my neighbours, and a fear to mine acquaintance: they that did see me without fled from me.—11.

I am forgotten as a dead man out of mind: I am like a broken vessel.—12.

For I have heard the slander of many: fear was on every side...13.

PRAYER IN TROUBLE.

My times are in thy hand: deliver me from the hand of mine enemies, and from them that persecute me.—*Ps*. xxxi. 15.

Make thy face to shine upon thy servant: save me for thy mercies' sake.—16.

For I said in my haste, I am cut off from before thine eyes: nevertheless thou heardest the voice of my supplications when I cried unto thee.—22.

For day and night thy hand was heavy upon me... *Ps*. xxxii. 4.

O Lord, rebuke me not in thy wrath: neither chasten me in thy hot displeasure.—*Ps*. xxxviii. 1.

For thine arrows stick fast in me, and thy hand presseth me sore.—2.

I am troubled; I am bowed down greatly; I go mourning all the day long.—6.

I am feeble and sore broken: I have roared by reason of the disquietness of my heart.—8.

My heart panteth, my strength faileth me: as for the light of mine eyes, it also is gone from me.—10.

My lovers and my friends stand aloof from my sore; and my kinsmen stand afar off.—11.

But I, as a deaf man, heard not; and I was as a dumb man that openeth not his mouth.—13.

For in thee, O Lord, do I hope: thou wilt hear, O Lord my God.—15.

For I am ready to halt, and my sorrow is continually before me.—17.

Forsake me not, O Lord: O my God, be not far from me.—*Ps.* xxxviii. 21.

Make haste to help me, O Lord my salvation.—22.

And now, Lord, what wait I for? my hope is in thee.—*Ps.* xxxix. 7.

I was dumb, I opened not my mouth; because thou didst it.—9.

Remove thy stroke away from me: I am consumed by the blow of thine hand.—10.

Hear my prayer, O Lord, and give ear unto my cry; hold not thy peace at my tears...12.

For innumerable evils have compassed me about: ...therefore my heart faileth me.—*Ps.* xl. 12.

Be pleased, O Lord, to deliver me: O Lord, make haste to help me.—13.

My tears have been my meat day and night, while they continually say unto me, Where is thy God?—*Ps.* xlii. 3.

When I remember these things, I pour out my soul in me...4.

O my God, my soul is cast down within me.—6.

I will say unto God my rock, Why hast thou forgotten me? why go I mourning because of the oppression of the enemy?—9.

Wherefore hidest thou thy face, and forgettest our affliction and our oppression?—*Ps.* xliv. 24.

For our soul is bowed down to the dust...25.

Arise for our help, and redeem us for thy mercies' sake.—26.

Make me to hear joy and gladness; that the bones which thou hast broken may rejoice.—*Ps.* li. 8.

Give ear to my prayer, O God; and hide not thyself from my supplication.—*Ps.* lv. 1.

Attend unto me, and hear me: I mourn in my complaint…2.

My heart is sore pained within me:…4.

Fearfulness and trembling are come upon me, and horror hath overwhelmed me.—5.

And I said, Oh that I had wings like a dove! for then would I fly away, and be at rest.—6.

For it was not an enemy that reproached me; then I could have borne it: neither was it he that hated me that did magnify himself against me; then I would have hid myself from him:—12.

But it was thou, a man mine equal, my guide, and mine acquaintance.—13.

Thou tellest my wanderings: put thou my tears into thy bottle: are they not in thy book?—*Ps.* lvi. 8.

…My soul is bowed down.—*Ps.* lvii. 6.

…Defend me from them that rise up against me.—*Ps.* lix. 1.

O God, thou hast cast us off, thou hast scattered us, thou hast been displeased; O turn thyself to us again.—*Ps.* lx. 1.

…Save with thy right hand, and hear me.—5.

Give us help from trouble: for vain is the help of man.—11.

PRAYER IN TROUBLE.

Hear my cry, O God; attend unto my prayer.—*Ps.* lxi. 1.

From the end of the earth will I cry unto thee, when my heart is overwhelmed: lead me to the rock that is higher than I.—2.

My soul, wait thou only upon God; for my expectation is from him.—*Ps.* lxii. 5.

Save me, O God; for the waters are come in unto my soul.—*Ps.* lxix. 1.

I sink in deep mire, where there is no standing: I am come into deep waters, where the floods overflow me.—2.

I am weary of my crying: my throat is dried: mine eyes fail while I wait for my God.—3.

Reproach hath broken my heart; and I am full of heaviness: and I looked for some to take pity, but there was none; and for comforters, but I found none.—20.

Make haste, O God, to deliver me; make haste to help me, O Lord.—*Ps.* lxx. 1.

I am poor and needy: make haste unto me, O God: thou art my help and my deliverer; O Lord, make no tarrying.—5.

Deliver me in thy righteousness, and cause me to escape: incline thine ear unto me, and save me.—*Ps.* lxxi. 2.

Be thou my strong habitation, whereunto I may continually resort: thou hast given commandment to save me; for thou art my rock and my fortress.—3.

PRAYER IN TROUBLE.

In the day of my trouble I sought the Lord : my sore ran in the night, and ceased not : my soul refused to be comforted.—*Ps.* lxxvii. 2.

I remembered God, and was troubled : I complained, and my spirit was overwhelmed.—3.

Thou holdest mine eyes waking : I am so troubled that I cannot speak.—4.

Will the Lord cast off for ever ? and will he be favourable no more ?—7.

Is his mercy clean gone for ever ? doth his promise fail for evermore ?—8.

Hath God forgotten to be gracious ? hath he in anger shut up his tender mercies ?—9.

...This is my infirmity : but I will remember the years of the right hand of the most High.—10.

How long, Lord ? wilt thou be angry for ever ?... *Ps.* lxxix. 5.

Let the sighing of the prisoner come before thee ; according to the greatness of thy power preserve thou those that are appointed to die.—11.

Turn us again, O God of hosts, and cause thy face to shine ; and we shall be saved.—*Ps.* lxxx. 7.

Turn us, O God of our salvation, and cause thine anger toward us to cease.—*Ps.* lxxxv. 4.

Wilt thou be angry with us for ever ?...5.

Wilt thou not revive us again : that thy people may rejoice in thee ?—6.

Shew us thy mercy, O Lord, and grant us thy salvation.—7.

PRAYER IN TROUBLE.

Bow down thine ear, O Lord, hear me: for I am poor and needy.—*Ps.* lxxxvi. 1.

Be merciful unto me, O Lord: for I cry unto thee daily.—3.

In the day of my trouble I will call upon thee: for thou wilt answer me.—7.

Shew me a token for good...17.

O Lord God of my salvation, I have cried day and night before thee:—*Ps.* lxxxviii. 1.

Let my prayer come before thee: incline thine ear unto my cry;—2.

For my soul is full of troubles...3.

Thou hast laid me in the lowest pit, in darkness, in the deeps.—6.

Thy wrath lieth hard upon me, and thou hast afflicted me with all thy waves.—7.

Thou hast put away mine acquaintance far from me...8.

Mine eye mourneth by reason of affliction: Lord, I have called daily upon thee, I have stretched out my hands unto thee.—9.

Lord, why castest thou off my soul? why hidest thou thy face from me?—14.

I am afflicted and ready to die from my youth up...15.

Lover and friend hast thou put far from me, and mine acquaintance into darkness.—18.

Make us glad according to the days wherein thou

hast afflicted us, and the years wherein we have seen evil.—*Ps.* xc. 15.

Hear my prayer, O Lord, and let my cry come unto thee.—*Ps.* cii. 1.

Hide not thy face from me in the day when I am in trouble; incline thine ear unto me: in the day when I call answer me speedily.—2.

For my days are consumed like smoke, and my bones are burned as an hearth.—3.

My heart is smitten, and withered like grass; so that I forget to eat my bread.—4.

By reason of the voice of my groaning my bones cleave to my skin.—5.

I watch, and am as a sparrow alone upon the house top.—7.

Mine enemies reproach me all the day…8.

I said, O my God, take me not away in the midst of my days…24.

For I am poor and needy, and my heart is wounded within me.—*Ps.* cix. 22.

I am gone like the shadow when it declineth : I am tossed up and down as the locust.—23.

My knees are weak through fasting; and my flesh faileth of fatness.—24.

I became also a reproach unto them: when they looked upon me they shaked their heads.—25.

Help me, O Lord my God: O save me according to thy mercy :—26.

PRAYER IN TROUBLE.

That they may know that this is thy hand; that thou, Lord, hast done it.—*Ps.* cix. 27.

Remove from me reproach and contempt; for I have kept thy testimonies.—*Ps.* cxix. 22.

My soul melteth for heaviness: strengthen thou me according unto thy word.—28.

Turn away my reproach which I fear: for thy judgments are good.—39.

Let, I pray thee, thy merciful kindness be for my comfort, according to thy word unto thy servant.—76.

Mine eyes fail for thy word, saying, When wilt thou comfort me?—82.

For I am become like a bottle in the smoke...83.

The proud have digged pits for me, which are not after thy law.—85.

I am thine, save me; for I have sought thy precepts.—94.

I am afflicted very much...107.

Hold thou me up, and I shall be safe...117.

Mine eyes fail for thy salvation...123.

I cried with my whole heart; hear me, O Lord...145.

I prevented the dawning of the morning, and cried: I hoped in thy word.—147.

Consider mine affliction, and deliver me.—153.

Let my cry come near before thee, O Lord:—169.

Let thine hand help me...173.

In my distress I cried unto the Lord, and he heard me.—*Ps.* cxx. 1.

I will lift up mine eyes unto the hills, from whence cometh my help.—*Ps.* cxxi. 1.

Out of the depths have I cried unto thee, O Lord.—*Ps.* cxxx. 1.

Lord, hear my voice: let thine ears be attentive to the voice of my supplications.—2.

I wait for the Lord, my soul doth wait, and in his word do I hope.—5.

Lord, remember David, and all his afflictions.—*Ps.* cxxxii. 1.

I cried unto the Lord with my voice; with my voice unto the Lord did I make my supplication.—*Ps.* cxlii. 1.

I poured out my complaint before him; I shewed before him my trouble.—2.

When my spirit was overwhelmed within me, then thou knewest my path...3.

Attend unto my cry; for I am brought very low...6.

Bring my soul out of prison, that I may praise thy name.—7.

Therefore is my spirit overwhelmed within me; my heart within me is desolate.—*Ps.* cxliii. 4.

Hear me speedily, O Lord: my spirit faileth: hide not thy face from me...7.

Teach me to do thy will; for thou art my God...10.

Send thine hand from above; rid me, and deliver me out of great waters.—*Ps.* cxliv. 7.

Like a crane or a swallow, so did I chatter: I did mourn as a dove: mine eyes fail with looking upward: O Lord, I am oppressed; undertake for me.—*Isa.* xxxviii. 14.

...I shall go softly all my years in the bitterness of my soul.—15.

Be not wroth very sore, O Lord, neither remember iniquity for ever: behold, see, we beseech thee, we are all thy people.—*Isa.* lxiv. 9.

Wilt thou refrain thyself for these things, O Lord? wilt thou hold thy peace, and afflict us very sore?—12.

O Lord, correct me, but with judgment; not in thine anger, lest thou bring me to nothing.—*Jer.* x. 24.

O Lord, behold my affliction...*Lam.* i. 9.

Behold, O Lord; for I am in distress...mine heart is turned within me...20.

...For my sighs are many, and my heart is faint.—22.

Waters flowed over mine head; then I said, I am cut off.—*Lam.* iii. 54.

I called upon thy name, O Lord, out of the low dungeon.—55.

Thou hast heard my voice: hide not thine ear at my breathing, at my cry.—56.

O Lord, thou hast seen my wrong: judge thou my cause.—59.

Remember, O Lord, what is come upon us: consider, and behold our reproach.—*Lam.* v. 1.

The joy of our heart is ceased; our dance is turned into mourning.—15.

For this our heart is faint; for these things our eyes are dim.—17.

Wherefore dost thou forget us for ever, and forsake us so long time?—*Lam.* v. 20.

Turn thou us unto thee, O Lord, and we shall be turned; renew our days as of old.—21.

O Lord, revive thy work in the midst of the years, in the midst of the years make known; in wrath remember mercy.—*Habak.* iii. 2.

COMFORT AND SUPPORT IN AFFLICTION.

...The Lord hath heard thy affliction.—*Gen.* xvi. 11.
...Fear not; for God hath heard the voice of the lad where he is.—*Gen.* xxi. 17.

And the Lord said, I have surely seen the affliction of my people which are in Egypt, and have heard their cry...I know their sorrows.—*Ex.* iii. 7.

...And when they heard that the Lord had visited the children of Israel, and that he had looked upon their affliction, then they bowed their heads and worshipped.—*Ex.* iv. 31.

And when we cried unto the Lord God of our fathers, the Lord heard our voice, and looked on our affliction, and our labour, and our oppression. —*Deut.* xxvi. 7.

The eternal God is thy refuge, and underneath are the everlasting arms...*Deut.* xxxiii. 27.

It may be that the Lord will look on mine affliction, and that the Lord will requite me good... 2 *Sam.* xvi. 12.

In my distress I called upon the Lord, and cried

to my God: and he did hear my voice out of his temple, and my cry did enter into his ears.— 2 Sam. xxii. 7.

They prevented me in the day of my calamity: but the Lord was my stay.—19.

And the afflicted people thou wilt save...28.

Behold, happy is the man whom God correcteth: therefore despise not thou the chastening of the Almighty:—Job v. 17.

For he maketh sore, and bindeth up: he woundeth, and his hands make whole.—18.

He shall deliver thee in six troubles: yea, in seven there shall no evil touch thee.—19.

...Thou shalt forget thy misery, and remember it as waters that pass away.—Job xi. 16.

And thou shalt be secure, because there is hope...18.

Are the consolations of God small with thee?— Job xv. 11.

For he will not lay upon man more than right; that he should enter into judgment with God.— Job xxxiv. 23.

Many there be which say of my soul, There is no help for him in God.—Ps. iii. 2.

But thou, O Lord, art a shield for me; my glory, and the lifter up of mine head.—3.

I cried unto the Lord with my voice, and he heard me out of his holy hill.—4.

...Thou hast enlarged me when I was in distress. —Ps. iv. 1.

...The Lord hath heard the voice of my weeping.— Ps. vi. 8.

The Lord also will be a refuge for the oppressed, a refuge in times of trouble.—Ps. ix. 9.

I have set the Lord always before me : because he is at my right hand, I shall not be moved.—Ps. xvi. 8.

For he hath not despised nor abhorred the affliction of the afflicted; neither hath he hid his face from him; but when he cried unto him, he heard. —Ps. xxii. 24.

...I will fear no evil: for thou art with me; thy rod and thy staff they comfort me.—Ps. xxiii. 4.

Weeping may endure for a night, but joy cometh in the morning.—Ps. xxx. 5.

...Thou hast considered my trouble; thou hast known my soul in adversities.—Ps. xxxi. 7.

Thou art my hiding place; thou shalt preserve me from trouble; thou shall compass me about with songs of deliverance.—Ps. xxxii. 7.

Our soul waiteth for the Lord: he is our help and our shield.—Ps. xxxiii. 20.

This poor man cried, and the Lord heard him out of all his troubles.—Ps. xxxiv. 6.

The righteous cry, and the Lord heareth, and delivereth them out of all their troubles.—17.

The Lord is nigh unto them that are of a broken heart...18.

Many are the afflictions of the righteous: but the Lord delivereth him out of them all.—19.

He keepeth all his bones : not one of them is broken.—*Ps.* xxxiv. 20.

The salvation of the righteous is of the Lord: he is their strength in the time of trouble.—*Ps.* xxxvii. 39.

And the Lord shall help them, and deliver them…40.

I waited patiently for the Lord; and he inclined unto me, and heard my cry.—*Ps.* xl. 1.

Why art thou cast down, O my soul? and why art thou disquieted in me? hope thou in God: for I shall yet praise him for the help of his countenance.—*Ps.* xlii. 5.

God is our refuge and strength, a very present help in trouble.—*Ps.* xlvi. 1.

Therefore will not we fear, though the earth be removed, and though the mountains be carried into the midst of the sea.—2.

The Lord of hosts is with us; the God of Jacob is our refuge.—7.

And call upon me in the day of trouble: I will deliver thee, and thou shalt glorify me.—*Ps.* l. 15.

For he hath delivered me out of all trouble—*Ps.* liv. 7.

Cast thy burden upon the Lord, and he shall sustain thee: he shall never suffer the righteous to be moved.—*Ps.* lv. 22.

…In the shadow of thy wings will I make my refuge, until these calamities be overpast.—*Ps.* lvii. 1.

My soul, wait thou only upon God; for my expectation is from him.—*Ps.* lxii. 5.

He only is my rock and my salvation: he is my defence; I shall not be moved.—*Ps.* lxii. 6.
...The rock of my strength, and my refuge, is in God.—7.
...God is a refuge for us.—8.
Because thou hast been my help, therefore in the shadow of thy wings will I rejoice.—*Ps.* lxiii. 7.
Thou, which hast shewed me great and sore troubles, shalt quicken me again, and shalt bring me up again from the depths of the earth.—*Ps.* lxxi. 20.
Thou shalt increase my greatness, and comfort me on every side.—21.
In the day of my trouble I will call upon thee: for thou wilt answer me.—*Ps.* lxxxvi. 7.
...Thou, Lord, hast holpen me, and comforted me.—17.
He shall call upon me, and I will answer him: I will be with him in trouble.—*Ps.* xci. 15.
Blessed is the man whom thou chastenest, O Lord...*Ps.* xciv. 12.
That thou mayest give him rest from the days of adversity...13.
Unless the Lord had been my help, my soul had almost dwelt in silence.—17.
In the multitude of my thoughts within me thy comforts delight my soul.—19.
...He regarded their affliction, when he heard their cry.—*Ps.* cvi. 44.
I called upon the Lord in distress: the Lord answered me, and set me in a large place.—*Ps.* cxviii. 5.

The Lord hath chastened me sore: but he hath not given me over unto death.—*Ps.* cxviii. 18.

This is my comfort in my affliction: for thy word hath quickened me.—*Ps.* cxix. 50.

I remembered thy judgments of old, O Lord; and have comforted myself.—52.

...Thou in faithfulness hast afflicted me.—75.

Let, I pray thee, thy merciful kindness be for my comfort...76.

Unless thy law had been my delights, I should then have perished in mine affliction.—92.

Trouble and anguish have taken hold on me: yet thy commandments are my delights.—143.

In my distress I cried unto the Lord, and he heard me.—*Ps.* cxx. 1.

My help cometh from the Lord, which made heaven and earth.—*Ps.* cxxi. 2.

The Lord is thy keeper: the Lord is thy shade upon thy right hand.—5.

The Lord shall preserve thee from all evil.—7.

They that sow in tears shall reap in joy.—*Ps.* cxxvi. 5.

He that goeth forth and weepeth, bearing precious seed, shall doubtless come again with rejoicing, bringing his sheaves with him.—6.

Though I walk in the midst of trouble, thou wilt revive me...*Ps.* cxxxviii. 7.

I know that the Lord will maintain the cause of the afflicted...*Ps.* cxl. 12.

I cried unto thee, O Lord: I said, Thou art my

refuge and my portion in the land of the living. —*Ps.* cxlii. 5.

If thou faint in the day of adversity, thy strength is small.—*Prov.* xxiv. 10.

...In the day of adversity consider.—*Eccl.* vii. 14.

And though the Lord give you the bread of adversity, and the water of affliction, yet shall not thy teachers be removed into a corner any more, but thine eyes shall see thy teachers.—*Isa.* xxx. 20.

...I have heard thy prayer, I have seen thy tears...
Isa. xxxviii. 5.

Fear thou not; for I am with thee: be not dismayed; for I am thy God: I will strengthen thee; yea, I will help thee; yea, I will uphold thee with the right hand of my righteousness.—*Isa.* xli. 10.

For I the Lord thy God will hold thy right hand, saying unto thee, Fear not; I will help thee.—13.

When thou passest through the waters, I will be with thee; and through the rivers, they shall not overflow thee: when thou walkest through the fire, thou shalt not be burned; neither shall the flame kindle upon thee.—*Isa.* xliii. 2.

Look unto me, and be ye saved, all the ends of the earth: for I am God, and there is none else. —*Isa.* xlv. 22.

...I have chosen thee in the furnace of affliction. —*Isa.* xlviii. 10.

...Sorrow and mourning shall flee away.—*Isa.* li. 11.

I, even I, am he that comforteth you...12.

I have seen his ways, and will heal him: I will lead him also, and restore comforts unto him and to his mourners.—*Isa*. lvii. 18.

Behold, the Lord's hand is not shortened, that it cannot save; neither his ear heavy, that it cannot hear.—*Isa*. lix. 1.

In all their affliction he was afflicted, and the angel of his presence saved them...*Isa*. lxiii. 9.

O Lord, my strength, and my fortress, and my refuge in the day of affliction....*Jer*. xvi. 19.

Thus saith the Lord; Refrain thy voice from weeping, and thine eyes from tears: for thy work shall be rewarded.—*Jer*. xxxi. 16.

This I recall to my mind, therefore have I hope.—*Lam*. iii. 21.

For the Lord will not cast off for ever:—31.

But though he cause grief, yet will he have compassion according to the multitude of his mercies.—32.

For he doth not afflict willingly nor grieve the children of men.—33.

The Lord is good, a strong hold in the day of trouble;...*Nah*. i. 7.

FAITH IN GOD.
BELIEVE AND TRUST IN HIM.

———o———

...Fear not, Abram : I am thy shield, and thy exceeding great reward.—*Gen.* xv. 1.

And he believed in the Lord ; and he counted it to him for righteousness.—6.

And the angel of the Lord called unto Abraham out of heaven the second time,—*Gen.* xxii. 15.

And said,...for because thou hast done this thing, and hast not withheld thy son, thine only son :—16.

That in blessing I will bless thee, and in multiplying I will multiply thy seed as the stars of the heaven...17.

And in thy seed shall all the nations of the earth be blessed ; because thou hast obeyed my voice.—18.

...Fear not, for I am with thee...*Gen.* xxvi. 24.

...I am God, the God of thy father : fear not to go down into Egypt ; for I will there make of thee a great nation.—*Gen.* xlvi. 3.

That they may believe that the Lord God of their fathers,...hath appeared unto thee.—*Ex.* iv. 5.

And the people believed : and when they heard

that the Lord had visited the children of Israel, and that he had looked upon their affliction, then they bowed their heads and worshipped.—*Ex.* iv. 31.

Behold, to-morrow about this time I will cause it to rain a very grievous hail...*Ex.* ix. 18.

Send therefore now, and gather thy cattle, and all that thou hast in the field: for upon every man and beast which shall be found in the field, and shall not be brought home, the hail shall come down upon them, and they shall die.—19.

He that feared the word of the Lord among the servants of Pharaoh made his servants and his cattle flee into the houses:—20.

And he that regarded not the word of the Lord left his servants and his cattle in the field.—21.

...And the Lord sent thunder and hail, and the fire ran along upon the ground;...23.

And the hail smote throughout all the land of Egypt all that was in the field, both man and beast...25.

Fear ye not, stand still, and see the salvation of the Lord, which he will shew you to day...*Ex.* xiv. 13.

...Speak unto the children of Israel, that they go forward.—15.

...And the people feared the Lord, and believed the Lord, and his servant Moses.—31.

...Dread not, neither be afraid of them.—*Deut.* i. 29.

The Lord your God which goeth before you, he shall fight for you...30.

BELIEVE AND TRUST IN HIM.

Yet in this thing ye did not believe the Lord your God.—*Deut.* i. 32.

But ye that did cleave unto the Lord your God are alive every one of you this day.—*Deut.* iv. 4.

...Let not your hearts faint, fear not, and do not tremble, neither be ye terrified...*Deut.* xx. 3.

For the Lord your God is he that goeth with you ...to save you.—4.

Be strong and of a good courage, fear not, nor be afraid of them: for the Lord thy God, he it is that doth go with thee; he will not fail thee, nor forsake thee.—*Deut.* xxxi. 6.

The Lord recompense thy work, and a full reward be given thee of the Lord God of Israel, under whose wings thou art come to trust.—*Ruth* ii. 12.

...It may be that the Lord will work for us: for there is no restraint to the Lord to save by many or by few.—1 *Sam.* xiv. 6.

...The Lord that delivered me out of the paw of the lion, and out of the paw of the bear, he will deliver me out of the hand of this Philistine.—1 *Sam.* xvii. 37.

Thou comest to me with a sword, and with a spear, and with a shield: but I come to thee in the name of the Lord of hosts, the God of the armies of Israel, whom thou hast defied.—45.

And all this assembly shall know that the Lord saveth not with sword and spear...47.

The Lord is my rock, and my fortress, and my deliverer;—2 *Sam.* xxii. 2.

The God of my rock; in him will I trust...
2 *Sam.* xxii. 3.

...He is a buckler to all them that trust in him.—31.

He (Hezekiah) trusted in the Lord God of Israel...
2 *Kings* xviii. 5.

...Now on whom dost thou trust, that thou rebellest against me?—20.

Now, behold, thou trustest upon the staff of this bruised reed, even upon Egypt, on which if a man lean, it will go into his hand, and pierce it: so is Pharaoh king of Egypt unto all that trust on him.—21.

But if ye say unto me, We trust in the Lord our God: is not that he whose high places and whose altars Hezekiah hath taken away, and hath said to Judah and Jerusalem, Ye shall worship before this altar in Jerusalem?—22.

Lord, it is nothing with thee to help, whether with many, or with them that have no power: help us, O Lord our God; for we rest on thee, and in thy name we go against this multitude...2 *Ch.* xiv. 11.

...Because thou hast relied on the king of Syria, and not relied on the Lord thy God, therefore is the host of the king of Syria escaped out of thine hand.—2 *Ch.* xvi. 7.

Were not the Ethiopians and the Lubims a huge host, with very many chariots and horsemen? yet, because thou didst rely on the Lord, he delivered them into thine hand.—8.

Be not afraid nor dismayed by reason of this great

multitude; for the battle is not your's, but God's.—2 *Ch.* xx. 15.

Ye shall not need to fight in this battle: set yourselves, stand ye still, and see the salvation of the Lord with you;...fear not, nor be dismayed; to-morrow go out against them: for the Lord will be with you.—17.

...Believe in the Lord your God, so shall ye be established...20.

Be strong and courageous, be not afraid nor dismayed for the king of Assyria, nor for all the multitude that is with him: for there be more with us than with him:—2 *Ch.* xxxii. 7.

With him is an arm of flesh; but with us is the Lord our God to help us, and to fight our battles...8.

...Be not ye afraid of them: remember the Lord... *Neh.* iv. 14.

Though he slay me, yet will I trust in him... *Job* xiii. 15.

I laid me down and slept; I awaked; for the Lord sustained me.—*Ps.* iii. 5.

I will not be afraid of ten thousands of people, that have set themselves against me round about.—6.

Salvation belongeth unto the Lord...8.

I will both lay me down in peace, and sleep: for thou, Lord, only makest me dwell in safety.—*Ps.* iv. 8.

Let all those that put their trust in thee rejoice... *Ps.* v. 11.

O Lord my God, in thee do I put my trust... *Ps.* vii. 1.

And they that know thy name will put their trust in thee: for thou, Lord, hast not forsaken them that seek thee.—*Ps.* ix. 10.

In the Lord put I my trust...*Ps.* xi. 1.

Preserve me, O God: for in thee do I put my trust.—*Ps.* xvi. 1.

Shew thy marvellous lovingkindness, O thou that savest by thy right hand them which put their trust in thee...*Ps.* xvii. 7.

Some trust in chariots, and some in horses: but we will remember the name of the Lord our God.—*Ps.* xx. 7.

For the king trusteth in the Lord, and through the mercy of the most High he shall not be moved.—*Ps.* xxi. 7.

Our fathers trusted in thee: they trusted, and thou didst deliver them.—*Ps.* xxii. 4.

He trusted on the Lord that he would deliver him...8.

O my God, I trust in thee: let me not be ashamed. ...*Ps.* xxv. 2.

...I have trusted also in the Lord; therefore I shall not slide.—*Ps.* xxvi. 1.

The Lord is my light and my salvation; whom shall I fear?...*Ps.* xxvii. 1.

Though an host should encamp against me, my heart shall not fear...3.

The Lord is my strength and my shield; my heart trusted in him, and I am helped...*Ps.* xxviii. 7.

BELIEVE AND TRUST IN HIM.

...I trust in the Lord.—*Ps.* xxxi. 6.

...Fear was on every side: while they took counsel together against me, they devised to take away my life :—13.

But I trusted in thee, O Lord: I said, thou art my God.—14.

My times are in thy hand...15.

Oh how great is thy goodness, which thou hast laid up for them that fear thee; which thou has wrought for them that trust in thee before the sons of men!—19.

...He that trusteth in the Lord, mercy shall compass him about.—*Ps.* xxxii. 10.

For our heart shall rejoice in him, because we have trusted in his holy name.—*Ps.* xxxiii. 21.

O taste and see that the Lord is good: blessed is the man that trusteth in him.—*Ps.* xxxiv. 8.

...And none of them that trust in him shall be desolate.—22.

How excellent is thy lovingkindness, O God! therefore the children of men put their trust under the shadow of thy wings.—*Ps.* xxxvi. 7.

Trust in the Lord, and do good; so shalt thou dwell in the land, and verily thou shalt be fed.—*Ps.* xxxvii. 3.

Commit thy way unto the Lord; trust also in him; and he shall bring it to pass.—5.

Rest in the Lord, and wait patiently for him...7.

...Those that wait upon the Lord, they shall inherit the earth.—9.

And the Lord shall help them, and deliver them: ...and save them, because they trust in him.—*Ps.* xxxvii. 40.

And now, Lord, what wait I for? my hope is in thee.—*Ps.* xxxix. 7.

And he hath put a new song in my mouth, even praise unto our God: many shall see it, and fear, and shall trust in the Lord.—*Ps.* xl. 3.

Blessed is that man that maketh the Lord his trust...4.

For I will not trust in my bow, neither shall my sword save me.—*Ps.* xliv. 6.

...I trust in the mercy of God for ever and ever.—*Ps.* lii. 8.

As for me, I will call upon God; and the Lord shall save me.—*Ps.* lv. 16.

Cast thy burden upon the Lord, and he shall sustain thee...22.

What time I am afraid, I will trust in thee.—*Ps.* lvi. 3.

In God I will praise his word, in God I have put my trust; I will not fear what flesh can do unto me.—4.

In God have I put my trust: I will not be afraid what man can do unto me.—11.

Be merciful unto me, O God, be merciful unto me: for my soul trusteth in thee: yea, in the shadow of thy wings will I make my refuge, until these calamities be overpast.—*Ps.* lvii. 1.

BELIEVE AND TRUST IN HIM.

...I will trust in the covert of thy wings.—*Ps.* lxi 4.

Truly my soul waiteth upon God: from him cometh my salvation.—*Ps.* lxii. 1.

He only is my rock and my salvation; he is my defence; I shall not be greatly moved.—2.

My soul, wait thou only upon God; for my expectation is from him.—5.

Trust in him at all times; ye people, pour out your heart before him: God is a refuge for us.—8.

The righteous shall be glad in the Lord, and shall trust in him...*Ps.* lxiv. 10.

...O God of our salvation; who art the confidence of all the ends of the earth, and of them that are afar off upon the sea.—*Ps.* lxv. 5.

In thee, O Lord, do I put my trust...*Ps.* lxxi. 1.

For thou art my hope, O Lord God: thou art my trust from my youth.—5.

But it is good for me to draw near to God: I have put my trust in the Lord God, that I may declare all thy works.—*Ps.* lxxiii. 28.

O Lord of hosts, blessed is the man that trusteth in thee.—*Ps.* lxxxiv. 12.

...O thou my God, save thy servant that trusteth in thee.—*Ps.* lxxxvi. 2.

I will say of the Lord, He is my refuge and my fortress: my God; in him will I trust.—*Ps.* xci. 2.

He shall cover thee with his feathers, and under his wings shalt thou trust: his truth shall be thy shield and buckler.—4.

Thou shalt not be afraid for the terror by night; nor for the arrow that flieth by day;—*Ps.* xci. 5.

A thousand shall fall at thy side, and ten thousand at thy right hand; but it shall not come nigh thee.—7.

Because thou hast made the Lord, which is my refuge, even the most High, thy habitation;—9.

There shall no evil befall thee, neither shall any plague come nigh thy dwelling.—10.

For he shall give his angels charge over thee, to keep thee in all thy ways.—11.

He (a good man) shall not be afraid of evil tidings: his heart is fixed, trusting in the Lord.—*Ps.* cxii. 7.

Ye that fear the Lord, trust in the Lord: he is their help and their shield.—*Ps.* cxv. 11.

The Lord is on my side; I will not fear: what can man do unto me?—*Ps.* cxviii. 6.

It is better to trust in the Lord than to put confidence in man.—8.

It is better to trust in the Lord than to put confidence in princes.—9.

I will lift up mine eyes unto the hills, from whence cometh my help.—*Ps.* cxxi. 1.

My help cometh from the Lord, which made heaven and earth.—2.

They that trust in the Lord shall be as mount Zion, which cannot be removed, but abideth for ever.—*Ps.* cxxv. 1.

Let Israel hope in the Lord: for with the Lord

there is mercy, and with him is plenteous redemption.—*Ps.* cxxx. 7.

But mine eyes are unto thee, O God the Lord: in thee is my trust...*Ps.* cxli. 8.

Cause me to hear thy lovingkindness in the morning; for in thee do I trust.—*Ps.* cxliii. 8.

My goodness, and my fortress; my high tower, and my deliverer; my shield, and he in whom I trust...*Ps.* cxliv. 2.

Happy is that people, whose God is the Lord.—15.

Put not your trust in princes, nor in the son of man, in whom there is no help.—*Ps.* cxlvi. 3.

Happy is he that hath the God of Jacob for his help, whose hope is in the Lord his God.—5.

Trust in the Lord with all thine heart; and lean not unto thine own understanding.—*Prov.* iii. 5.

Be not afraid of sudden fear,...25.

For the Lord shall be thy confidence, and shall keep thy foot from being taken.—26.

...Whoso trusteth in the Lord, happy is he.— *Prov.* xvi. 20.

The name of the Lord is a strong tower: the righteous runneth into it, and is safe.—*Prov.* xviii. 10.

...Whoso putteth his trust in the Lord shall be safe.—*Prov.* xxix. 25.

Every word of God is pure: he is a shield unto them that put their trust in him.—*Prov.* xxx. 5.

Behold, God is my salvation; I will trust, and not be afraid; for the Lord JEHOVAH is my strength and my song; he also is become my salvation.—*Isa*. xii. 2.

...This is our God; we have waited for him, and he will save us: this is the Lord; we will be glad and rejoice in his salvation.—*Isa*. xxv. 9.

Thou wilt keep him in perfect peace, whose mind is stayed on thee: because he trusteth in thee.—*Isa*. xxvi. 3.

Trust ye in the Lord for ever: for in the Lord JEHOVAH is everlasting strength.—4.

...The Lord is a God of judgment: blessed are all they that wait for him.—*Isa*. xxx. 18.

O Lord, be gracious unto us; we have waited for thee: be thou their arm every morning, our salvation also in the time of trouble.—*Isa*. xxxiii. 2.

For the Lord is our judge, the Lord is our lawgiver, the Lord is our king; he will save us.—22.

Fear thou not; for I am with thee: be not dismayed; for I am thy God...*Isa*. xli. 10.

For I the Lord thy God will hold thy right hand, saying unto thee, Fear not; I will help thee.—13.

Fear not: for I am with thee...*Isa*. xliii. 5.

...Know and believe me, and understand that I am he: before me there was no God formed, neither shall there be after me.—10.

I, even I, am the Lord; and beside me there is no saviour.—11.

Yea, before the day was I am he; and there is none that can deliver out of my hand...13.

I am the Lord, your Holy One...*Isa.* xliii. 15.

Fear ye not, neither be afraid: have not I told thee from that time, and have declared it? ye are even my witnesses. Is there a God beside me? yea, there is no God; I know not any.—*Isa.* xliv. 8.

Look unto me, and be ye saved, all the ends of the earth: for I am God, and there is none else. —*Isa.* xlv. 22.

...Is my hand shortened at all, that it cannot redeem? or have I no power to deliver?...*Isa.* l. 2.

Behold, the Lord God will help me...9.

Who is among you that feareth the Lord?...let him trust in the name of the Lord, and stay upon his God.—10.

...All the ends of the earth shall see the salvation of our God.—*Isa.* lii. 10.

Be not afraid of their faces: for I am with thee to deliver thee, saith the Lord.—*Jer.* i. 8.

Truly in vain is salvation hoped for from the hills, and from the multitude of mountains: truly in the Lord our God is the salvation of Israel.—*Jer.* iii. 23.

Thus saith the Lord, Let not the wise man glory in his wisdom, neither let the mighty man glory in his might, let not the rich man glory in his riches: —*Jer.* ix. 23.

But let him that glorieth glory in this, that he understandeth and knoweth me, that I am the Lord...24.

Blessed is the man that trusteth in the Lord, and whose hope the Lord is.—*Jer.* xvii. 7.

Heal me, O Lord, and I shall be healed; save me, and I shall be saved: for thou art my praise. —*Jer.* xvii. 14.

...I will surely deliver thee...because thou hast put thy trust in me, saith the Lord.—*Jer.* xxxix. 18.

Whether it be good, or whether it be evil, we will obey the voice of the Lord our God....*Jer.* xlii. 6.

...Our God whom we serve is able to deliver us from the burning fiery furnace, and he will deliver us out of thine hand, O king.—*Dan.* iii. 17.

Then Nebuchadnezzar spake, and said, Blessed be the God of Shadrach, Meshach, and Abednego, who hath sent his angel, and delivered his servants that trusted in him...that they might not serve nor worship any god, except their own God.—28.

...Because there is no other God that can deliver after this sort.—29.

All the presidents of the kingdom, the governors, and the princes, the counsellors, and the captains, have consulted together to establish a royal statute, and to make a firm decree, that whosoever shall ask a petition of any God or man for thirty days, save of thee, O king, he shall be cast into the den of lions. —*Dan.* vi. 7.

Now when Daniel knew that the writing was signed, he went into his house; and his windows being opened in his chamber toward Jerusalem, he kneeled upon his knees three times a day, and

BELIEVE AND TRUST IN HIM.

prayed, and gave thanks before his God, as he did aforetime.—*Dan.* vi. 10.

Then the king commanded, and they brought Daniel, and cast him into the den of lions. Now the king spake and said unto Daniel, Thy God whom thou servest continually, he will deliver thee.—16.

Then said Daniel unto the king,...21.

My God hath sent his angel, and hath shut the lions' mouths, that they have not hurt me...22.

So Daniel was taken up out of the den, and no manner of hurt was found upon him, because he belived in his God.—23.

For all people will walk every one in the name of his God, and we will walk in the name of the Lord our God for ever and ever.—*Micah* iv. 5.

The Lord is good, a stronghold in the day of trouble; and he knoweth them that trust in him. —*Nah.* i. 7.

...The just shall live by his faith.—*Habak.* ii. 4.

Although the fig tree shall not blossom, neither shall fruit be in the vines; the labour of the olive shall fail, and the fields shall yield no meat; the flock shall be cut off from the fold, and there shall be no herd in the stalls:—*Habak.* iii. 17.

Yet I will rejoice in the Lord, I will joy in the God of my salvation.—18.

GOD OUR BEST FRIEND: SEEK COUNSEL AND GUIDANCE OF HIM.

...God is with thee in all that thou doest.—*Gen.* xxi. 22.

And he said, O Lord God...send me good speed this day, and shew kindness unto my master.—*Gen.* xxiv. 12.

...I being in the way, the Lord led me to the house of my master's brethren.—27.

And he said unto me, The Lord, before whom I walk, will send his angel with thee, and prosper thy way...40.

And I bowed down my head, and worshipped the Lord, and blessed the Lord God of my master Abraham, which had led me in the right way to take my master's brother's daughter unto his son.—48.

And he said unto them, Hinder me not, seeing the Lord hath prospered my way...56.

...And she went to enquire of the Lord.—*Gen.* xxv. 22.

And Moses cried unto the Lord, saying, What shall I do unto this people?...*Ex.* xvii. 4.

...The people come unto me to enquire of God.—*Ex.* xviii. 15.

Hearken now unto my voice, I will give thee counsel, and God shall be with thee: Be thou for the people God-ward, that thou mayest bring the causes unto God.—*Ex.* xviii. 19.

...And it came to pass, that every one which sought the Lord went out unto the tabernacle of the congregation, which was without the camp.—*Ex.* xxxiii. 7.

...If from thence thou shalt seek the Lord thy God, thou shalt find him, if thou seek him with all thy heart and with all thy soul.—*Deut.* iv. 29.

And he said unto him, Oh my Lord, wherewith shall I save Israel?...*Judg.* vi. 15.

And the Lord said unto him, Surely I will be with thee...16.

And they said unto him, Ask counsel, we pray thee, of God, that we may know whether our way which we go shall be prosperous.—*Judg.* xviii. 5.

And the children of Israel arose, and went up to the house of God, and asked counsel of God, and said, Which of us shall go up first to the battle against the children of Benjamin? And the Lord said, Judah shall go up first.—*Judg.* xx. 18.

And the children of Israel enquired of the Lord, (for the ark of the covenant of God was there in those days,—27.

And Phinehas, the son of Eleazar, the son of Aaron, stood before it in those days,) saying, Shall I yet again go out to battle against the children of Benjamin my brother, or shall I cease?...28.

And Saul asked counsel of God, Shall I go down after the Philistines? wilt thou deliver them into the hand of Israel.—1 *Sam.* xiv. 37.

And David went thence to Mizpeh of Moab: and he said unto the king of Moab, Let my father and my mother, I pray thee, come forth, and be with you, till I know what God will do for me.—1 *Sam.* xxii. 3.

And he enquired of the Lord for him…10.

Then David enquired of the Lord yet again. And the Lord answered him and said, Arise, go down to Keilah;…1 *Sam.* xxiii. 4.

Then said David…10.

Will Saul come down as thy servant hath heard? O Lord God of Israel, I beseech thee, tell thy servant. And the Lord said, He will come down.—11.

Then said David, Will the men of Keilah deliver me and my men into the hand of Saul? And the Lord said, They will deliver thee up.—12.

And David was greatly distressed;…but…encouraged himself in the Lord his God.—1 *Sam.* xxx. 6.

And David enquired at the Lord, saying, Shall I pursue after this troop? shall I overtake them? And he answered him, Pursue: for thou shalt surely overtake them, and without fail recover all.—8.

…The angel of the Lord said to Elijah the Tishbite, Arise, go up to meet the messengers of the king of Samaria, and say unto them, Is it not because there is not a God in Israel, that ye go to enquire of Baalzebub the god of Ekron?—2 *Kings* i. 3.

SEEK COUNSEL & GUIDANCE of HIM.

And the king said unto Hazael,...go, meet the man of God, and enquire of the Lord by him, saying, Shall I recover of this disease?—2 *Kings* viii. 8.

Go ye, enquire of the Lord for me, and for the people, and for all Judah, concerning the words of this book that is found...2 *Kings* xxii. 13.

So Saul died for his transgression which he committed against the Lord, even against the word of the Lord, which he kept not, and also for asking counsel of one that had a familiar spirit, to enquire of it;—1 *Ch.* x. 13.

And enquired not of the Lord...14.

And David enquired of God, saying, Shall I go up against the Philistines? and wilt thou deliver them into mine hand? And the Lord said unto him, Go up; for I will deliver them into thine hand.—1 *Ch.* xiv. 10.

And the Philistines yet again spread themselves abroad in the valley.—13.

Therefore David enquired again of God; and God said unto him, Go not up after them...14.

David therefore did as God commanded him.—16. ...Thus the Lord preserved David whithersoever he went.—1 *Ch.* xviii. 13.

Is not the Lord your God with you? and hath he not given you rest on every side?...1 *Ch.* xxii. 18.

And he (Rehoboam) did evil, because he prepared not his heart to seek the Lord.—2 *Ch.* xii. 14.

...Because we have sought the Lord our God, we

have sought him, and he hath given us rest on every side.—2 *Ch.* xiv. 7.

And they entered into a covenant to seek the Lord God of their fathers with all their heart and with all their soul.—2 *Ch.* xv. 12.

And the Lord was with Jehoshaphat, because he walked in the first ways of his father David, and sought not unto Baalim;—2 *Ch.* xvii. 3.

But sought to the Lord God of his father...4.

And Ahab king of Israel said unto Jehoshaphat king of Judah, Wilt thou go with me to Ramoth-gilead? And he answered him, I am as thou art, and my people as thy people...2 *Ch.* xviii. 3.

And Jehoshaphat said unto the king of Israel, Enquire, I pray thee, at the word of the Lord to day.—4.

Then there came some that told Jehoshaphat, saying, There cometh a great multitude against thee from beyond the sea on this side Syria...2 *Ch.* xx. 2.

And Jehoshaphat feared, and set himself to seek the Lord...3.

And Judah gathered themselves together, to ask help of the Lord: even out of all the cities of Judah they came to seek the Lord.—4.

So the realm of Jehoshaphat was quiet: for his God gave him rest round about.—30.

And he (Uzziah) sought God...and as long as he sought the Lord, God made him to prosper.— 2 *Ch.* xxvi. 5.

And in every work that he (Hezekiah) began in the service of the house of God, and in the law, and in the commandments, to seek his God, he did it with all his heart, and prospered.—2 *Ch.* xxxi. 21.

...In the eighth year of his (Josiah's) reign, while he was yet young, he began to seek after the God of David his father...2 *Ch.* xxxiv. 3.

...I proclaimed a fast there, at the river Ahaba, that we might afflict ourselves before our God, to seek of him a right way for us, and for our little ones, and for all our substance.—*Ezra* viii. 21.

...The hand of our God is upon all them for good that seek him...22.

So we fasted and besought our God for this: and he was intreated of us.—23.

I would seek unto God, and unto God would I commit my cause.—*Job* v. 8.

If thou wouldest seek unto God betimes, and make thy supplication to the Almighty;—*Job* viii. 5.

Though thy beginning was small, yet thy latter end should greatly increase.—7.

...Thou, Lord, has not forsaken them that seek thee.—*Ps.* ix. 10.

The wicked, through the pride of his countenance, will not seek after God: God is not in all his thoughts.—*Ps.* x. 4.

The Lord looked down from heaven upon the children of men, to see if there were any that did understand, and seek God.—*Ps.* xiv. 2.

I will bless the Lord, who hath given me counsel. …*Ps.* xvi. 7.

Shew me thy ways, O Lord; teach me thy paths. —*Ps.* xxv. 4.

Teach me thy way, O Lord, and lead me in a plain path.—*Ps.* xxvii. 11.

…For thy name's sake lead me, and guide me… *Ps.* xxxi. 3.

I will instruct thee and teach thee in the way which thou shalt go: I will guide thee with mine eye.— *Ps.* xxxii. 8.

The young lions do lack, and suffer hunger: but they that seek the Lord shall not want any good thing.—*Ps.* xxxiv. 10.

Let all those who seek thee rejoice and be glad in thee…*Ps.* xl. 16.

O God, thou art my God; early will I seek thee. …*Ps.* lxiii. 1.

…Your heart shall live that seek God.—*Ps.* lxix. 32.

Thou shalt guide me with thy counsel…*Ps.* lxxiii. 24.

When he slew them, then they sought him: and they returned and enquired early after God.— *Ps.* lxxviii. 34.

…Let the heart of them rejoice that seek the Lord. —*Ps.* cv. 3.

Seek the Lord, and his strength: seek his face evermore.—4.

…They waited not for his counsel.—*Ps.* cvi. 13.

…I will walk at liberty; for I seek thy precepts. —*Ps.* cxix. 45.

In all thy ways acknowledge him, and he shall direct thy paths.—*Prov.* iii. 6.

Counsel is mine, and sound wisdom...*Prov.* viii. 14.

Commit thy works unto the Lord...*Prov.* xvi. 3.

There are many devices in a man's heart; nevertheless the counsel of the Lord, that shall stand. —*Prov.* xix. 21.

...Let the counsel of the Holy One of Israel draw nigh and come, that we may know it!—*Isa.* v. 19.

And when they shall say unto you, Seek unto them that have familiar spirits,...should not a people seek unto their God?...*Isa.* viii. 19.

To the law and to the testimony: if they speak not according to this word, it is because there is no light in them.—20.

For the people turneth not unto him that smiteth them, neither do they seek the Lord of hosts.— *Isa.* ix. 13.

...The Lord of hosts, which is wonderful in counsel, and excellent in working.—*Isa.* xxviii. 29.

Woe unto them that seek deep to hide their counsel from the Lord...*Isa.* xxix. 15.

Woe to the rebellious children, saith the Lord, that take counsel, but not of me; and that cover with a covering, but not of my spirit, that they may add sin to sin...*Isa.* xxx. 1.

That walk to go down into Egypt, and have not asked at my mouth...2.

Woe to them that go down to Egypt for help;

...but they look not unto the Holy One of Israel, neither seek the Lord!—*Isa.* xxxi. 1.

...O Lord, I am oppressed; undertake for me.—*Isa.* xxxviii. 14.

...I said not unto the seed of Jacob, Seek ye me in vain...*Isa.* xlv. 19.

...I am the Lord thy God, which teacheth thee to profit, which leadeth thee by the way that thou shouldest go.—*Isa.* xlviii. 17.

Seek ye the Lord while he may be found, call ye upon him while he is near.—*Isa.* lv. 6.

O Lord, I know that the way of man is not in himself: it is not in man that walketh to direct his steps.—*Jer.* x. 23.

And ye shall seek me, and find me, when ye shall search for me with all your heart.—*Jer.* xxix. 13.

That the Lord thy God may shew us the way wherein we may walk, and the thing that we may do.—*Jer.* xlii. 3.

In those days, and in that time, saith the Lord,... they shall go, and seek the Lord their God.—*Jer.* l. 4.

They shall ask the way to Zion with their faces thitherward, saying, Come, and let us join ourselves to the Lord in a perpetual covenant that shall not be forgotten.—5.

For thus saith the Lord unto the house of Israel, Seek ye me, and ye shall live.—*Amos* v. 4.

Seek ye the Lord, all ye meek of the earth... *Zeph.* ii. 2.

THE FAVOUR OF GOD A SHIELD AND A BLESSING.

—o—

...Noah found grace in the eyes of the Lord.—*Gen.* vi. 8.

And I will make of thee a great nation, and I will bless thee, and make thy name great; and thou shalt be a blessing.—*Gen.* xii. 2.

...The Lord hath blessed my master greatly; and he is become great...*Gen.* xxiv. 35.

And Isaac said unto them, Wherefore come ye to me, seeing ye hate me, and have sent me away from you?—*Gen.* xxvi. 27.

And they said, We saw certainly that the Lord was with thee: and we said, Let there be now an oath betwixt us, even betwixt us and thee;...28.

That thou wilt do us no hurt,...as we have done unto thee nothing but good, and have sent thee away in peace: thou art now the blessed of the Lord.—29.

And Jacob sent and called Rachel and Leah to the field unto his flock,—*Gen.* xxxi. 4.

And said unto them, I see your father's countenance, that it is not toward me as before; but the God of my father hath been with me.—5.

And your father hath deceived me, and changed my wages ten times; but God suffered him not to hurt me.—*Gen.* xxxi. 7.

And Laban said to Jacob,...26.

It is in the power of my hand to do you hurt: but the God of your father spake unto me yesternight, saying, Take thou heed that thou speak not to Jacob either good or bad.—29.

Except the God of my father, the God of Abraham, and the fear of Isaac, had been with me, surely thou hadst sent me away now empty. God hath seen mine affliction and the labour of my hands, and rebuked thee yesternight.—42.

And the Lord was with Joseph, and he was a prosperous man...*Gen.* xxxix. 2.

And his master saw that the Lord was with him, and that the Lord made all that he did to prosper in his hand.—3.

And Joseph found grace in his sight, and he served him...4.

And Joseph's master took him, and put him into the prison, a place where the king's prisoners were bound: and he was there in the prison.—20.

But the Lord was with Joseph, and shewed him mercy, and gave him favour in the sight of the keeper of the prison.—21.

And the keeper of the prison committed to Joseph's hand all the prisoners that were in the prison; and whatsoever they did there, he was the doer of it.—22.

The keeper of the prison looked not to anything that was under his hand; because the Lord was with him, and that which he did, the Lord made it to prosper.—*Gen.* xxxix. 23.

And Pharaoh said unto his servants, Can we find such a one as this is, a man in whom the spirit of God is?—*Gen.* xli. 38.

And God looked upon the children of Israel, and God had respect unto them.—*Ex.* ii. 25.

And I will give this people favour in the sight of the Egyptians...*Ex.* iii. 21.

The Lord shall fight for you, and ye shall hold your peace.—*Ex.* xiv. 14.

...The Egyptians said, Let us flee from the face of Israel; for the Lord fighteth for them against the Egyptians.—25.

And the Lord said unto Moses, I will do this thing also that thou hast spoken: for thou hast found grace in my sight, and I know thee by name.—*Ex.* xxxiii. 17.

And they shall put my name upon the children of Israel; and I will bless them.—*Num.* vi. 27.

If the Lord delight in us, then he will bring us into this land, and give it us; a land which floweth with milk and honey.—*Num.* xiv. 8.

...The Lord is with us: fear them not.—9.

...They have heard that thou Lord art among this people...14.

And God said unto Balaam, Thou shalt not go

with them ; thou shalt not curse the people: for they are blessed.—*Num.* xxii. 12.

And Balak said unto Balaam, What hast thou done unto me ? I took thee to curse mine enemies, and, behold, thou hast blessed them altogether.— *Num.* xxiii. 11.

And he answered and said, Must I not take heed to speak that which the Lord hath put in my mouth ?—12.

Behold, I have received commandment to bless : and he hath blessed ; and I cannot reverse it.—20.

For the Lord thy God hath blessed thee in all the works of thy hand : he knoweth thy walking through this great wilderness : these forty years the Lord thy God hath been with thee ; thou hast lacked nothing. —*Deut.* ii. 7.

And because he loved thy fathers, therefore he chose their seed after them...*Deut.* iv. 37.

The Lord did not set his love upon you, nor choose you, because ye were more in number than any people; for ye were the fewest of all people :—*Deut.* vii. 7.

But because the Lord loved you, and because he would keep the oath which he had sworn unto your fathers...8.

Only the Lord had a delight in thy fathers to love them...*Deut.* x. 15.

...The Lord thy God would not hearken unto Balaam; but the Lord thy God turned the curse into a blessing

unto thee, because the Lord thy God loved thee.—
Deut. xxiii. 5.

...The beloved of the Lord shall dwell in safety by him; and the Lord shall cover him all the day long, and he shall dwell between his shoulders.—
Deut. xxxiii. 12.

...Who is like unto thee, O people saved by the Lord, the shield of thy help!...29.

On that day the Lord magnified Joshua in the sight of all Israel....*Josh.* iv. 14.

And the child Samuel grew on, and was in favour both with the Lord, and also with men.—1 *Sam.* ii. 26.

And Saul saw and knew that the Lord was with David...1 *Sam.* xviii. 28.

...And Saul sought him every day, but God delivered him not into his hand.—1 *Sam.* xxiii. 14.

And when David heard that Nabal was dead, he said, Blessed be the Lord that hath pleaded the cause of my reproach from the hand of Nabal, and hath kept his servant from evil.—1 *Sam.* xxv. 39.

And the king said unto Zadok, Carry back the ark of God into the city: if I shall find favour in the eyes of the Lord, he will bring me again, and shew me both it, and his habitation.—2 *Sam.* xv. 25.

They prevented me in the day of my calamity: but the Lord was my stay.—2 *Sam.* xxii. 19.

He brought me forth into a large place: he delivered me, because he delighted in me.—20.

And Solomon the son of David was strengthened

in his kingdom, and the Lord his God was with him, and magnified him exceedingly.—2 *Ch.* i. 1.

...They fell to him out of Israel in abundance, when they saw that the Lord his God was with him.— 2 *Ch.* xv. 9.

...They compassed about him to fight: but Jehoshaphat cried out, and the Lord helped him; and God moved them to depart from him.—2 *Ch.* xviii. 31.

...And the king granted me, according to the good hand of my God upon me.—*Neh.* ii. 8.

Then I told them of the hand of my God, which was good upon me...18.

Then answered I them, and said unto them, The God of heaven, he will prosper us...20.

...They met not the children with bread and with water, but hired Balaam against them, that he should curse them: howbeit our God turned the curse into a blessing.—*Neh.* xiii. 2.

Thou hast granted me life and favour, and thy visitation hath preserved my spirit.—*Job* x. 12.

But thou, O Lord, art a shield for me; my glory, and the lifter up of mine head.—*Ps.* iii. 3.

...Thy blessing is upon thy people.—8.

For thou, Lord, wilt bless the righteous; with favour wilt thou compass him as with a shield.— *Ps.* v. 12.

...In his favour is life...*Ps.* xxx. 5.

Lord, by thy favour thou hast made my mountain to stand strong.—7.

A SHIELD AND A BLESSING.

By this I know that thou favourest me, because mine enemy doth not triumph over me.—*Ps.* xli. 11.

...Neither did their own arm save them: but thy right hand, and thine arm, and the light of thy countenance, because thou hadst a favour unto them.—*Ps.* xliv. 3.

...Grace is poured into thy lips: therefore God hath blessed thee for ever.—*Ps.* xlv. 2.

When I cry unto thee, then shall mine enemies turn back: this I know; for God is for me.—*Ps.* lvi. 9.

For the Lord God is a sun and shield: the Lord will give grace and glory:...*Ps.* lxxxiv. 11.

Lord, thou hast been favourable unto thy land. ...*Ps.* lxxxv. 1.

...In thy favour our horn shall be exalted.—*Ps.* lxxxix. 17.

I intreated thy favour with my whole heart... *Ps.* cxix. 58.

If it had not been the Lord who was on our side, when men rose up against us:—*Ps.* cxxiv. 2.

Then they had swallowed us up quick, when their wrath was kindled against us.—3.

Except the Lord build the house, they labour in vain that build it: except the Lord keep the city, the watchman waketh but in vain.—*Ps.* cxxvii. 1.

Let not mercy and truth forsake thee:...*Prov.* iii. 3.

So shalt thou find favour and good understanding in the sight of God and man.—4.

Whoso findeth me (Wisdom) findeth life, and shall obtain favour of the Lord.—*Prov.* viii. 35.

Blessings are upon the head of the just.—*Prov.* x. 6.

The blessing of the Lord, it maketh rich, and he addeth no sorrow with it.—22.

...The desire of the righteous shall be granted.—24.

He that diligently seeketh good procureth favour. —*Prov.* xi. 27.

A good man obtaineth favour of the Lord.— *Prov.* xii. 2.

When a man's ways please the Lord, he maketh even his enemies to be at peace with him.—*Prov.* xvi. 7.

...In my wrath I smote thee, but in my favour have I had mercy on thee.—*Isa.* lx. 10.

And I will make thee unto this people a fenced brasen wall: and they shall fight against thee, but they shall not prevail against thee: for I am with thee to save thee and to deliver thee, saith the Lord. —*Jer.* xv. 20.

GRATITUDE TO GOD.
PRAISE AND THANKSGIVING.

—o—

...And the man bowed down his head, and worshipped the Lord.—*Gen.* xxiv. 26.

And he said, Blessed be the Lord God of my master Abraham, who hath not left destitute my master of his mercy and his truth...27.

Then Jacob said unto his household,...*Gen.* xxxv. 2. ...Let us arise, and go up to Beth-el; and I will make there an altar unto God, who answered me in the day of my distress, and was with me in the way which I went.—3.

And when ye will offer a sacrifice of thanksgiving unto the Lord, offer it at your own will.—*Lev.* xxii. 29.

When thou hast eaten and art full, then thou shalt bless the Lord thy God for the good land which he hath given thee.—*Deut.* viii. 10.

...Thou shalt remember the Lord thy God: for it is he that giveth thee power to get wealth...18.

And thou shalt keep the feast of weeks unto the Lord thy God with a tribute of a freewill offering thine hand, which thou shalt give unto the Lord thy God, according as the Lord thy God hath blessed thee.—*Deut.* xvi. 10.

Only fear the Lord, and serve him in truth with all your heart : for consider how great things he hath done for you.—1 *Sam.* xii. 24.

The Lord liveth; and blessed be my rock; and exalted be the God of the rock of my salvation.— 2 *Sam.* xxii. 47.

Therefore I will give thanks unto thee, O Lord, among the heathen, and I will sing praises unto thy name.—50.

And he (David) appointed certain of the Levites to minister before the ark of the Lord, and to record, and to thank and praise the Lord God of Israel.—1 *Ch.* xvi. 4.

Give thanks unto the Lord, call upon his name, make known his deeds among the people.—8.

For great is the Lord, and greatly to be praised...25.

Glory and honour are in his presence...27.

Give unto the Lord the glory due unto his name...29.

O give thanks unto the Lord; for he is good; for his mercy endureth for ever.—34.

Save us, O God of our salvation,...that we may give thanks to thy holy name, and glory in thy praise,—35.

Blessed be the Lord God of Israel for ever and ever. And all the people said, Amen, and praised the Lord.—36.

...Stand every morning to thank and praise the Lord, and likewise at even.—1 *Ch.* xxiii. 30.

Wherefore David blessed the Lord before all the congregation : and David said, Blessed be thou, Lord God of Israel our father, for ever and ever. —1 *Ch.* xxix. 10.

Thine, O Lord, is the greatness, and the power, and the glory, and the victory, and the majesty : for all that is in the heaven and in the earth is thine ; thine is the kingdom, O Lord, and thou art exalted as head above all.—11.

Now therefore, our God, we thank thee, and praise thy glorious name.—13.

And David said to all the congregation, Now bless the Lord your God. And all the congregation blessed the Lord God of their fathers, and bowed down their heads, and worshipped the Lord.—20.

And when all the children of Israel saw how the fire came down, and the glory of the Lord upon the house, they bowed themselves with their faces to the ground upon the pavement, and worshipped, and praised the Lord, saying, For he is good ; for his mercy endureth for ever.—2 *Ch.* vii. 3.

And the Levites...stood up to praise the Lord God of Israel with a loud voice on high.—2 *Ch.* xx. 19.

Moreover Hezekiah the king and the princes commanded the Levites to sing praise unto the Lord... And they sang praises with gladness, and they bowed their heads and worshipped.—2 *Ch.* xxix. 30.

And Hezekiah appointed the courses of the priests and the Levites after their courses, every man according to his service...to give thanks, and to praise in the gates of the tents of the Lord.—2 Ch. xxxi. 2.

And they sang together by course in praising and giving thanks unto the Lord; because he is good, for his mercy endureth for ever toward Israel. And all the people shouted with a great shout when they praised the Lord, because the foundation of the house of the Lord was laid.—Ezra iii. 11.

And Ezra blessed the Lord, the great God. And all the people answered, Amen, Amen, with lifting up their hands: and they bowed their heads, and worshipped the Lord with their faces to the ground. —Neh. viii. 6.

...Stand up and bless the Lord your God for ever and ever: and blessed be thy glorious name, which is exalted above all blessing and praise.—Neh. ix. 5.

And Mattaniah...was the principal to begin the thanksgiving in prayer...Neh. xi. 17.

For in the days of David and Asaph of old there were chief of the singers, and songs of praise and thanksgiving unto God.—Neh. xii. 46.

I will praise the Lord according to his righteousness: and will sing praise to the name of the Lord most high.—Ps. vii. 17.

O Lord our Lord, how excellent is thy name in all the earth!—Ps. viii. 9.

PRAISE AND THANKSGIVING.

I will praise thee, O Lord, with my whole heart... *Ps.* ix. 1.

I will sing unto the Lord, because he hath dealt bountifully with me.—*Ps.* xiii. 6.

I will bless the Lord, who hath given me counsel. ...*Ps.* xvi. 7.

Therefore will I give thanks unto thee, O Lord... *Ps.* xviii. 49.

My praise shall be of thee in the great congregation...*Ps.* xxii. 25.

...They shall praise the Lord that seek him...26.

I will wash mine hands in innocency: so will I compass thine altar, O Lord:—*Ps.* xxvi. 6.

That I may publish with the voice of thanksgiving, and tell of all thy wondrous works.—7.

Sing unto the Lord, O ye saints of his, and give thanks at the remembrance of his holiness.—*Ps.* xxx. 4.

To the end that my glory may sing praise to thee, and not be silent. O Lord my God, I will give thanks unto thee for ever.—12.

Blessed be the Lord: for he hath shewed me his marvellous kindness in a strong city.—*Ps.* xxxi. 21.

Rejoice in the Lord, O ye righteous: for praise is comely for the upright.—*Ps.* xxxiii. 1.

I will give thee thanks in the great congregation: I will praise thee among much people.—*Ps.* xxxv. 18

According to thy name, O God, so is thy praise unto the ends of the earth...*Ps.* xlviii. 10.

Offer unto God thanksgiving; and pay thy vows unto the most High.--*Ps.* l. 14.

O Lord, open thou my lips; and my mouth shall shew forth thy praise.—*Ps.* li. 15.

I will praise thee for ever, because thou hast done it...*Ps.* lii. 9.

...I will praise thy name, O Lord; for it is good.— *Ps.* liv. 6.

Blessed be the Lord, who daily loadeth us with benefits, even the God of our salvation.—*Ps.* lxviii. 19.

I will praise the name of God with a song, and will magnify him with thanksgiving.—*Ps.* lxix. 30.

My mouth shall shew forth thy righteousness and thy salvation all the day...*Ps.* lxxi. 15.

Unto thee, O God, do we give thanks, unto thee do we give thanks: for that thy name is near thy wondrous works declare.—*Ps.* lxxv. 1.

So we thy people and sheep of thy pasture will give thee thanks for ever: we will shew forth thy praise to all generations.—*Ps.* lxxix. 13.

I will praise thee, O Lord, my God with all my heart: and I will glorify thy name for evermore.— *Ps.* lxxxvi. 12.

It is a good thing to give thanks unto the Lord, and to sing praises unto thy name, O most High.— *Ps.* xcii. 1.

To shew forth thy lovingkindness in the morning, and thy faithfulness every night.—2.

Let us come before his presence with thanksgiving...*Ps.* xcv. 2.

Enter into his gates with thanksgiving, and into his courts with praise: be thankful unto him, and bless his name.—*Ps.* c. 4.

Bless the Lord, O my soul: and all that is within me, bless his holy name.—*Ps.* ciii. 1.

Bless the Lord, O my soul, and forget not all his benefits:—2.

Who redeemeth thy life from destruction; who crowneth thee with lovingkindness and tender mercies;—4.

Who satisfieth thy mouth with good things; so that thy youth is renewed like the eagle's.—5.

O give thanks unto the Lord; call upon his name: make known his deeds among the people.—*Ps.* cv. 1.

Oh that men would praise the Lord for his goodness, and for his wonderful works to the children of men!—*Ps.* cvii. 31.

Let them exalt him also in the congregation of the people, and praise him in the assembly of the elders.—32.

O God, my heart is fixed; I will sing and give praise even with my glory.—*Ps.* cviii. 1.

I will praise thee, O Lord, among the people: and I will sing praises unto thee among the nations.—3.

Be thou exalted, O God, above the heavens: and thy glory above all the earth.—5.

What shall I render unto the Lord for all his benefits toward me?—*Ps.* cxvi. 12.

I will offer to thee the sacrifice of thanksgiving, and will call upon the name of the Lord—17.

O praise the Lord, all ye nations: praise him all ye people.—*Ps.* cxvii. 1.

For his merciful kindness is great toward us: and the truth of the Lord endureth for ever. Praise ye the Lord.—2.

O give thanks unto the Lord; for he is good: because his mercy endureth for ever.—*Ps.* cxviii. 1.

I will praise thee: for thou hast heard me, and art become my salvation.—21.

I will praise thee with uprightness of heart... *Ps.* cxix. 7.

At midnight I will rise to give thanks unto thee because of thy righteous judgments.—62.

Seven times a day do I praise thee because of thy righteous judgments.—164.

My lips shall utter praise, when thou has taught me thy statutes.—171.

I will worship toward thy holy temple, and praise thy name for thy lovingkindness and for thy truth: for thou hast magnified thy word above all thy name.—*Ps.* cxxxviii. 2.

I will extol thee, my God, O king; and I will bless thy name for ever and ever.—*Ps.* cxlv. 1.

Every day will I bless thee;...2.

My mouth shall speak the praise of the Lord: and let all flesh bless his holy name for ever and ever.—*Ps.* cxlv. 21.

While I live will I praise the Lord: I will sing praises unto my God while I have any being.—*Ps.* cxlvi. 2.

Praise ye the Lord from the heavens: praise him in the heights.—*Ps.* cxlviii. 1.

Praise ye him, all his angels: praise ye him, all his hosts.—2.

Praise ye him, sun and moon: praise him, all ye stars of light.—3.

Let them praise the name of the Lord: for he commanded, and they were created.—5.

Both young men, and maidens; old men, and children:—12.

Let them praise the name of the Lord: for his name alone is excellent; his glory is above the earth and heaven.—13.

Let every thing that hath breath praise the Lord. Praise ye the Lord.—*Ps.* cl. 6.

Honour the Lord with thy substance, and with the first fruits of all thine increase.—*Prov.* iii. 9.

The living, the living, he shall praise thee, as I do this day...*Isa.* xxxviii. 19.

Sing unto the Lord a new song, and his praise from the end of the earth, ye that go down to the sea, and all that is therein; the isles, and the inhabitants thereof.—*Isa.* xlii. 10.

Let them give glory unto the Lord, and declare his praise in the islands.—*Isa.* xlii. 12.

I will mention the lovingkindnesses of the Lord, and the praises of the Lord, according to all that the Lord hath bestowed on us...*Isa.* lxiii. 7.

...Then Daniel blessed the God of heaven.—*Dan.* ii. 19.

...And said, Blessed be the name of God for ever and ever: for wisdom and might are his.—20.

I thank thee, and praise thee, O thou God of my fathers, who hast given me wisdom and might, and hast made known unto me now what we desired of thee...23.

...I Nebuchadnezzar lifted up mine eyes unto heaven, and mine understanding returned unto me, and I blessed the most High, and I praised and honoured him that liveth for ever...*Dan.* iv. 34.

Now when Daniel knew that the writing was signed, he went into his house...and prayed, and gave thanks before his God, as he did aforetime.—*Dan.* vi. 10.

And ye shall eat in plenty, and be satisfied, and praise the name of the Lord your God, that hath dealt wondrously with you...*Joel* ii. 26.

...I will sacrifice unto thee with the voice of thanksgiving; I will pay *that* that I have vowed. Salvation is of the Lord.—*Jonah* ii. 9.

THE WICKEDNESS OF INGRATITUDE TO GOD.

Because thou servedst not the Lord thy God with joyfulness, and with gladness of heart, for the abundance of all things;—*Deut.* xxviii. 47.

Therefore shalt thou serve thine enemies which the Lord shall send against thee...48.

Do ye thus requite the Lord, O foolish people and unwise? is not he thy father that hath bought thee? hath he not made thee, and established thee? —*Deut.* xxxii. 6.

...He forsook God which made him, and lightly esteemed the Rock of his salvation.—15.

Of the Rock that begat thee thou art unmindful, and hast forgotten God that formed thee.—18.

And the children of Israel remembered not the Lord their God, who had delivered them out of the hands of all their enemies on every side.—*Judg.* viii. 34.

Did not I deliver you from the Egyptians, and from the Amorites?....*Judg.* x. 11.

Yet ye have forsaken me, and served other gods: wherefore I will deliver you no more.—13.

Go and cry unto the gods which ye have chosen; let them deliver you in the time of your tribulation.—*Judg.* x. 14.

...Ye have this day rejected your God, who himself saved you out of all your adversities and your tribulations...1 *Sam.* x. 19.

None saith, Where is God my maker, who giveth songs in the night;—*Job* xxxv. 10.

Who teacheth us more than the beasts of the earth, and maketh us wiser than the fowls of heaven?—11.

They (the children of Ephraim) kept not the covenant of God, and refused to walk in his law;—*Ps.* lxxviii. 10.

And forgat his works, and his wonders that he had shewed them.—11.

He clave the rocks in the wilderness, and gave them drink as out of the great depths.—15.

And they sinned yet more against him by provoking the most High in the wilderness.—17.

Yea, they spake against God; they said, Can God furnish a table in the wilderness?—19.

Behold, he smote the rock, that the waters gushed out, and the streams overflowed; can he give bread also? can he provide flesh for his people?—20.

Therefore the Lord heard this, and was wroth...21.

Because they believed not in God, and trusted not in his salvation.—22.

They forgat God their saviour, which had done great things in Egypt.—*Ps.* cvi. 21.

INGRATITUDE TO GOD.

Yea, they despised the pleasant land, they believed not his word.—*Ps.* cvi. 24.

Thus they provoked him to anger with their inventions…29.

Hear, O heavens, and give ear, O earth: for the Lord hath spoken, I have nourished and brought up children, and they have rebelled against me.—*Isa.* i. 2.

The ox knoweth his owner, and the ass his master's crib: but Israel doth not know, my people doth not consider.—3.

…They have forsaken the Lord, they have provoked the Holy One of Israel to anger, they are gone away backward.—4.

I, even I, am he that comforteth you: who art thou, that thou shouldest be afraid of a man,…*Isa.* li. 12.

And forgettest the Lord thy maker, that hath stretched forth the heavens, and laid the foundations of the earth.—13.

For he said, Surely they are my people, children that will not lie: so he was their Saviour.—*Isa.* lxiii. 8.

In all their affliction he was afflicted, and the angel of his presence saved them: in his love and in his pity he redeemed them; and he bare them, and carried them all the days of old.—9.

But they rebelled, and vexed his holy Spirit…10.

Thus saith the Lord, What iniquity have your fathers found in me, that they are gone far from me, and have walked after vanity, and are become vain?—*Jer.* ii. 5.

Neither said they, Where is the Lord that brought us up out of the land of Egypt, that led us through the wilderness...*Jer.* ii. 6.

For my people have committed two evils; they have forsaken me the fountain of living waters, and hewed them out cisterns, broken cisterns, that can hold no water.—13.

Hast thou not procured this unto thyself, in that thou hast forsaken the Lord thy God, when he led thee by the way?—17.

...Know therefore and see that it is an evil thing and bitter, that thou hast forsaken the Lord thy God, and that my fear is not in thee, saith the Lord of hosts.—19.

THE JUSTICE AND JUDGMENT OF GOD.

———o———

And Abraham drew near, and said, Wilt thou also destroy the righteous with the wicked?—*Gen.* xviii. 23.

That be far from thee to do after this manner, to slay the righteous with the wicked: and that the righteous should be as the wicked, that be far from thee: Shall not the Judge of all the earth do right?—25.

The Lord is long-suffering, and of great mercy, forgiving iniquity and transgression, and by no means clearing the guilty...*Num.* xiv. 18.

For the Lord your God is God of gods, and Lord of lords...which regardeth not persons, nor taketh reward:—*Deut.* x. 17.

He doth execute the judgment of the fatherless and widow, and loveth the stranger, in giving him food and raiment.—18.

He is the Rock, his work is perfect: for all his ways are judgment: a God of truth and without iniquity, just and right is he...*Deut.* xxxii. 4.

For the Lord shall judge his people...36.

...The Lord is a God of knowledge, and by him actions are weighed.—1 *Sam.* ii. 3.

He is the Lord our God; his judgments are in all the earth.—1 *Ch.* xvi. 14.

Howbeit thou art just in all that is brought upon us; for thou hast done right, but we have done wickedly.—*Neh.* ix. 33.

...Who ever perished, being innocent? or where were the righteous cut off?—*Job* iv. 7.

Even as I have seen, they that plow iniquity, and sow wickedness, reap the same—8.

Doth God pervert judgment? or doth the Almighty pervert justice?—*Job* viii. 3.

Shall any teach God knowledge? seeing he judgeth those that are high.—*Job* xxi. 22.

For the work of a man shall he render unto him, and cause every man to find according to his ways.—*Job* xxxiv. 11.

...Wilt thou condemn him that is most just?—17.

...Him that accepteth not the persons of princes, nor regardeth the rich more than the poor? for they all are the work of his hands.—19.

For he will not lay upon man more than right; that he should enter into judgment with God.—23.

Touching the Almighty, we cannot find him out: he is excellent in power, and in judgment, and in plenty of justice...*Job* xxxvii. 23.

Therefore the ungodly shall not stand in the

JUDGMENT OF GOD.

judgment, nor sinners in the congregation of the righteous.—*Ps.* i. 5.

God judgeth the righteous, and God is angry with the wicked every day.—*Ps.* vii. 11.

For thou hast maintained my right and my cause; thou satest in the throne judging right.—*Ps.* ix. 4.

...He hath prepared his throne for judgment.—7.

And he shall judge the world in righteousness, he shall minister judgment to the people in uprightness.—8.

The Lord is known by the judgment which he executeth: the wicked is snared in the work of his own hands.—16.

...Thou wilt cause thine ear to hear:—*Ps.* x. 17.

To judge the fatherless and the oppressed, that the man of the earth may no more oppress.—18.

...The judgments of the Lord are true and righteous altogether.—*Ps.* xix. 9.

Judge me, O Lord; for I have walked in mine integrity...*Ps.* xxvi. 1.

He shall call to the heavens from above, and to the earth, that he may judge his people.—*Ps.* l. 4.

And the heavens shall declare his righteousness: for God is judge himself.—6.

Save me, O God, by thy name, and judge me by thy strength.—*Ps.* liv. 1.

...Verily there is a reward for the righteous: verily there is a God that judgeth in the earth.—*Ps.* lviii. 11.

O let the nations be glad and sing for joy: for thou

shalt judge the people righteously, and govern the nations upon earth.—*Ps.* lxvii. 4.

Thou, even thou, art to be feared: and who may stand in thy sight when once thou art angry?—*Ps.* lxxvi. 7.

Thou didst cause judgment to be heard from heaven; the earth feared, and was still,—8.

When God arose to judgment, to save all the meek of the earth.—9.

God standeth in the congregation of the mighty; he judgeth among the gods.—*Ps.* lxxxii. 1.

Arise, O God, judge the earth: for thou shalt inherit all nations.—8.

Justice and judgment are the habitation of thy throne: mercy and truth shall go before thy face.—*Ps.* lxxxix. 14.

For the Lord will not cast off his people, neither will he forsake his inheritance.—*Ps.* xciv. 14.

But judgment shall return unto righteousness...15.

Say among the heathen that the Lord reigneth: the world also shall be established that it shall not be moved: he shall judge the people righteously.—*Ps.* xcvi. 10.

Let the heavens rejoice, and let the earth be glad...11.

Before the Lord: for he cometh, for he cometh to judge the earth: he shall judge the world with righteousness, and the people with his truth.—13.

Clouds and darkness are round about him:

righteousness and judgment are the habitation of his throne.—*Ps.* xcvii. 2.

The Lord executeth righteousness and judgment for all that are oppressed.—*Ps.* ciii. 6.

Remember his marvellous works that he hath done; his wonders, and the judgments of his mouth; —*Ps.* cv. 5.

He is the Lord our God: his judgments are in all the earth.—7.

I know, O Lord, that thy judgments are right, and that thou in faithfulness hast afflicted me.—*Ps.* cxix. 75.

Righteous art thou, O Lord, and upright are thy judgments.—137.

For the rod of the wicked shall not rest upon the lot of the righteous.....*Ps.* cxxv. 3.

For the ways of man are before the eyes of the Lord, and he pondereth all his goings.—*Prov.* v. 21.

His own iniquities shall take the wicked himself, and he shall be holden with the cords of his sins.—22.

Though hand join in hand, the wicked shall not be unpunished: but the seed of the righteous shall be delivered.—*Prov.* xi. 21.

...Doth not he that pondereth the heart consider it? and he that keepeth thy soul, doth not he know it? and shall not he render to every man according to his works?—*Prov.* xxiv. 12.

...Walk in the ways of thine heart, and in the sight of thine eyes: but know thou, that for all these things God will bring thee into judgment.—*Eccl.* xi. 9.

For God shall bring every work into judgment, with every secret thing, whether it be good, or whether it be evil.—*Eccl.* xii. 14.

The Lord of hosts shall be exalted in judgment, and God that is holy shall be sanctified in righteousness.—*Isa.* v. 16.

...For when thy judgments are in the earth, the inhabitants of the world will learn righteousness.—*Isa.* xxvi. 9.

...The Lord is a God of judgment: blessed are all they that wait for him.—*Isa.* xxx. 18.

There is no God else beside me; a just God and a Saviour.—*Isa.* xlv. 21.

...I am the Lord which exercise lovingkindness, judgment, and righteousness in the earth: for in these things I delight, saith the Lord.—*Jer.* ix. 24.

Great in counsel, and mighty in work: for thine eyes are open upon all the ways of the sons of men: to give every one according to his ways, and according to the fruit of his doings.—*Jer.* xxxii. 19.

I will do unto them after their way, and according to their deserts will I judge them; and they shall know that I am the Lord.—*Ezek.* vii. 27.

The soul that sinneth, it shall die. The son shall not bear the iniquity of the father, neither shall the father bear the iniquity of the son: the righteousness of the righteous shall be upon him, and the wickedness of the wicked shall be upon him.—*Ezek.* xviii. 20.

...Is not my way equal? are not your ways unequal?—*Ezek.* xviii. 25.

...Honour the king of heaven, all whose works are truth, and his ways judgment...*Dan.* iv. 37.

The just Lord...will not do iniquity: every morning doth he bring his judgment to light, he faileth not. ...*Zeph.* iii. 5.

And I will come near to you to judgment; and I will be a swift witness against the sorcerers,...and against false swearers,...and against those that oppress the hireling in his wages, the widow, and the fatherless, and that turn aside the stranger from his right, and fear not me, saith the Lord of hosts.—*Mal.* iii. 5.

Then shall ye return, and discern between the righteous and the wicked, between him that serveth God and him that serveth him not.—18.

CONSCIENCE.
SELF-EXAMINATION.

———o———

And David's heart smote him after that he had numbered the people. And David said unto the Lord, I have sinned greatly in that I have done: and now, I beseech thee, O Lord, take away the iniquity of thy servant; for I have done very foolishly.—2 *Sam.* xxiv. 10.

If I justify myself, mine own mouth shall condemn me: if I say, I am perfect, it shall also prove me perverse.—*Job* ix. 20.

Though I were perfect, yet would I not know my soul.—21.

If thou prepare thine heart, and stretch out thine hands toward him;—*Job* xi. 13.

If iniquity be in thine hand, put it far away...14.

For then shalt thou lift up thy face without spot; yea, thou shalt be stedfast, and shalt not fear.—15.

How many are mine iniquities and sins? make me to know my transgression and my sin.—*Job* xiii. 23.

...My heart shall not reproach me so long as I live.—*Job* xxvii. 6.

That which I see not teach thou me: if I have done iniquity I will do no more.—*Job* xxxiv. 32.

Stand in awe, and sin not: commune with your own heart upon your bed, and be still.—*Ps.* iv. 4.

...My reins also instruct me in the night seasons.—*Ps.* xvi. 7.

Thou hast proved mine heart; thou hast visited me in the night; thou hast tried me, and shalt find nothing; I am purposed that my mouth shall not transgress.—*Ps.* xvii. 3.

I have kept the ways of the Lord, and have not wickedly departed from my God.—*Ps.* xviii. 21.

Who can understand his errors? cleanse thou me from secret faults.—*Ps.* xix. 12.

Let the words of my mouth, and the meditation of my heart be acceptable in thy sight, O Lord, my strength, and my redeemer.—14.

Examine me, O Lord, and prove me; try my reins and my heart.—*Ps.* xxvi. 2.

I said, I will take heed to my ways, that I sin not with my tongue.—*Ps.* xxxix. 1.

Behold, thou desirest truth in the inward parts: and in the hidden part thou shalt make me to know wisdom.—*Ps.* li. 6.

...I commune with mine own heart: and my spirit made diligent search.—*Ps.* lxxvii. 6.

And I said, This is my infirmity...10.

Wherewithal shall a young man cleanse his way? by taking heed thereto according to thy word.—*Ps.* cxix. 9.

Thy word have I hid in mine heart, that I might not sin against thee.—*Ps.* cxix. 11.

I thought on my ways, and turned my feet unto thy testimonies.—59.

Let my heart be sound in thy statutes; that I be not ashamed.—80.

I have refrained my feet from every evil way, that I might keep thy word.—101.

Search me, O God, and know my heart: try me, and know my thoughts:—*Ps.* cxxxix. 23.

And see if there be any wicked way in me, and and lead me in the way everlasting.—24.

Set a watch, O Lord, before my mouth; keep the door of my lips.—*Ps.* cxli. 3.

Keep thy heart with all diligence; for out of it are the issues of life.—*Prov.* iv. 23.

Ponder the path of thy feet, and let all thy ways be established.—26.

The spirit of man is the candle of the Lord, searching all the inward parts.—*Prov.* xx. 27.

The heart is deceitful above all things, and desperately wicked: who can know it.—*Jer.* xvii. 9.

Let us search and try our ways, and turn again to the Lord.—*Lam.* iii. 40.

Let us lift up our heart with our hands unto God in the heavens.—41.

Thus saith the Lord of hosts; Consider your ways.—*Hagg.* i. 7.

REPENTANCE.
GOD IS WILLING TO PARDON.

———o———

The Lord is long-suffering, and of great mercy, forgiving iniquity and transgression....*Num.* xiv. 18.

And it shall come to pass, when all these things are come upon thee, the blessing and the curse, which I have set before thee, and thou shalt call them to mind,...*Deut.* xxx. 1.

And shalt return unto the Lord thy God, and shalt obey his voice according to all that I command thee this day, thou and thy children, with all thine heart, and with all thy soul;—2.

That then the Lord thy God will turn thy captivity, and have compassion upon thee, and will return and gather thee from all the nations, whither the Lord thy God hath scattered thee.—3.

...If ye do return unto the Lord with all your hearts, ...then put away the strange gods...from among you, and prepare your hearts unto the Lord, and serve him only...1 *Sam.* vii. 3.

And they cried unto the Lord, and said, We have sinned, because we have forsaken the Lord... 1 *Sam.* xii. 10.

...Fear not: ye have done all this wickedness: yet turn not aside from following the Lord, but serve the Lord with all your heart.—1 *Sam.* xii. 20.

And David said unto Nathan, I have sinned against the Lord. And Nathan said...The Lord also hath put away thy sin, thou shalt not die.—2 *Sam.* xii. 13.

And the word of the Lord came to Elijah,...saying,—1 *Kings* xxi. 28.

Seest thou how Ahab humbleth himself before me? because he humbleth himself before me, I will not bring the evil in his days...29.

If my people, which are called by my name, shall humble themselves, and pray, and seek my face, and turn from their wicked ways; then will I hear from heaven, and will forgive their sin, and will heal their land.—2 *Ch.* vii. 14.

...For the Lord your God is gracious and merciful, and will not turn away his face from you, if ye return unto him.—2 *Ch.* xxx. 9.

Because thine heart was tender, and thou didst humble thyself before God, when thou heardest his words against this place,...and humbledst thyself before me, and didst rend thy clothes, and weep before me; I have even heard thee also, saith the Lord.—2 *Ch.* xxxiv. 27.

...Thou art a God ready to pardon, gracious and merciful, slow to anger, and of great kindness... *Neh.* ix. 17.

GOD IS WILLING TO PARDON.

...Know therefore that God exacteth of thee less than thine iniquity deserveth.—*Job* xi. 6.

How many are mine iniquities and sins? make me to know my transgression and my sin.—*Job* xiii. 23.

If thou return to the Almighty, thou shalt be built up, thou shalt put away iniquity far from thy tabernacles.—*Job* xxii. 23.

He looketh upon men, and if any say, I have sinned, and perverted that which was right, and it profited me not;—*Job* xxxiii. 27.

He will deliver his soul from going into the pit, and his life shall see the light.—28.

Lo, all these things worketh God oftentimes with man,—29.

To bring back his soul from the pit, to be enlightened with the light of the living.—30.

Surely it is meet to be said unto God, I have borne chastisement, I will not offend any more: —*Job* xxxiv. 31.

That which I see not teach thou me: if I have done iniquity, I will do no more.—32.

Who can understand his errors? cleanse thou me from secret faults.—*Ps.* xix. 12.

Remember not the sins of my youth, nor my transgressions: according to thy mercy remember thou me for thy goodness' sake, O Lord.—*Ps.* xxv. 7.

For thy name's sake, O Lord, pardon mine iniquity; for it is great.—11.

Look upon mine affliction and my pain; and forgive all my sins.—*Ps.* xxv. 18.

Blessed is he whose transgression is forgiven, whose sin is covered.—*Ps.* xxxii. 1.

Blessed is the man unto whom the Lord imputeth not iniquity, and in whose spirit there is no guile.—2.

I acknowledged my sin unto thee, and mine iniquity have I not hid. I said, I will confess my transgressions unto the Lord; and thou forgavest the iniquity of my sin.—5.

The Lord is nigh unto them that are of a broken heart; and saveth such as be of a contrite spirit. —*Ps.* xxxiv. 18.

O Lord, rebuke me not in thy wrath: neither chasten me in thy hot displeasure.—*Ps.* xxxviii. 1.

For mine iniquities are gone over mine head: as an heavy burden they are too heavy for me.—4.

For I will declare my iniquity; I will be sorry for my sin.—18.

Deliver me from all my transgressions...*Ps.* xxxix. 8.

For innumerable evils have compassed me about: mine iniquities have taken hold upon me, so that I am not able to look up; they are more than the hairs of mine head: therefore my heart faileth me.—*Ps.* xl. 12.

I said, Lord, be merciful unto me: heal my soul; for I have sinned against thee.—*Ps.* xli. 4.

Have mercy upon me, O God, according to thy lovingkindness: according unto the multitude of thy tender mercies blot out my transgressions.—*Ps.* li. 1.

GOD IS WILLING TO PARDON.

Wash me thoroughly from mine iniquity, and cleanse me from my sin.—*Ps.* li. 2.

For I acknowledge my transgressions: and my sin is ever before me.—3.

Against thee, thee only, have I sinned, and done this evil in thy sight: that thou mightest be justified when thou speakest, and be clear when thou judgest.—4.

Hide thy face from my sins, and blot out all mine iniquities.—9.

Create in me a clean heart, O God; and renew a right spirit within me.—10.

Then will I teach transgressors thy ways; and sinners shall be converted unto thee.—13.

The sacrifices of God are a broken spirit: a broken and a contrite heart, O God, thou wilt not despise.—17.

If I regard iniquity in my heart, the Lord will not hear me.—*Ps.* lxvi. 18.

Thou hast forgiven the iniquity of thy people, thou hast covered all their sin.—*Ps.* lxxxv. 2.

Turn us, O God of our salvation, and cause thine anger toward us to cease.—4.

For thou, Lord, art good, and ready to forgive: and plenteous in mercy unto all them that call upon thee.—*Ps.* lxxxvi. 5.

Bless the Lord, O my soul, and forget not all his benefits:—*Ps.* ciii. 2.

Who forgiveth all thine iniquities...3.

He will not always chide; neither will he keep his anger for ever.—*Ps.* ciii. 9.

He hath not dealt with us after our sins; nor rewarded us according to our iniquities.—10.

As far as the east is from the west, so far hath he removed our transgressions from us.—12.

I have gone astray like a lost sheep; seek thy servant; for I do not forget thy commandments.—*Ps.* cxix. 176.

If thou, Lord, shouldest mark iniquities, O Lord, who shall stand?—*Ps.* cxxx. 3.

But there is forgiveness with thee, that thou mayest be feared.—4.

Let Israel hope in the Lord: for with the Lord there is mercy, and with him is plenteous redemption.—7.

And he shall redeem Israel from all his iniquities.—8.

...See if there be any wicked way in me, and lead me in the way everlasting.—*Ps.* cxxxix. 24.

...Enter not into judgment with thy servant: for in thy sight shall no man living be justified.—*Ps.* cxliii. 2.

He that covereth his sins shall not prosper: but whoso confesseth and forsaketh them shall have mercy.—*Prov.* xxviii. 13.

Wash you, make you clean; put away the evil of your doings from before mine eyes; cease to do evil.—*Isa.* i. 16.

Come now, and let us reason together, saith the Lord: though your sins be as scarlet, they shall be

GOD IS WILLING TO PARDON.

as white as snow; though they be red like crimson, they shall be as wool.—*Isa.* i. 18.

I have blotted out, as a thick cloud, thy transgressions, and, as a cloud, thy sins: return unto me; for I have redeemed thee.—*Isa.* xliv. 22.

"Let the wicked forsake his way, and the unrighteous man his thoughts: and let him return unto the Lord, and he will have mercy upon him; and to our God, for he will abundantly pardon.—*Isa.* lv. 7.

For thus saith the high and lofty One that inhabiteth eternity, whose name is Holy; I dwell in the high and holy place, with him also that is of a contrite and humble spirit, to revive the spirit of the humble, and to revive the heart of the contrite ones.—*Isa.* lvii. 15.

For our transgressions are multiplied before thee, and our sins testify against us: for our transgressions are with us; and as for our iniquities, we know them;—*Isa.* lix. 12.

Only acknowledge thine iniquity, that thou hast transgressed against the Lord thy God...*Jer.* iii. 13.

Turn, O backsliding children, saith the Lord...14.

If thou wilt return, O Israel, saith the Lord, return unto me...*Jer.* iv. 1.

O Jerusalem, wash thine heart from wickedness, that thou mayest be saved. How long shall thy vain thoughts lodge within thee?—14.

...Amend your ways and your doings, and I will cause you to dwell in this place.—*Jer.* vii. 3.

O Lord, correct me, but with judgment; not in thine anger, lest thou bring me to nothing.—*Jer.* x. 24.

We acknowledge, O Lord, our wickedness:..for we have sinned against thee.—*Jer.* xiv. 20.

...Return ye now every one from his evil way, and make your ways and your doings good.—*Jer.* xviii. 11.

Therefore now amend your ways and your doings, and obey the voice of the Lord your God; and the Lord will repent him of the evil that he hath pronounced against you.—*Jer.* xxvi. 13.

...For I will forgive their iniquity, and I will remember their sin no more.—*Jer.* xxxi. 34.

And I will cleanse them from all their iniquity, whereby they have sinned against me; and I will pardon all their iniquities, whereby they have sinned, and whereby they have transgressed against me.—*Jer.* xxxiii. 8.

...If the wicked will turn from all his sins that he hath committed, and keep all my statutes, and do that which is lawful and right, he shall surely live, he shall not die.—*Ezek.* xviii. 21.

All his transgressions that he hath committed, they shall not be mentioned unto him: in his righteousness that he hath done he shall live.—22.

Have I any pleasure at all that the wicked should die? saith the Lord God: and not that he should return from his ways, and live?—23.

Again, when the wicked man turneth away from his wickedness that he hath committed, and doeth

GOD IS WILLING TO PARDON. 245

that which is lawful and right, he shall save his soul alive.—*Ezek.* xviii. 27.

Because he considereth, and turneth away from all his transgressions that he hath committed...28.

...Repent, and turn yourselves from all your transgressions; so iniquity shall not be your ruin.—30.

Cast away from you all your transgressions, whereby ye have transgressed; and make you a new heart and a new spirit...31.

And I set my face unto the Lord God, to seek by prayer and supplications, with fasting:...*Dan.* ix. 3.

And I prayed unto the Lord my God, and made my confession, and said, O Lord,...4.

We have sinned, and have committed iniquity, and have done wickedly, and have rebelled, even by departing from thy precepts and from thy judgments.—5.

O Lord, righteousness belongeth unto thee, but unto us confusion of faces, as at this day...7.

...Because we have sinned against thee.—8.

To the Lord our God belong mercies and forgivenesses, though we have rebelled against him;—9.

Neither have we obeyed the voice of the Lord our God, to walk in his laws, which he set before us by his servants the prophets.—10.

...Yet made we not our prayer before the Lord our God, that we might turn from our iniquities, and understand thy truth.—13.

...The Lord our God is righteous in all his works which he doeth : for we obeyed not his voice.—*Dan.* ix. 14.

...We have sinned, we have done wickedly.—15.

...Fear not, Daniel: for from the first day that thou didst set thine heart to understand, and to chasten thyself before thy God, thy words were heard, and I am come for thy words.—*Dan.* x. 12.

I will go and return to my place, till they acknowledge their offence, and seek my face...*Hosea* v. 15.

Come, and let us return unto the Lord: for he hath torn, and he will heal us; he hath smitten, and he will bind us up.—*Hosea* vi. 1.

I will heal their backsliding, I will love them freely: for mine anger is turned away from him.—*Hosea* xiv. 4.

Therefore also now, saith the Lord, turn ye even to me with all your heart, and with fasting, and with weeping, and with mourning :—*Joel* ii. 12.

And rend your heart, and not your garments, and turn unto the Lord your God: for he is gracious and merciful, slow to anger, and of great kindness, and repenteth him of the evil.—13.

Who knoweth if he will return and repent, and leave a blessing behind him ?...14.

But let man and beast be covered with sackcloth, and cry mightily unto God: yea, let them turn every one from his evil way...*Jon.* iii. 8.

And God saw their works, that they turned from their evil way; and God repented of the evil, that

GOD IS WILLING TO PARDON.

he had said that he would do unto them; and he did it not.—*Jon.* iii. 10.

Who is a God like unto thee, that pardoneth iniquity, and passeth by the transgression of the remnant of his heritage? he retaineth not his anger for ever, because he delighteth in mercy.—*Mic.* vii. 18.

He will turn again, he will have compassion upon us; he will subdue our iniquities; and thou wilt cast all their sins into the depths of the sea.—19.

...Return unto me, and I will return unto you, saith the Lord of hosts.—*Mal.* iii. 7.

PRAYER.
GOD HEARETH AND ANSWERETH.

---o---

...Then began men to call upon the name of the Lord.—*Gen.* iv. 26.

So Abraham prayed unto God...*Gen.* xx. 17.

...Jacob said unto his household,...*Gen.* xxxv. 2.

...Let us arise, and go up to Beth-el; and I will make there an altar unto God, who answered me in the day of my distress...3.

...I turned, and came down from the mount,...and the two tables of the covenant were in my two hands.—*Deut.* ix. 15.

...And, behold, ye had sinned against the Lord your God, and had made you a molten calf:...16.

And I fell down before the Lord, as at the first, forty days and forty nights:...18.

For I was afraid of the anger and hot displeasure, wherewith the Lord was wroth against you to destroy you. But the Lord hearkened unto me at that time also.—19.

And the Lord was very angry with Aaron to have destroyed him: and I prayed for Aaron also the same time.—20.

PRAYER.

And she (Hannah) was in bitterness of soul, and prayed unto the Lord, and wept sore.—1 *Sam.* i. 10.
...And said, O Lord of hosts, if thou wilt indeed look on the affliction of thine handmaid, and remember me, and not forget thine handmaid, but wilt give unto thine handmaid a man child, then I will give him unto the Lord all the days of his life...11.

Now Hannah, she spake in heart; only her lips moved, but her voice was not heard...13.
...And the Lord remembered her.—19.

And she said, Oh my lord,...I am the woman that stood by thee here, praying unto the Lord.—26.

For this child I prayed; and the Lord hath given me my petition which I asked of him:—27.

Therefore also I have lent him to the Lord; as long as he liveth he shall be lent to the Lord.—28.

And Hannah prayed, and said, My heart rejoiceth in the Lord, mine horn is exalted in the Lord;... because I rejoice in thy salvation.—1 *Sam.* ii. 1.

And the children of Israel said to Samuel, Cease not to cry unto the Lord our God for us, that he will save us out of the hand of the Philistines.—1 *Sam.* vii. 8.
...And Samuel cried unto the Lord for Israel; and the Lord heard him.--9.
...The Lord thundered...on that day upon the Philistines, and discomfited them...10.

In my distress I called upon the Lord, and cried to

my God: and he did hear my voice out of his temple, and my cry did enter into his ears.—2 *Sam.* xxii. 7.

...And God said, Ask what I shall give thee.— 1 *Kings* iii. 5.

And Solomon said, Thou hast shewed unto thy servant David my father great mercy, according as he walked before thee in truth, and in righteousness, and in uprightness of heart with thee; and thou hast kept for him this great kindness, that thou hast given him a son to sit on his throne, as it is this day.—6.

And now, O Lord my God, thou hast made thy servant king:...and I am but a little child: I know not how to go out or come in.—7.

Give therefore thy servant an understanding heart to judge thy people, that I may discern between good and bad.—9.

And God said unto him,...11.

Behold, I have done according to thy words: lo, I have given thee a wise and an understanding heart...12.

And Solomon stood before the altar of the Lord in the presence of all the congregation of Israel, and spread forth his hands toward heaven:—1 *Kings* viii. 22.

And he said, Lord God of Israel, there is no God like thee, in heaven above, or on earth beneath:...23.

...Have thou respect unto the prayer of thy servant, and to this supplication, O Lord my God, to hearken unto the cry and to the prayer, which thy servant prayeth before thee to day:—1 *Kings* viii. 28.

That thine eyes may be open toward this house night and day,...29.

And hearken thou to the supplication of thy servant, and of thy people Israel, when they shall pray toward this place; and hear thou in heaven thy dwelling place: and when thou hearest, forgive.—30.

What prayer and supplication soever be made by any man, or by all thy people Israel, which shall know every man the plague of his own heart:...38.

Then hear thou in heaven thy dwelling place, and forgive, and do, and give to every man according to his ways, whose heart thou knowest; (for thou, even thou only, knowest the hearts of all the children of men;)—39.

If they sin against thee, (for there is no man that sinneth not,) and thou be angry with them;...46.

Yet if they shall bethink themselves,...and repent, and make supplication unto thee...saying, We have sinned, and done perversely, we have committed wickedness;—47.

And so return unto thee with all their heart, and with all their soul,...48.

Then hear thou their prayer and their supplication in heaven thy dwelling place, and maintain their cause,—49.

And forgive thy people that have sinned against thee...50.

...When Solomon had made an end of praying all this prayer and supplication unto the Lord, he arose ...from kneeling on his knees with his hands spread up to heaven.—1 *Kings* viii. 54.

And he stood, and blessed all the congregation of Israel with a loud voice...55.

The Lord our God be with us, as he was with our fathers: let him not leave us nor forsake us.—57.

And the Lord said unto him, I have heard thy prayer and thy supplication, that thou hast made before me: I have hallowed this house,...and mine eyes and mine heart shall be there perpetually.— 1 *Kings* ix. 3.

And he (Elijah)...cried unto the Lord, and said, O Lord my God, I pray thee, let this child's soul come into him again.—1 *Kings* xvii. 21.

And the Lord heard the voice of Elijah; and the soul of the child came into him again, and he revived.—22.

And Hezekiah prayed before the Lord, and said,... 2 *Kings* xix. 15.

Lord, bow down thine ear, and hear: open, Lord, thine eyes, and see: and hear the words of Sennacherib which hath sent him to reproach the living God.—16.

Now therefore, O Lord our God, I beseech thee, save thou us out of his hand, that all the kingdoms of the earth may know that thou art the Lord God, even thou only.—19.

GOD HEARETH AND ANSWERETH. 253

...Thus saith the Lord God of Israel, That which thou hast prayed to me against Sennacherib king of Assyria I have heard.—2 *Kings* xix. 20.
...He shall not come into this city, nor shoot an arrow there;...32.
—By the way that he came, by the same shall he return;...33.
For I will defend this city, to save it, for mine own sake, and for my servant David's sake.—34.
In those days was Hezekiah sick unto death, And the prophet Isaiah...said unto him, Thus saith the Lord, Set thine house in order; for thou shalt die, and not live.—2 *Kings* xx. 1.
Then he turned his face to the wall, and prayed unto the Lord, saying,—2.
I beseech thee, O Lord, remember now how I have walked before thee in truth and with a perfect heart, and have done that which is good in thy sight. And Hezekiah wept sore.—3.
And it came to pass, afore Isaiah was gone out into the middle court, that the word of the Lord came to him, saying,—4.
Turn again, and tell Hezekiah,...Thus saith the Lord, the God of David thy father, I have heard thy prayer, I have seen thy tears: behold, I will heal thee...5.
And I will add unto thy days fifteen years...6.
And Jabez called on the God of Israel, saying, Oh that thou wouldest bless me indeed, and enlarge

my coast, and that thine hand might be with me, and that thou wouldest keep me from evil, that it may not grieve me! And God granted him that which he requested.—1 Ch. iv. 10.

...They cried to God in the battle, and he was intreated of them; because they put their trust in him. —1 Ch. v. 20.

And Asa cried unto the Lord his God, and said,... help us, O Lord our God; for we rest on thee, and in thy name we go against this multitude. O Lord, thou art our God; let not man prevail against thee. —2 Ch. xiv. 11.

So the Lord smote the Ethiopians before Asa, and before Judah; and the Ethiopians fled.—12.

And when he (Manasseh) was in affliction, he besought the Lord his God, and humbled himself greatly before the God of his fathers,—2 Ch. xxxiii. 12.

And prayed unto him: and he was intreated of him, and heard his supplication and brought him again to Jerusalem into his kingdom...13.

Thou shalt make thy prayer unto him, and he shall hear thee, and thou shalt pay thy vows.— Job xxii. 27.

He shall pray unto God, and he will be favourable unto him...Job xxxiii. 26.

I cried unto the Lord with my voice, and he heard me out of his holy hill.—Ps. iii. 4.

...The Lord will hear when I call unto him.—Ps. iv. 3.

My voice shalt thou hear in the morning, O Lord;

in the morning will I direct my prayer unto thee, and will look up.—*Ps.* v. 3.

The Lord hath heard my supplication; the Lord will receive my prayer.—*Ps.* vi. 9.

Hear the right, O Lord, attend unto my cry, give ear unto my prayer, that goeth not out of feigned lips.—*Ps.* xvii. 1.

In my distress I called upon the Lord, and cried unto my God: he heard my voice out of his temple, and my cry came before him, even into his ears.—*Ps.* xviii. 6.

Blessed be the Lord, because he hath heard the voice of my supplications.—*Ps.* xxviii. 6.

O Lord my God, I cried unto thee, and thou hast healed me.—*Ps.* xxx. 2.

For this shall every one that is godly pray unto thee in a time when thou mayest be found...*Ps.* xxxii. 6.

I sought the Lord, and he heard me, and delivered me from all my fears.—*Ps.* xxxiv. 4.

I waited patiently for the Lord; and he inclined unto me, and heard my cry.—*Ps.* xl. 1.

Call upon me in the day of trouble: I will deliver thee, and thou shalt glorify me.—*Ps.* l. 15.

As for me, I will call upon God;—*Ps.* lv. 16.

Evening, and morning, and at noon, will I pray, and cry aloud: and he shall hear my voice.—17.

...Ye people, pour out your heart before him.—*Ps.* lxii. 8.

O thou that hearest prayer, unto thee shall all flesh come.—*Ps.* lxv. 2.

...Verily God hath heard me; he hath attended to the voice of my prayer.—*Ps.* lxvi. 19.

Blessed be God, which hath not turned away my prayer, nor his mercy from me.—20.

...As for me, my prayer is unto thee, O Lord, in an acceptable time...*Ps.* lxix. 13.

I cried unto God with my voice, even unto God with my voice; and he gave ear unto me.—*Ps.* lxxvii. 1.

...Unto thee have I cried, O Lord; and in the morning shall my prayer prevent thee.—*Ps.* lxxxviii. 13.

He shall call upon me, and I will answer him. *Ps.* xci. 15.

O come, let us worship and bow down: let us kneel before the Lord our maker.—*Ps.* xcv. 6.

Moses and Aaron among his priests, and Samuel among them that call upon his name; they called upon the Lord, and he answered them.—*Ps.* xcix. 6.

He will regard the prayer of the destitute, and not despise their prayer.—*Ps.* cii. 17.

...I give myself unto prayer.—*Ps.* cix. 4.

I love the Lord, because he hath heard my voice and my supplications.—*Ps.* cxvi. 1.

Because he hath inclined his ear unto me, therefore will I call upon him as long as I live.—2.

In my distress I cried unto the Lord, and he heard me.—*Ps.* cxx. 1.

The Lord is nigh unto all them that call upon him, to all that call upon him in truth.—*Ps.* cxlv. 18.

...The prayer of the upright is his delight.—*Prov.* xv. 8.

The Lord is far from the wicked: but he heareth the prayer of the righteous.—*Prov.* xv. 29.

...He will be very gracious unto thee at the voice of thy cry; when he shall hear it, he will answer thee.—*Isa.* xxx. 19.

Seek ye the Lord while he may be found, call ye upon him while he is near.—*Isa.* lv. 6.

Then shalt thou call, and the Lord shall answer; thou shalt cry, and he shall say, Here I am.—*Isa.* lviii. 9.

And it shall come to pass, that before they call, I will answer; and while they are yet speaking, I will hear.—*Isa.* lxv. 24.

Then shall ye call upon me, and ye shall go and pray unto me, and I will hearken unto you.—*Jer.* xxix. 12.

Thus saith the Lord,...*Jer.* xxxiii. 2.

Call unto me, and I will answer thee...3.

I called upon thy name, O Lord, out of the low dungeon.—*Lam.* iii. 55.

Thou hast heard my voice...56.

...He (Daniel) kneeled upon his knees three times a day and prayed, and gave thanks before his God...*Dan.* vi. 10.

...These men assembled, and found Daniel praying and making supplication before his God.—11.

And I set my face unto the Lord God, to seek by prayer and supplications...*Dan.* ix. 3.

And I prayed unto the Lord my God, and made my confession...4.

Take with you words, and turn to the Lord: say unto him, Take away all iniquity, and receive us graciously...*Hosea* xiv. 2.

...What meanest thou, O sleeper? arise, call upon thy God...*Jonah* i. 6.

Then Jonah prayed unto the Lord his God...*Jon.* ii. 1.

When my soul fainted within me I remembered the Lord: and my prayer came in unto thee, into thine holy temple.—7.

...Then will I turn to the people a pure language, that they may all call upon the name of the Lord, to serve him with one consent.—*Zeph.* iii. 9.

...They shall call on my name, and I will hear them: I will say, It is my people: and they shall say, The Lord is my God.—*Zech.* xiii. 9.

IT IS GOOD TO BLESS AND PRAY FOR EACH OTHER.

———o———

And God said unto him in a dream,...*Gen.* xx. 6.

Restore the man (Abraham) his wife; for he is a prophet, and he shall pray for thee, and thou shalt live...7.

And Esau said unto his father, Hast thou but one blessing, my father? bless me, even me also... *Gen.* xxvii. 38.

And Isaac called Jacob, and blessed him ... *Gen.* xxviii. 1.

And early in the morning Laban rose up, and kissed his sons and his daughters, and blessed them. ...*Gen.* xxxi. 55.

And Joseph said unto his father, They are my sons, whom God hath given me in this place. And he said, Bring them, I pray thee, unto me, and I will bless them.—*Gen.* xlviii. 9.

And he blessed Joseph, and said, God, before whom my fathers...did walk, the God which fed me all my life long unto this day,—15.

The Angel which redeemed me from all evil, bless the lads...16.

The blessings of thy father have prevailed above the blessings of my progenitors unto the utmost bound of the everlasting hills: they shall be on the head of Joseph.—*Gen.* xlix. 26.

...Every one according to his blessing he blessed them.—28.

And Moses returned unto the Lord, and said, Oh, this people have sinned a great sin, and have made them gods of gold.—*Ex.* xxxii. 31.

Yet now, if thou wilt forgive their sin—; and if not, blot me, I pray thee, out of thy book which thou hast written.—32.

The Lord bless thee, and keep thee:—*Num.* vi. 24.

The Lord make his face shine upon thee, and be gracious unto thee:—25.

The Lord lift up his countenance upon thee, and give thee peace.—26.

...Behold, Miriam became leprous,...*Num.* xii. 10.

And Moses cried unto the Lord, saying, Heal her now, O God, I beseech thee.—13.

Behold, Boaz came from Beth-lehem, and said unto the reapers, The Lord be with you. And they answered him, The Lord bless thee.—*Ruth* ii. 4.

The Lord recompense thy work, and a full reward be given thee of the Lord God of Israel...12.

And Samuel said...1 *Sam.* xii. 20.

As for me, God forbid that I should sin against the Lord in ceasing to pray for you...23.

PRAY FOR EACH OTHER.

And the king turned his face, and blessed the whole congregation of Israel...2 *Ch.* vi. 3.

...There were many in the congregation that were not sanctified :—2 *Ch.* xxx. 17.

...Yet did they eat the passover otherwise than it was written. But Hezekiah prayed for them, saying, The good Lord pardon every one —18.

That prepareth his heart to seek God...19.

And the Lord hearkened to Hezekiah...20.

And his sons went and feasted in their houses, every one his day ;...*Job* i. 4.

And it was so, when the days of their feasting were gone about, that Job sent and sanctified them, and rose up early in the morning, and offered burnt offerings according to the number of them all: for Job said, It may be that my sons have sinned...in their hearts. Thus did Job continually.—5.

And the Lord turned the captivity of Job, when he prayed for his friends.—*Job* xlii. 10.

The Lord hear thee in the day of trouble ; the name of the God of Jacob defend thee ;—*Ps.* xx. 1.

Send thee help from the sanctuary, and strengthen thee out of Zion ;—2.

Grant thee according to thine own heart, and fulfil all thy counsel.—4.

O let not the oppressed return ashamed : let the poor and needy praise thy name.—*Ps.* lxxiv. 21.

Let the sighing of the prisoner come before thee ;

according to the greatness of thy power preserve thou those that are appointed to die.—*Ps.* lxxix. 11.

Do good, O Lord unto those that be good, and to them that are upright in their hearts.—*Ps.* cxxv. 4.

Let the righteous smite me; it shall be a kindness: and let him reprove me;...for yet my prayer also shall be in their calamities.—*Ps.* cxli. 5.

Give heed to me, O Lord,...*Jer.* xviii. 19.

...Remember that I stood before thee to speak good for them, and to turn away thy wrath from them.—20.

SPIRITUAL LONGINGS.
JOYS FOR THE GODLY-MINDED.

———o———

And Enoch walked with God: and he was not; for God took him.—*Gen.* v. 24.

If...thou shalt seek the Lord thy God, thou shalt find him, if thou seek him with all thy heart and with all thy soul.—*Deut.* iv. 29.

The beloved of the Lord shall dwell in safety by him; and the Lord shall cover him all the day long, and he shall dwell between his shoulders. —*Deut.* xxxiii. 12.

...Let them that love him be as the sun when he goeth forth in his might...*Judg.* v. 31.

...Let us draw near hither unto God.—1 *Sam.* xiv. 36.

Acquaint now thyself with him, and be at peace: thereby good shall come unto thee.—*Job* xxii. 21.

For then shalt thou have thy delight in the Almighty, and shalt lift up thy face unto God.—26.

Oh that I knew where I might find him! that I might come even to his seat!—*Job* xxiii. 3.

...Know that the Lord hath set apart him that is godly for himself...*Ps.* iv. 3.

...Lord, lift thou up the light of thy countenance upon us...Ps. iv. 6.

My heart shall rejoice in thy salvation.—Ps. xiii. 5.

...Thou art my Lord: my goodness extendeth not to thee;—Ps. xvi. 2.

But to the saints that are in the earth, and to the excellent, in whom is all my delight.—3.

I have set the Lord always before me: because he is at my right hand, I shall not be moved.—8.

Therefore my heart is glad, and my glory rejoiceth.—9.

Hold up my goings in thy paths, that my footsteps slip not.—Ps. xvii. 5.

Keep me as the apple of the eye, hide me under the shadow of thy wings.—8.

With the pure thou wilt shew thyself pure... Ps. xviii. 26.

...The Lord my God will enlighten my darkness.—28.

The secret of the Lord is with them that fear him. —Ps. xxv. 14.

Mine eyes are ever toward the Lord.—15.

One thing have I desired of the Lord, that will I seek after; that I may dwell in the house of the Lord all the days of my life, to behold the beauty of the Lord, and to enquire in his temple.—Ps. xxvii. 4.

When thou saidst, Seek ye my face; my heart said unto thee, Thy face, Lord, will I seek.—8.

Hide not thy face far from me:...thou hast been my

help; leave me not, neither forsake me, O God of my salvation.—*Ps.* xxvii. 9.

I had fainted, unless I had believed to see the goodness of the Lord in the land of the living.—13.

Unto thee will I cry, O Lord my rock; be not silent to me...*Ps.* xxviii. 1.

I will extol thee, O Lord; for thou hast lifted me up...*Ps.* xxx. 1.

O love the Lord, all ye his saints: for the Lord preserveth the faithful.—*Ps.* xxxi. 23.

For this shall every one that is godly pray unto thee in a time when thou mayest be found.—*Ps.* xxxii 6.

Thou art my hiding place...7.

Be glad in the Lord, and rejoice, ye righteous: and shout for joy, all ye that are upright in heart.—11.

Our soul waiteth for the Lord: he is our help and our shield.—*Ps.* xxxiii. 20.

Let thy mercy, O Lord, be upon us, according as we hope in thee.—22.

My soul shall make her boast in the Lord: the humble shall hear thereof, and be glad.—*Ps.* xxxiv. 2.

Delight thyself also in the Lord; and he shall give thee the desires of thine heart.—*Ps.* xxxvii. 4.

Lord, all my desire is before thee...*Ps.* xxxviii. 9.

For in thee O Lord do I hope: thou wilt hear, O Lord my God.—15.

And now, Lord, what wait I for? my hope is in thee.—*Ps.* xxxix. 7.

As the hart panteth after the water brooks, so panteth my soul after thee, O God.—*Ps.* xlii. 1.

My soul thirsteth for God, for the living God: when shall I come and appear before God?—2.

O send out thy light and thy truth: let them lead me: let them bring me unto thy holy hill, and to thy tabernacles.—*Ps.* xliii. 3.

Then will I go unto the altar of God, unto God my exceeding joy...4.

In God we boast all the day long, and praise thy name for ever.—*Ps.* xliv. 8.

Cast me not away from thy presence; and take not thy holy spirit from me.—*Ps.* li. 11.

Restore unto me the joy of thy salvation; and uphold me with thy free spirit.—12.

My soul, wait thou only upon God; for my expectation is from him.—*Ps.* lxii. 5.

He only is my rock and my salvation; he is my defence; I shall not be moved.—6.

In God is my salvation and my glory.—7.

O God, thou art my God; early will I seek thee: my soul thirsteth for thee, my flesh longeth for thee in a dry and thirsty land, where no water is.—*Ps.* lxiii. 1.

To see thy power and thy glory, so as I have seen thee in the sanctuary.—2.

Because thy lovingkindness is better than life, my lips shall praise thee.—3.

Thus will I bless thee while I live: I will lift up my hands in thy name.—4.

Because thou hast been my help, therefore in the shadow of thy wings will I rejoice.—*Ps.* lxiii. 7.

My soul followeth hard after thee: thy right hand upholdeth me.—8.

Come, and hear, all ye that fear God, and I will declare what he hath done for my soul.—*Ps.* lxvi. 16.

Let the righteous be glad; let them rejoice before God: yea, let them exceedingly rejoice.—*Ps.* lxviii. 3.

Draw nigh unto my soul, and redeem it...*Ps.* lxix. 18.

Whom have I in heaven but thee? and there is none upon earth I desire beside thee.—*Ps.* lxxiii. 25.

It is good for me to draw near to God...28.

Turn us again, O God of hosts, and cause thy face to shine; and we shall be saved.—*Ps.* lxxx. 7.

How amiable are thy tabernacles, O Lord of hosts!—*Ps.* lxxxiv. 1.

My soul longeth, yea, even fainteth for the courts of the Lord: my heart and my flesh crieth out for the living God.—2.

Blessed are they that dwell in thy house: they will be still praising thee.—4.

For a day in thy courts is better than a thousand. I had rather be a doorkeeper in the house of my God, than to dwell in the tents of wickedness.—10.

For the Lord God is a sun and shield: the Lord will give grace and glory: no good thing will he withhold from them that walk uprightly.—11.

Blessed is the people that know the joyful sound:

they shall walk, O Lord, in the light of thy countenance.—*Ps.* lxxxix. 15.

In thy name shall they rejoice all the day: and in thy righteousness shall they be exalted.—16.

Because he hath set his love upon me, therefore will I deliver him: I will set him on high, because he hath known my name.—*Ps.* xci. 14.

He shall call upon me, and I will answer him: I will be with him in trouble; I will deliver him, and honour him.—15.

With long life will I satisfy him, and shew him my salvation.—16.

In the multitude of my thoughts within me thy comforts delight my soul.—*Ps.* xciv. 19.

Light is sown for the righteous, and gladness for the upright in heart.—*Ps.* xcvii. 11.

Rejoice in the Lord, ye righteous: and give thanks at the remembrance of his holiness.—12.

For he satisfieth the longing soul, and filleth the hungry soul with goodness.—*Ps.* cvii. 9.

The righteous shall see it, and rejoice…42.

Whoso is wise, and will observe these things, even they shall understand the lovingkindness of the Lord.—43.

Unto the upright there ariseth light in the darkness…*Ps.* cxii. 4.

I will praise thee: for thou hast heard me, and art become my salvation.—*Ps.* cxviii. 21.

God is the Lord, which hath shewed us light…27.

With my whole heart have I sought thee.—*Ps.* cxix. 10.

My soul breaketh for the longing that it hath unto thy judgment at all times.—20.

Behold, I have longed after thy precepts: quicken me in thy righteousness.—40.

My soul fainteth for thy salvation: but I hope in thy word.—81.

Quicken me after thy lovingkindness…88.

Mine eyes fail for thy salvation, and for the word of thy righteousness.—123.

I opened my mouth, and panted: for I longed for thy commandments.—131.

I have longed for thy salvation, O Lord; and thy law is my delight.—174.

Let my soul live, and it shall praise thee…175.

My soul waiteth for the Lord more than they that watch for the morning: I say, more than they that watch for the morning.—*Ps.* cxxx. 6.

How precious also are thy thoughts unto me, O God! how great is the sum of them!—*Ps.* cxxxix. 17.

If I should count them, they are more in number than the sand: when I awake, I am still with thee.—18.

Mine eyes are unto thee, O God the Lord…*Ps.* cxli. 8.

Bring my soul out of prison, that I may praise thy name.—*Ps.* cxlii. 7.

…Happy is that people, whose God is the Lord.—*Ps.* cxliv. 15.

The hope of the righteous shall be gladness. ...*Prov.* x. 28.

He that followeth after righteousness and mercy findeth life, righteousness, and honour.—*Prov.* xxi. 21.

...They that seek the Lord understand all things. —*Prov.* xxviii. 5.

...This is our God; we have waited for him, and he will save us: this is the Lord; we have waited for him, we will be glad and rejoice in his salvation. —*Isa.* xxv. 9.

Thou wilt keep him in perfect peace, whose mind is staid on thee...*Isa.* xxvi. 3.

...The desire of our soul is to thy name, and to the remembrance of thee.—8.

With my soul have I desired thee in the night; yea, with my spirit within me will I seek thee early...9.

...Blessed are all they that wait for him.—*Isa.* xxx. 18.

For ye shall go out with joy, and be led forth with peace...*Isa.* lv. 12.

...The sons of the stranger, that join themselves to the Lord, to serve him, and to love the name of the Lord, to be his servants;...*Isa.* lvi. 6.

Even them will I bring to my holy mountain, and make them joyful in my house of prayer...7.

Then shalt thou delight thyself in the Lord. ...*Isa.* lviii. 14.

...The Lord shall be unto thee an everlasting light, and thy God thy glory.—*Isa.* lx. 19.

I will greatly rejoice in the Lord, my soul shall be

joyful in my God; for he hath clothed me with the garments of salvation.—*Isa.* lxi. 10.

The Lord is my portion, saith my soul; therefore will I hope in him.—*Lam.* iii. 24.

Let us lift up our heart with our hands unto God in the heavens.—41.

...I will betroth thee unto me in righteousness, and in judgment, and in lovingkindness, and in mercies.—*Hosea* ii. 19.

...Wait on thy God continually.—*Hosea* xii. 6.

When my soul fainted within me I remembered the Lord: and my prayer came in unto thee, into thine holy temple.—*Jonah* ii. 7.

Therefore I will look unto the Lord; I will wait for the God of my salvation: my God will hear me.—*Micah* vii. 7.

RELIGIOUS ZEAL.

Then Moses stood in the gate of the camp, and said, Who is on the Lord's side? let him come unto me. And all the sons of Levi gathered themselves together unto him.—*Ex.* xxxii. 26.

And they came, every one whose heart stirred him up, and every one whom his spirit made willing, and they brought the Lord's offering to the work of the tabernacle of the congregation, and for all his service, and for the holy garments.—*Ex.* xxxv. 21.

And Moses said unto him, (Joshua) Enviest thou for my sake? would God that all the Lord's people were prophets, and that the Lord would put his spirit upon them!—*Num.* xi. 29.

And the Lord spake unto Moses, saying,—*Num.* xxv. 10.

Phineas, the son of Eleazar...hath turned my wrath away from the children of Israel, while he was zealous for my sake among them...11.

Wherefore say, Behold, I give unto him my covenant of peace:—12.

And he shall have it, and his seed after him, even the covenant of an everlasting priesthood; because he was zealous for his God.—13.

RELIGIOUS ZEAL.

And Elijah came unto all the people, and said, How long halt ye between two opinions? if the Lord be God, follow him: but if Baal, then follow him. And the people answered him not a word.— 1 *Kings* xviii. 21.

Then said Elijah unto the people, I, even I only, remain a prophet of the Lord; but Baal's prophets are four hundred and fifty men.—22.

...Call ye on the name of your gods, and I will call on the name of the Lord: and the God that answereth by fire, let him be God. And all the people answered and said, It is well spoken.—24.

And it came to pass at the time of the offering of the evening sacrifice, that Elijah the prophet came near, and said, Lord God of Abraham, Isaac, and of Israel, let it be known this day that thou art God in Israel, and that I am thy servant, and that I have done all these things at thy word.—36.

Hear me, O Lord, hear me, that this people may know that thou art the Lord God...37.

Then the fire of the Lord fell, and consumed the burnt sacrifice, and the wood, and the stones, and the dust...38.

And when all the people saw it, they fell on their faces: and they said, The Lord, he is the God; the Lord, he is the God.—39.

And he (Elijah) said, I have been very jealous for the Lord God of hosts...1 *Kings* xix. 10.

And he (Jehu) said, Come with me, and see my zeal for the Lord...2 *Kings* x. 16.

And they entered into a covenant to seek the Lord God...with all their heart and with all their soul;—2 *Ch.* xv. 12.

And they sware unto the Lord with a loud voice, and with shouting, and with trumpets, and with cornets.—14.

And all Judah rejoiced at the oath: for they had sworn with all their heart, and sought him with their whole desire; and he was found of them...15.

And they taught in Judah, and had the book of the law of the Lord with them, and went about throughout all the cities of Judah, and taught the people.—2 *Ch.* xvii. 9.

And the fear of the Lord fell upon all the kingdoms of the lands...10.

And in every work that he (Hezekiah) began in the service of the house of God, and in the law, and in the commandments, to seek his God, he did it with all his heart.—2 *Ch.* xxxi. 21.

...I have not concealed the words of the Holy One.—*Job* vi. 10.

I will give thee thanks in the great congregation: I will praise thee among much people.—*Ps.* xxxv. 18.

I have preached righteousness in the great congregation: lo, I have not refrained my lips, O Lord, thou knowest.—*Ps.* xl. 9.

I have not hid thy righteousness within my heart;

I have declared thy faithfulness and thy salvation : I have not concealed thy lovingkindness and thy truth from the great congregation.—*Ps.* xl. 10.

I will make thy name to be remembered in all generations :...*Ps.* xlv. 17.

...Then will I teach transgressors thy ways; and sinners shall be converted unto thee.—*Ps.* li. 13.

Thou hast given a banner to them that fear thee, that it may be displayed because of the truth.—*Ps.* lx. 4.

My mouth shall shew forth thy righteousness and thy salvation all the day...*Ps.* lxxi. 15.

O God, thou hast taught me from my youth : and hitherto have I declared thy wondrous works.—17.

Now also when I am old and greyheaded, O God, forsake me not; until I have shewed thy strength unto this generation, and thy power to every one that is to come.—18.

O Give thanks unto the Lord; call upon his name: make known his deeds among the people.—*Ps.* cv. 1. ...Talk ye of all his wondrous works.—2.

My zeal hath consumed me, because mine enemies have forgotten thy words.—*Ps.* cxix. 139.

Moreover because the preacher was wise, he still taught the people knowledge; yea, he gave good heed, and sought out, and set in order many proverbs.—*Eccl.* xii. 9.

...Many people shall go and say, Come ye, and let us go up to the mountain of the Lord, to the house of Jacob...*Isa.* ii. 3.

I heard the voice of the Lord, saying, Whom shall I send, and who will go for us? Then said I, Here am I; send me.—*Isa.* vi. 8.

For Zion's sake will I not hold my peace, and for Jerusalem's sake I will not rest, until the righteousness thereof go forth as brightness, and the salvation thereof as a lamp that burneth.—*Isa.* lxii. 1.

...They are not valiant for the truth upon the earth.—*Jer.* ix. 3.

...Know that for thy sake I have suffered rebuke.—*Jer.* xv. 15.

...I am in derision daily, every one mocketh me.—*Jer.* xx. 7.

For since I spake, I cried out, I cried violence and spoil; because the word of the Lord was made a reproach unto me, and a derision, daily.—8.

Then I said, I will not make mention of him, nor speak any more in his name. But his word was in mine heart as a burning fire shut up in my bones, and I was weary with forbearing, and I could not stay.—9.

...The inhabitants of one city shall go to another, saying, Let us go speedily to pray before the Lord, and to seek the Lord of hosts: I will go also.—*Zech.* viii. 21.

Yea, many people and strong nations shall come to seek the Lord of hosts in Jerusalem, and to pray before the Lord.—22.

My covenant was with him (Levi) of life and peace; and I gave them to him for the fear wherewith he feared me...*Mal.* ii. 5.

The law of truth was in his mouth, and iniquity was not found in his lips: he walked with me in peace and equity, and did turn many away from iniquity.—6.

GOD GIVES US STRENGTH.

The archers have sorely grieved him, (Joseph) and shot at him:...*Gen.* xlix. 23.

But his bow abode in strength, and the arms of his hands were made strong by the hands of the mighty God of Jacob.—24.

The Lord is my strength and song, and he is become my salvation...*Ex.* xv. 2.

...The Lord spake unto Joshua,...*Josh.* i. 1.

Have not I commanded thee? Be strong and of a good courage; be not afraid, neither be thou dismayed: for the Lord thy God is with thee whithersoever thou goest.—9.

And Saul said to David, Thou art not able to go against this Philistine to fight with him: for thou art but a youth...1 *Sam.* xvii. 33.

David said,...The Lord that delivered me out of the paw of the lion, and out of the paw of the bear, he will deliver me out of the hand of this Philistine. And Saul said unto David, Go, and the Lord be with thee.—37.

So David...smote the Philistine...50.

And Jonathan, Saul's son arose, and went to

David into the wood, and strengthened his hand in God.—1 *Sam.* xxiii. 16.

...David encouraged himself in the Lord his God.— 1 *Sam.* xxx. 6.

God is my strength and power: and he maketh my way perfect.—2 *Sam.* xxii. 33.

For thou hast girded me with strength to battle...40.

Seek the Lord and his strength, seek his face continually.—1 *Ch.* xvi. 11.

...Deal courageously, and the Lord shall be with the good.—2 *Ch.* xix. 11.

...And I was strengthened as the hand of the Lord my God was upon me...*Ezra* vii. 28.

Will he plead against me with his great power? No; but he would put strength in me.—*Job* xxiii. 6.

It is God that girdeth me with strength...*Ps.* xviii. 32.

The king shall joy in thy strength, O Lord. ...*Ps.* xxi. 1.

Be not thou far from me, O Lord: O my strength, haste thee to help me.—*Ps.* xxii. 19.

...The Lord is the strength of my life; of whom shall I be afraid?—*Ps.* xxvii. 1.

Though an host should encamp against me, my heart shall not fear: though war should rise against me, in this will I be confident.—3.

Wait on the Lord: be of good courage, and he shall strengthen thine heart: wait, I say, on the Lord.—14.

GOD GIVES US STRENGTH.

The Lord is my strength and my shield; my heart trusted in him, and I am helped...*Ps.* xxviii. 7.

The Lord is their strength, and he is the saving strength of his anointed.—8.

The Lord will give strength unto his people; the Lord will bless his people with peace.—*Ps.* xxix. 11.

Be of good courage, and he shall strengthen your heart, all ye that hope in the Lord.—*Ps.* xxxi. 24.

The salvation of the righteous is of the Lord: he is their strength in the time of trouble.—*Ps.* xxxvii. 39.

Blessed is he that considereth the poor:...*Ps.* xli. 1.

The Lord will strengthen him upon the bed of languishing...3.

God is our refuge and strength...*Ps.* xlvi. 1.

Why boastest thou thyself in mischief, O mighty man?...*Ps.* lii. 1.

Thou lovest evil more than good;...3.

Lo, this is the man that made not God his strength: but trusted in the abundance of his riches, and strengthened himself in his wickedness.—7.

Through God we shall do valiantly...*Ps.* lx. 12.

...The God of Israel is he that giveth strength and power unto his people.—*Ps.* lxviii. 35.

I will go in the strength of the Lord God: I will make mention of thy righteousness, even of thine only.—*Ps.* lxxi. 16.

My flesh and my heart faileth: but God is the strength of my heart, and my portion for ever.—*Ps.* lxxiii. 26.

Blessed is the man whose strength is in thee. ...*Ps.* lxxxiv. 5.

My soul melteth for heaviness: strengthen thou me according unto thy word.—*Ps.* cxix. 28.

In the day when I cried thou answeredst me, and strengthenedst me with strength in my soul. —*Ps.* cxxxviii. 3.

The way of the Lord is strength to the upright. ...*Prov.* x. 29.

In the fear of the Lord is strong confidence: and his children shall have a place of refuge.—*Prov.* xiv. 26.

The name of the Lord is a strong tower: the righteous runneth into it, and is safe.—*Prov.* xviii. 10.

For thou hast been a strength to the poor, a strength to the needy in his distress, a refuge from the storm...*Isa.* xxv. 4.

Trust ye in the Lord for ever: for in the Lord JEHOVAH is everlasting strength.—*Isa.* xxvi. 4.

Strengthen ye the weak hands, and confirm the feeble knees.—*Isa.* xxxv. 3.

Say to them that are of a fearful heart, Be strong, fear not: behold, your God will come;...he will come and save you.—4.

He giveth power to the faint; and to them that have no might he increaseth strength.—*Isa.* xl. 29.

Even the youths shall faint and be weary, and the young men shall utterly fall:—30.

But they that wait upon the Lord shall renew their strength; they shall mount up with wings as eagles;

they shall run, and not be weary; and they shall walk, and not faint.—*Isa.* xl. 31.

Fear thou not; for I am with thee: be not dismayed; for I am thy God: I will strengthen thee; yea, I will help thee; yea, I will uphold thee with the right hand of my righteousness.—*Isa.* xli. 10.

The Lord God is my strength, and he will make my feet like hinds' feet, and he will make me to walk upon high places...*Habak.* iii. 19.

And I will strengthen them in the Lord; and they shall walk up and down in his name, saith the Lord. —*Zech.* x. 12.

GOD REQUIRES OF US JUSTICE AND JUDGMENT.

Thou shalt not wrest the judgment of thy poor in his cause.—*Ex.* xxiii. 6.

Keep thee far from a false matter; and the innocent and righteous slay thou not: for I will not justify the wicked.—7.

Ye shall do no unrighteousness in judgment: thou shalt not respect the person of the poor, nor honour the person of the mighty: but in righteousness shalt thou judge thy neighbour.—*Lev.* xix. 15.

Ye shall do no unrighteousness in judgment, in meteyard, in weight, or in measure.—35.

Just balances, just weights, a just ephah, and a just hin, shall ye have: I am the Lord your God.—36.

Judges and officers shalt thou make thee in all thy gates:...and they shall judge the people with just judgment.—*Deut.* xvi. 18.

Thou shalt not wrest judgment; thou shalt not respect persons, neither take a gift: for a gift doth blind the eyes of the wise, and pervert the words of the righteous.—19.

That which is altogether just shalt thou follow,

that thou mayest live, and inherit the land which the Lord thy God giveth thee.—*Deut.* xvi. 20.

If a man have two wives, one beloved, and another hated, and they have born him children, both the beloved and the hated; and if the firstborn son be her's that was hated:—*Deut.* xxi. 15.

Then it shall be, when he maketh his sons to inherit that which he hath, that he may not make the son of the beloved firstborn before the son of the hated, which is indeed the firstborn :—16.

But he shall acknowledge the son of the hated for the firstborn, by giving him a double portion of all that he hath: for he is the beginning of his strength; the right of the firstborn is his.—17.

The fathers shall not be put to death for the children, neither shall the children be put to death for the fathers: every man shall be put to death for his own sin.—*Deut.* xxiv. 16.

Thou shalt not pervert the judgment of the stranger, nor of the fatherless; nor take a widow's raiment to pledge.—17.

Thou shalt not have in thy bag divers weights, a great and a small.—*Deut.* xxv. 13.

But thou shalt have a perfect and just weight, a perfect and just measure shalt thou have.—15.

For all that do such things, and all that do unrighteously, are an abomination unto the Lord thy God.—16.

And all Israel heard of the judgment which the

king had judged; and they feared the king: for they saw that the wisdom of God was in him, to do judgment.—1 *Kings* iii. 28.

Because the Lord loved Israel for ever, therefore made he thee king, to do judgment and justice.— 1 *Kings* x. 9.

And he (Jehoshaphat) set judges in the land throughout all the fenced cities of Judah, city by city,—2 *Ch.* xix. 5.

And said to the judges, Take heed what ye do: for ye judge not for man, but for the Lord, who is with you in the judgment.—6.

Wherefore now let the fear of the Lord be upon you; take heed and do it: for there is no iniquity with the Lord our God, nor respect of persons, nor taking of gifts.—7.

Give the king thy judgments, O God, and thy righteousness unto the king's son.—*Ps.* lxxii. 1.

He shall judge thy people with righteousness, and thy poor with judgment.—2.

How long will ye judge unjustly, and accept the persons of the wicked?—*Ps.* lxxxii. 2.

Defend the poor and fatherless: do justice to the afflicted and needy.—3.

Deliver the poor and needy: rid them out of the hand of the wicked.—4.

Blessed are they that keep judgment, and he that doeth righteousness at all times.—*Ps.* cvi. 3.

Withhold not good from them to whom it is due,

when it is in the power of thine hand to do it.—*Prov.* iii. 27.

Say not unto thy neighbour, Go, and come again, and to morrow I will give; when thou hast it by thee.—28.

Strive not with a man without cause, if he have done thee no harm.—30.

A just weight and balance are the Lord's... *Prov.* xvi. 11.

He that justifieth the wicked, and he that condemneth the just, even they both are abomination to the Lord.—*Prov.* xvii. 15.

He that is first in his own cause seemeth just; but his neighbour cometh and searcheth him.—*Prov.* xviii. 17.

The robbery of the wicked shall destroy them; because they refuse to do judgment.—*Prov.* xxi. 7.

It is joy to the just to do judgment.—15.

...It is not good to have respect of persons in judgment.—*Prov.* xxiv. 23.

Evil men understand not judgment: but they that seek the Lord understand all things.—*Prov.* xxviii. 5.

When the righteous are in authority, the people rejoice: but when the wicked beareth rule, the people mourn.—*Prov.* xxix. 2.

Many seek the ruler's favour; but every man's judgment cometh from the Lord.—26.

Open thy mouth, judge righteously, and plead the cause of the poor and needy.—*Prov.* xxxi. 9.

Learn to do well; seek judgment, relieve the oppressed, judge the fatherless, plead for the widow. —*Isa.* i. 17.

Woe unto them that decree unrighteous decrees, and that write grievousness which they have prescribed;—*Isa.* x. 1.

To turn aside the needy from judgment, and to take away the right from the poor of my people, that widows may be their prey, and that they may rob the fatherless!—2.

And what will ye do in the day of visitation, and in the desolation which shall come from far; to whom will ye fly for help? and where will ye leave your glory?—3.

Without me they shall bow down under the prisoners, and they shall fall under the slain. For all this his anger is not turned away, but his hand is stretched out still.—4.

Take counsel, execute judgment.—*Isa.* xvi. 3.

The way of the just is uprightness: thou, most upright, dost weigh the path of the just.—*Isa.* xxvi. 7.

Thus saith the Lord, keep ye judgment, and do justice: for my salvation is near to come, and my righteousness to be revealed.—*Isa.* lvi. 1.

None calleth for justice, nor any pleadeth for truth:...*Isa.* lix. 4.

The way of peace they know not; and there is no judgment in their goings: they have made them crooked paths: whosoever goeth therein shall not know peace.—8.

Therefore is judgment far from us, neither doth justice overtake us: we wait for light, but behold obscurity; for brightness, but we walk in darkness.—9.

In transgressing and lying against the Lord, and departing away from our God,...13.

...Judgment is turned away backward, and justice standeth afar off:...14.

Yea, truth faileth; and he that departeth from evil maketh himself a prey: and the Lord saw it, and it displeased him that there was no judgment.—15.

For I the Lord love judgment...*Isa.* lxi. 8.

Run ye to and fro through the streets of Jerusalem, and see now, and know, and seek in the broad places thereof, if ye can find a man, if there be any that executeth judgment, that seeketh the truth; and I will pardon it.—*Jer.* v. 1.

...If ye thoroughly execute judgment between a man and his neighbour;—*Jer.* vii. 5.

If ye oppress not the stranger, the fatherless, and the widow, and shed not innocent blood...6.

Then will I cause you to dwell in...the land that I gave to your fathers, for ever and ever.—7.

Thus saith the Lord; Execute ye judgment and righteousness, and deliver the spoiled out of the hand of the oppressor...*Jer.* xxii. 3.

...Did not thy father...do judgment and justice, and then it was well with him?—15.

He judged the cause of the poor and needy; then it was well with him: was not this to know me? saith the Lord.—16.

...If a man be just, and do that which is lawful and right,—*Ezek.* xviii. 5.

And hath not oppressed any, but hath restored to the debtor his pledge, hath spoilt none by violence,...7.

He that hath not given forth upon usury, neither hath taken any increase, that hath withdrawn his hand from iniquity, hath executed true judgment between man and man,—8.

Hath walked in my statutes, and hath kept my judgments, to deal truly; he is just, he shall surely live, saith the Lord God.—9.

Turn thou to thy God; keep mercy and judgment, and wait on thy God continually.—*Hosea* xii. 6.

I know your manifold transgressions and your mighty sins: they afflict the just, they take a bribe, and they turn aside the poor in the gate from their right.—*Amos* v. 12.

Hate the evil, and love the good, and establish judgment in the gate...15.

...Let judgment run down as waters, and righteousness as a mighty stream.—24.

He hath shewed thee, O man, what is good; and what doth the Lord require of thee, but to do justly, and to love mercy, and to walk humbly with thy God?—*Micah* vi. 8.

Thus speaketh the Lord of hosts, saying, Execute true judgment, and shew mercy and compassions every man to his brother.—*Zech.* vii. 9.

BE TRUTHFUL AND UPRIGHT, HONEST AND FAITHFUL.

---o---

Thou shalt not bear false witness against thy neighbour.—*Ex.* xx. 16.

Thou shalt not raise a false report: put not thine hand with the wicked to be an unrighteous witness.—*Ex.* xxiii. 1.

If a soul sin,...and lie unto his neighbour in that which was delivered him to keep,...*Lev.* vi. 2.

Or have found that which was lost, and lieth concerning it, and sweareth falsely; in any of all these that a man doeth, sinning therein:—3.

Then it shall be, because he hath sinned, and is guilty, that he shall restore that which he took...4.

Ye shall not steal, neither deal falsely, neither lie one to another.—*Lev.* xix. 11.

Thou shalt not defraud thy neighbour, neither rob him: the wages of him that is hired shall not abide with thee all night until the morning.—13.

If thou wilt walk before me, as David thy father walked, in integrity of heart, and in uprightness, to do according to all that I have commanded thee,...1 *Kings* ix. 4.

Then I will establish the throne of thy kingdom upon Israel for ever...1 *Kings* ix. 5.

...Judge me, O Lord, according to my righteousness, and according to mine integrity that is in me.—*Ps.* vii. 8.

My defence is of God, which saveth the upright in heart.—10.

For the righteous Lord loveth righteousness; his countenance doth behold the upright.—*Ps.* xi. 7.

Lord, who shall abide in thy tabernacle? who shall dwell in thy holy hill?—*Ps.* xv. 1.

He that walketh uprightly, and worketh righteousness, and speaketh the truth in his heart.—2.

...He that sweareth to his own hurt, and changeth not...4.

Let integrity and uprightness preserve me; for I wait on thee.—*Ps.* xxv. 21.

As for me, I will walk in mine integrity.—*Ps.* xxvi. 11.

...For the Lord preserveth the faithful...*Ps.* xxxi. 23.

Blessed is the man unto whom the Lord imputeth not iniquity, and in whose spirit there is no guile.—*Ps.* xxxii. 2.

...Shout for joy, all ye that are upright in heart.—11.

For praise is comely for the upright.—*Ps.* xxxiii. 1.

The wicked borroweth, and payeth not again... *Ps.* xxxvii. 21.

Behold, thou desirest truth in the inward parts... *Ps.* li. 6.

…The mouth of them that speak lies shall be stopped.—*Ps.* lxiii. 11.

…All the upright in heart shall glory.—*Ps.* lxiv. 10.

…No good thing will he withhold from them that walk uprightly.—*Ps.* lxxxiv. 11.

Mercy and truth are met together ; righteousness and peace have kissed each other.—*Ps.* lxxxv. 10.

Truth shall spring out of the earth…11.

…He that telleth lies shall not tarry in my sight.—*Ps.* ci. 7.

…The generation of the upright shall be blessed.—*Ps.* cxii. 2.

Unto the upright there ariseth light in the darkness…4.

Through thy precepts I get understanding: therefore I hate every false way.—*Ps.* cxix. 104.

…Lead me into the land of uprightness…*Ps.* cxliii. 10.

Let not mercy and truth forsake thee: bind them about thy neck; write them upon the table of thine heart:—*Prov.* iii. 3.

So shalt thou find favour and good understanding in the sight of God and man.—4.

My mouth shall speak truth…*Prov.* viii. 7.

He that walketh uprightly walketh surely.—*Prov.* x. 9.

The integrity of the upright shall guide them…*Prov.* xi. 3.

The righteousness of the upright shall deliver them…6.

…Such as are upright in their way are his delight.—20.

He that speaketh truth sheweth forth righteousness: but a false witness deceit.—*Prov.* xii. 17.

The lip of truth shall be established for ever: but a lying tongue is but for a moment.—19.

Lying lips are abomination to the Lord: but they that deal truly are his delight.—22.

A faithful witness will not lie: but a false witness will utter lies.—*Prov.* xiv. 5.

A true witness delivereth souls: but a deceitful witness speaketh lies.—25.

...A man of understanding walketh uprightly.—*Prov.* xv. 21.

By mercy and truth iniquity is purged...*Prov.* xvi. 6.

Better is the poor that walketh in his integrity, than he that is perverse in his lips, and is a fool.—*Prov.* xix. 1.

A false witness shall not be unpunished, and he that speaketh lies shall not escape.—5.

The just man walketh in his integrity: his children are blessed after him.—*Prov.* xx. 7.

Mercy and truth preserve the king: and his throne is upholden by mercy.—28.

The getting of treasures by a lying tongue is a vanity tossed to and fro of them that seek death. —*Prov.* xxi. 6.

Debate thy cause with thy neighbour himself; and discover not a secret to another.—*Prov.* xxv. 9.

Confidence in an unfaithful man in time of trouble is like a broken tooth, and a foot out of joint.—19.

A lying tongue hateth those that are afflicted by it; and a flattering mouth worketh ruin.—*Prov.* xxvi. 28.

Better is the poor that walketh in his uprightness, than he that is perverse in his ways, though he be rich.—*Prov.* xxviii. 6.

Whoso walketh uprightly shall be saved...18.

A faithful man shall abound with blessings...20.

Lo, this only have I found, that God hath made man upright; but they have sought out many inventions.—*Eccl.* vii. 29.

The way of the just is uprightness: thou, most upright, dost weigh the path of the just.—*Isa.* xxvi. 7.

Run ye to and fro through the streets of Jerusalem, and see now, and know,...if ye can find a man,... that seeketh the truth; and I will pardon it.—*Jer.* v. 1.

O Lord, are not thine eyes upon the truth?...3.

...Do not my words do good to him that walketh uprightly?—*Micah* ii. 7.

...Speak ye every man the truth to his neighbour; execute the judgment of truth and peace in your gates:...*Zech.* viii. 16.

...And love no false oath: for all these are things that I hate, saith the Lord.—17.

THE SIN OF DECEIT AND HYPOCRISY.

...Let not Pharaoh deal deceitfully any more in not letting the people go to sacrifice to the Lord.—*Ex.* viii. 29.

If a soul sin, and commit a trespass against the Lord, and lie unto his neighbour in that which was delivered him to keep,...or hath deceived his neighbour;—*Lev.* vi. 2.

Then it shall be, because he hath sinned, and is guilty, that he shall restore...the thing which he hath deceitfully gotten.—4.

...The hypocrite's hope shall perish.—*Job* viii. 13.

Will ye speak wickedly for God? and talk deceitfully for him?—*Job* xiii. 7.

Knowest thou not this of old, since man was placed upon earth,—*Job* xx. 4.

That the triumphing of the wicked is short, and the joy of the hypocrite but for a moment?—5.

All the while my breath is in me, and the spirit of God is in my nostrils;—*Job* xxvii. 3.

My lips shall not speak wickedness, nor my tongue utter deceit.—4.

For what is the hope of the hypocrite, though he hath gained, when God taketh away his soul?—8.

...The hypocrites in heart heap up wrath...*Job* xxxvi. 13.

...With flattering lips and with a double heart do they speak.—*Ps.* xii. 2.

Keep thy tongue from evil, and thy lips from speaking guile...*Ps.* xxxiv. 13.

...O deliver me from the deceitful and unjust man.—*Ps.* xliii. 1.

...Unto the wicked God saith, What hast thou to do to declare my statutes, or that thou shouldest take my covenant in thy mouth?—*Ps.* l. 16.

Thou givest thy mouth to evil, and thy tongue frameth deceit.—19.

Thou sittest and speakest against thy brother; thou slanderest thine own mother's son.—20.

The words of his mouth were smoother than butter, but war was in his heart: his words were softer than oil, yet were they drawn swords.—*Ps.* lv. 21.

He that worketh deceit shall not dwell within my house...*Ps.* ci. 7.

Deliver my soul, O Lord, from lying lips, and from a deceitful tongue.—*Ps.* cxx. 2.

An hypocrite with his mouth destroyeth his neighbour...*Prov.* xi. 9.

...The counsels of the wicked are deceit.—*Prov.* xii. 5.

Deceit is in the heart of them that imagine evil...20.

Bread of deceit is sweet to a man; but afterwards his mouth shall be filled with gravel.—*Prov.* xx. 17.

...Deceive not with thy lips.—*Prov.* xxiv. 28.

He that hateth dissembleth with his lips, and layeth up deceit within him;—*Prov.* xxvi. 24.

When he speaketh fair, believe him not: for there are seven abominations in his heart.—25.

Whose hatred is covered by deceit, his wickedness shall be shewed before the whole congregation.—26.

...The kisses of an enemy are deceitful.—*Prov.* xxvii. 6.

And they bend their tongues like their bow for lies: but they are not valiant for the truth upon the earth; for they proceed from evil to evil, and they know not me, saith the Lord.—*Jer.* ix. 3.

Take ye heed every one of his neighbour, and trust ye not in any brother: for every brother will utterly supplant, and every neighbour will walk with slanders.—4.

And they will deceive every one his neighbour, and will not speak the truth: they have taught their tongue to speak lies,...5.

Thine habitation is in the midst of deceit; through deceit they refuse to know me, saith the Lord.—6.

Their tongue is as an arrow shot out; it speaketh deceit: one speaketh peaceably to his neighbour with his mouth, but in heart he layeth his wait.—8.

Shall I not visit them for these things? saith the Lord...9.

The remnant of Israel shall not do iniquity, nor speak lies; neither shall a deceitful tongue be found in their mouth.—*Zeph.* iii. 13.

THE DUTY OF REPROVING SIN.

…Thou shalt in any wise rebuke thy neighbour, and not suffer sin upon him.—*Lev.* xix. 17.

And the Lord sent Nathan unto David. And he came unto him, and said unto him, There were two men in one city; the one rich, and the other poor.—2 *Sam.* xii. 1.

The rich man had exceeding many flocks and herds:—2.

But the poor man had nothing, save one little ewe lamb, which he had bought and nourished up: and it grew up together with him, and with his children ; it did eat of his own meat, and drank of his own cup, and lay in his bosom ;…3.

And there came a traveller unto the rich man, and he spared to take of his own flock and of his own herd,…but took the poor man's lamb,…4.

And David's anger was greatly kindled against the man ; and he said,…As the Lord liveth, the man that hath done this thing shall surely die:—5.

…Because he did this thing, and because he had no pity.—6.

And Nathan said to David, Thou art the man…7.

Wherefore hast thou despised the commandment of the Lord, to do evil in his sight?—2 *Sam.* xii. 9.

And David said,...I have sinned against the Lord. And Nathan said unto David, The Lord hath also put away thy sin; thou shalt not die.—13.

Howbeit, because by this deed thou hast given great occasion to the enemies of the Lord to blaspheme, the child also that is born unto thee shall surely die.—14.

...Uphold me with thy free spirit.—*Ps.* li. 12.

Then will I teach transgressors thy ways; and sinners shall be converted unto thee.—13.

Let the righteous smite me; it shall be a kindness: and let him reprove me; it shall be an excellent oil, which shall not break my head...*Ps.* cxli. 5.

...Reproofs of instruction are the way of life.—*Prov.* vi. 23.

...Rebuke a wise man, and he will love thee.—*Prov.* ix. 8.

...He that refuseth reproof erreth.—*Prov.* x. 17.

...He that regardeth reproof shall be honoured.—*Prov.* xiii. 18.

...He that regardeth reproof is prudent.—*Prov.* xv. 5.

The ear that heareth the reproof of life abideth among the wise.—31.

...He that heareth reproof getteth understanding.—32.

A reproof entereth more into a wise man than an hundred stripes into a fool.—*Prov.* xvii. 10.

THE DUTY OF REPROVING SIN.

...Reprove one that hath understanding, and he will understand knowledge.—*Prov.* xix. 25.

As an earring of gold, and an ornament of fine gold, so is a wise reprover upon an obedient ear.—*Prov.* xxv. 12.

Faithful are the wounds of a friend...*Prov.* xxvii. 6.

He that rebuketh a man afterwards shall find more favour than he that flattereth with the tongue.—*Prov.* xxviii. 23.

It is better to hear the rebuke of the wise, than for a man to hear the song of fools.—*Eccl.* vii. 5.

When I (the Lord) say unto the wicked, O wicked man, thou shalt surely die; if thou dost not speak to warn the wicked from his way, that wicked man shall die in his iniquity; but his blood will I require at thine hand.—*Ezek.* xxxiii. 8.

Nevertheless, if thou warn the wicked of his way to turn from it; if he do not turn from his way, he shall die in his iniquity; but thou hast delivered thy soul.—9.

GOD PROTECTS THE HELPLESS AND POOR, THE WIDOW AND FATHERLESS.

---o---

Thou shalt neither vex a stranger, nor oppress him...*Ex.* xxii. 21.

Ye shall not afflict any widow, or fatherless child.—22.

If thou afflict them in any wise, and they cry at all unto me, I will surely hear their cry;—23.

And my wrath shall wax hot, and I will kill you with the sword; and your wives shall be widows, and your children fatherless.—24.

For the Lord your God is God of gods, and Lord of lords, a great god:...*Deut.* x. 17.

He doth execute the judgment of the fatherless and widow, and loveth the stranger, in giving him food and raiment.—18.

When thou cuttest down thine harvest in thy field, and hast forgot a sheaf in the field, thou shalt not go again to fetch it: it shall be for the stranger, for the fatherless, and for the widow: that the Lord thy

God may bless thee in all the work of thine hands. —*Deut.* xxiv. 19.

When thou beatest thine olive tree, thou shalt not go over the boughs again: it shall be for the stranger, for the fatherless, and for the widow.—20.

When thou gatherest the grapes of thy vineyard, thou shalt not glean it afterward: it shall be for the stranger, for the fatherless, and for the widow.—21.

Cursed be he that perverteth the judgment of the stranger, fatherless, and widow. And all the people shall say, Amen.—*Deut.* xxvii. 19.

He disappointeth the devices of the crafty...*Job* v. 12.

But he saveth the poor from the sword, from their mouth, and from the hand of the mighty.—15.

So the poor hath hope...16.

Thou hast sent widows away empty, and the arms of the fatherless have been broken.—*Job* xxii. 9.

Therefore snares are round about thee, and sudden fear troubleth thee.—10.

Behold, God is mighty, and despiseth not any: —*Job* xxxvi. 5.

He...giveth right to the poor...6.

He delivereth the poor in his afiliction, and openeth their ears in oppression.—15.

For the needy shall not always be forgotten: the expectation of the poor shall not perish for ever.— *Ps.* ix. 18.

...The poor committeth himself unto thee; thou art the helper of the fatherless.—*Ps.* x. 14.

For the oppression of the poor, for the sighing of the needy, now will I arise, saith the Lord; I will set him in safety from him that puffeth at him.—*Ps.* xii. 5.

When my father and my mother forsake me, then the Lord will take me up.—*Ps.* xxvii. 10.

...Lord, who is like unto thee, who deliverest the poor from him that is too strong for him, yea, the poor and the needy from him that spoileth him?—*Ps.* xxxv. 10.

...I am poor and needy; yet the Lord thinketh upon me.—*Ps.* xl. 17.

A father of the fatherless, and a judge of the widows, is God in his holy habitation.—*Ps.* lxviii. 5.

...Thou, O God, hast prepared of thy goodness for the poor.—10.

For the Lord heareth the poor, and despiseth not his prisoners.—*Ps.* lxix. 33.

...He shall deliver the needy when he crieth; the poor also, and him that hath no helper.—*Ps.* lxxii. 12.

He shall spare the poor and needy, and shall save the souls of the needy.—13.

They (the wicked) slay the widow and the stranger, and murder the fatherless.—*Ps.* xciv. 6.

Yet they say, The Lord shall not see, neither shall the God of Jacob regard it.—7.

He will regard the prayer of the destitute, and not despise their prayer.—*Ps.* cii. 17.

...From heaven did the Lord behold the earth;—19.

To hear the groaning of the prisoner; to loose those that are appointed to death.—*Ps*. cii. 20.

...He shall stand at the right hand of the poor, to save him from those that condemn his soul.—*Ps*. cix. 31.

He raiseth up the poor out of the dust,...*Ps*. cxiii. 7.

That he may set him with princes, even with the princes of his people.—8.

I know that the Lord will maintain the cause of the afflicted, and the right of the poor.—*Ps*. cxl. 12.

Happy is he that hath the God of Jacob for his help, whose hope is in the Lord his God:—*Ps*. cxlvi. 5.

Which executeth judgment for the oppressed: which giveth food to the hungry. The Lord looseth the prisoners:—7.

The Lord openeth the eyes of the blind: the Lord raiseth them that are bowed down: the Lord loveth the righteous:—8.

The Lord preserveth the strangers; he relieveth the fatherless and widow: but the way of the wicked he turneth upside down.—9.

...He will establish the border of the widow.—*Prov*. xv. 25.

The rich and poor meet together: the Lord is the maker of them all.—*Prov*. xxii. 2.

For the Lord will plead their cause, and spoil the soul of those that spoiled them.—23.

Remove not the old landmark; and enter not into the fields of the fatherless:—*Prov*. xxiii. 10.

For their redeemer is mighty; he shall plead their cause with thee.—*Prov.* xxiii. 11.

If thou seest the oppression of the poor, and violent perverting of judgment and justice in a province, marvel not at the matter: for he that is higher than the highest regardeth; and there be higher than they.—*Eccl.* v. 8.

Thy princes are rebellious,...they judge not the fatherless, neither doth the cause of the widow come unto them.—*Isa.* i. 23.

Therefore saith the Lord, the Lord of hosts, the mighty One of Israel, Ah, I will ease me of mine adversaries...24.

And I will turn my hand upon thee...25.

The Lord standeth up to plead, and standeth to judge the people.—*Isa.* iii. 13.

The Lord will enter into judgment with the ancients of his people, and the princes thereof: for ye have eaten up the vineyard; the spoil of the poor is in your houses.—14.

What mean ye that ye beat my people to pieces, and grind the faces of the poor? saith the Lord God of hosts...15.

...The firstborn of the poor shall feed, and the needy shall lie down in safety...*Isa.* xiv. 30.

O Lord, thou art my God; I will exalt thee, I will praise thy name;...*Isa.* xxv. 1.

For thou hast been a strength to the poor, a

strength to the needy in his distress, a refuge from the storm, a shadow from the heat...*Isa.* xxv. 4.

Sing unto the Lord, praise ye the Lord: for he hath delivered the soul of the poor from the hand of evildoers.—*Jer.* xx. 13.

Leave thy fatherless children, I will preserve them alive; and let thy widows trust in me.—*Jer.* xlix. 11.

...In thee the fatherless findeth mercy.—*Hosea* xiv. 3.

Forasmuch therefore as your treading is upon the poor, and ye take from him burdens of wheat: ye have built houses of hewn stone, but ye shall not dwell in them; ye have planted pleasant vineyards, but ye shall not drink wine of them.—*Amos* v. 11.

Thus speaketh the Lord of hosts, saying, Execute true judgment, and shew mercy and compassions every man to his brother:—*Zech.* vii. 9.

And oppress not the widow, nor the fatherless, the stranger, nor the poor;...10.

BE CONSIDERATE TO THE POOR, THE SUFFERING AND HELPLESS.

———o———

If thou lend money to any of my people that is poor by thee, thou shalt not be to him as an usurer, neither shalt thou lay upon him usury.—*Ex.* xxii. 25.

If thou at all take thy neighbour's raiment to pledge, thou shalt deliver it unto him by that the sun goeth down :—26.

For that is his covering only, it is his raiment for his skin : wherein shall he sleep? and it shall come to pass, when he crieth unto me, that I will hear; for I am gracious.—27.

If thy brother be waxen poor, and fallen in decay with thee; then thou shalt relieve him : yea, though he be a stranger, or a sojourner; that he may live with thee.—*Lev.* xxv. 35.

Take thou no usury of him, or increase : but fear thy God; that thy brother may live with thee.—36.

And if thy brother that dwelleth by thee be waxen poor, and be sold unto thee; thou shalt not compel him to serve as a bondservant :—39.

Thou shalt not rule over him with rigour; but shalt fear thy God.—43.

If there be among you a poor man of one of thy brethren within any of thy gates in thy land which the Lord thy God giveth thee, thou shalt not harden thine heart, nor shut thine hand from thy poor brother:—*Deut.* xv. 7.

But thou shalt open thine hand wide unto him, and shalt surely lend him sufficient for his need, in that which he wanteth.—8.

Beware that there be not a thought in thy wicked heart, saying, The seventh year, the year of release, is at hand; and thine eye be evil against thy poor brother, and thou givest him nought; and he cry unto the Lord against thee, and it be sin unto thee.—9.

Thou shalt surely give him, and thine heart shall not be grieved when thou givest unto him: because that for this thing the Lord thy God shall bless thee in all thy works, and in all that thou puttest thine hand unto.—10.

For the poor shall never cease out of the land: therefore I command thee, saying, Thou shalt open thine hand wide unto thy brother, and to thy needy, in thy land.—11.

Every man shall give as he is able, according to the blessing of the Lord thy God which he hath given thee.—*Deut.* xvi. 17.

Thou shalt not oppress an hired servant that is poor and needy, whether he be of thy brethren, or of thy strangers that are in thy land within thy gates:—*Deut.* xxiv. 14.

At his day thou shalt give him his hire, neither shall the sun go down upon it; for he is poor, and setteth his heart upon it: lest he cry against thee unto the Lord, and it be sin unto thee.—*Deut.* xxiv. 15.

Cursed be he that maketh the blind to wander out of the way. And all the people shall say, Amen.— *Deut.* xxvii. 18.

Is not thy wickedness great? and thine iniquities infinite?—*Job* xxii. 5.

For thou hast taken a pledge from thy brother for nought, and stripped the naked of their clothing.—6.

Thou hast not given water to the weary to drink, and thou hast withholden bread from the hungry.—7.

Did not I weep for him that was in trouble? was not my soul grieved for the poor?—*Job* xxx. 25.

If I did despise the cause of my manservant or of my maidservant, when they contended with me;— *Job* xxxi. 13.

What then shall I do when God riseth up? and when he visiteth, what shall I answer him?—14.

If I have withheld the poor from their desire, or have caused the eyes of the widow to fail;—16.

Or have eaten my morsel myself alone, and the fatherless hath not eaten thereof;—17.

If I have seen any perish for want of clothing, or any poor without covering;—19.

If his loins have not blessed me, and if he were not warmed with the fleece of my sheep;—20.

If I have lifted up my hand against the fatherless, when I saw my help in the gate:—21.

Then let mine arm fall from my shoulder blade, and mine arm be broken from the bone.—*Job* xxxi. 22.

The wicked in his pride doth persecute the poor... *Ps.* x. 2.

The righteous sheweth mercy, and giveth.—*Ps.* xxxvii. 21.

He is ever merciful, and lendeth; and his seed is blessed.—26.

Blessed is he that considereth the poor: the Lord shall deliver him in time of trouble.—*Ps.* xli. 1.

The Lord will preserve him, and keep him alive; and he shall be blessed on the earth.—2.

There is that scattereth, and yet increaseth; and and there is that withholdeth more than is meet, but it tendeth to poverty.—*Prov.* xi. 24.

The liberal soul shall be made fat: and he that watereth shall be watered also himself.—25.

He that hath mercy on the poor, happy is he.— *Prov.* xiv. 21.

He that oppresseth the poor reproacheth his Maker: but he that honoureth him hath mercy on the poor.—31.

Whoso mocketh the poor reproacheth his Maker: and he that is glad at calamities shall not be unpunished.—*Prov.* xvii. 5.

He that hath pity upon the poor lendeth unto the Lord; and that which he hath given will he pay him again.—*Prov.* xix. 17.

Whoso stoppeth his ears at the cry of the poor, he also shall cry himself, but shall not be heard.— *Prov.* xxi. 13.

THE SUFFERING AND HELPLESS.

He that hath a bountiful eye shall be blessed; for he giveth of his bread to the poor.—*Prov.* xxii. 9.

He that oppresseth the poor to increase his riches, and he that giveth to the rich, shall surely come to want.—16.

Rob not the poor, because he is poor: neither oppress the afflicted in the gate:—22.

For the Lord will plead their cause, and spoil the soul of those that spoiled them.—23.

If thou hast nothing to pay, why should he take away thy bed from under thee?—27.

He that giveth unto the poor shall not lack. —*Prov.* xxviii. 27.

The righteous considereth the cause of the poor: but the wicked regardeth not to know it.—*Prov.* xxix. 7.

Is not this the fast that I have chosen? to loose the bands of wickedness, to undo the heavy burdens, and to let the oppressed go free, and that ye break every yoke?—*Isa.* lviii. 6.

Is it not to deal thy bread to the hungry, and that thou bring the poor that are cast out to thy house? when thou seest the naked, that thou cover him; and that thou hide not thyself from thine own flesh?—7.

And if thou draw out thy soul to the hungry, and satisfy the afflicted soul; then shall thy light rise in obscurity, and thy darkness be as the noon day.—10.

Break off thy sins by righteousness, and thine iniquities by shewing mercy to the poor...*Dan.* iv. 27.

SYMPATHISE AND BE KIND: RETURN GOOD FOR EVIL.

———o———

Forgive, I pray thee now, the trespass of thy brethren, and their sin;...*Gen.* l. 17.

And Joseph said unto them, Fear not: for am I in the place of God?—19.

But as for you, ye thought evil against me;...20.

Now therefore fear ye not: I will nourish you, and your little ones. And he comforted them, and spake kindly unto them.—21.

Thou shalt neither vex a stranger, nor oppress him: for ye were strangers in the land of Egypt.—*Ex.* xxii. 21.

If thou meet thine enemy's ox or his ass going astray, thou shalt surely bring it back to him again.—*Ex.* xxiii. 4.

If thou see the ass of him that hateth thee lying under his burden, and wouldest forbear to help him, thou shalt surely help with him.—5.

Also thou shalt not oppress a stranger: for ye know the heart of a stranger, seeing ye were strangers in the land of Egypt.—9.

Thou shalt not avenge, nor bear any grudge against the children of thy people, but thou shalt love thy neighbour as thyself: I am the Lord.—*Lev.* xix. 18.

If a stranger sojourn with thee in your land, ye shall not vex him.—33.

But the stranger that dwelleth with you shall be unto you as one born among you, and thou shalt love him as thyself; for ye were strangers in the land of Egypt: I am the Lord your God.—34.

Ye shall not therefore oppress one another; but thou shalt fear thy God.—*Lev.* xxv. 17.

Love ye the stranger: for ye were strangers in the land of Egypt.—*Deut.* x. 19.

Thou shalt not see thy brother's ox or his sheep go astray, and hide thyself from them: thou shalt in any case bring them again unto thy brother.—*Deut.* xxii. 1.

And if thy brother be not nigh unto thee, or if thou know him not, then thou shalt bring it into thine own house, and it shall be with thee until thy brother seek after it, and thou shalt restore it to him again.—2.

In like manner shalt thou do with his ass; and so shalt thou do with his raiment; and with all lost thing of thy brother's, which he hath lost, and thou hast found, shalt thou do likewise: thou mayest not hide thyself.—3.

Thou shalt not see thy brother's ox or his ass fall

down by the way, and hide thyself from them: thou shalt surely help him to lift them up again.—*Deut.* xxii. 4.

Thou shalt not abhor an Edomite; for he is thy brother: thou shalt not abhor an Egyptian; because thou wast a stranger in his land.—*Deut.* xxiii. 7.

When thou dost lend thy brother anything, thou shalt not go into his house to fetch his pledge.—*Deut.* xxiv. 10.

Then she (Ruth) said,...thou hast comforted me, and for that thou hast spoken friendly unto thine handmaid, though I be not like unto one of thine handmaidens.—*Ruth* ii. 13.

And the men of David said unto him, Behold the day of which the Lord said unto thee, Behold, I will deliver thine enemy into thine hand, that thou mayest do to him as it shall seem good unto thee. Then David...cut off the skirt of Saul's robe privily.— 1 *Sam.* xxiv. 4.

...But Saul rose up out of the cave, and went on his way.—7.

David also arose afterward, and went out of the cave, and cried after Saul, saying, My lord the king!...8.

...Wherefore hearest thou men's words, saying, Behold, David seeketh thy hurt?—9.

Behold, thine eyes have seen how that the Lord had delivered thee to day into mine hand in the cave: and some bade me kill thee: and I said, I will not put forth mine hand against my lord ; for he is the Lord's anointed.—1 *Sam.* xxiv. 10.

Moreover, my father, see, yea, see the skirt of thy robe in my hand : for in that I cut off the skirt of thy robe, and killed thee not, know thou and see that... I have not sinned against thee : yet thou huntest my soul to take it.—11.

...And Saul lifted up his voice, and wept.—16.

And he said to David, Thou art more righteous than I: for thou hast rewarded me good, whereas I have rewarded thee evil.—17.

To him that is afflicted pity should be shewed from his friend.—*Job* vi. 14.

I also could speak as ye do : if your soul were in my soul's stead, I could heap up words against you, and shake mine head at you.—*Job* xvi. 4.

But I would strengthen you with my mouth, and the moving of my lips should asswage your grief.—5.

Have pity upon me, have pity upon me, O ye my friends ; for the hand of God hath touched me.— *Job* xix. 21.

Did I not weep for him that was in trouble?... *Job* xxx. 25.

If I rejoiced at the destruction of him that hated me, or lifted up myself when evil found him :— *Job* xxxi. 29.

Neither have I suffered my mouth to sin by wishing a curse to his soul.—30.

The stranger did not lodge in the street: but I opened my doors to the traveller.—32.

...I have delivered him that without cause is mine enemy.—*Ps.* vii. 4.

With the merciful thou wilt shew thyself merciful.—*Ps.* xviii. 25.

...The righteous sheweth mercy and giveth.—*Ps.* xxxvii. 21.

He is ever merciful, and lendeth.—26.

Withhold not good from them to whom it is due, when it is in the power of thine hand to do it.—*Prov.* iii. 27.

Say not unto thy neighbour, Go, and come again, and to morrow I will give; when thou hast it by thee.—28.

Love covereth all sins.—*Prov.* x. 12.

He that is void of wisdom despiseth his neighbour.—*Prov.* xi. 12.

The merciful man doeth good to his own soul...17.

The discretion of a man deferreth his anger; and it is his glory to pass over a transgression.—*Prov.* xix. 11.

He that despiseth his neighbour sinneth...*Prov.* xiv. 21.

Say not thou, I will recompense evil; but wait on the Lord, and he shall save thee.—*Prov.* xx. 22.

Mercy and truth preserve the king: and his throne is upholden by mercy.—28.

...The righteous giveth and spareth not.—*Prov.* xxi. 26.

If thou forbear to deliver them that are drawn unto death, and those that are ready to be slain;—*Prov.* xxiv. 11.

If thou sayest, Behold, we know it not; doth not he that pondereth the heart consider it? and he that keepeth thy soul, doth not he know it? and shall not he render to every man according to his works?—12.

Rejoice not when thine enemy falleth, and let not thine heart be glad when he stumbleth:—17.

Lest the Lord see it, and it displease him...18.

Be not a witness against thy neighbour without cause...28.

Say not, I will do so to him as he hath done to me: I will render to the man according to his work.—29.

If thine enemy be hungry, give him bread to eat; and if he be thirsty, give him water to drink.— *Prov.* xxv. 21.

...In her tongue is the law of kindness.—*Prov.* xxxi. 26.

Cast thy bread upon the waters: for thou shalt find it after many days.—*Eccl.* xi. 1.

Give a portion to seven, and also to eight...2.

And what doth the Lord require of thee, but to do justly, and to love mercy, and to walk humbly with thy God?—*Micah* vi. 8.

Thus speaketh the Lord of hosts, saying,...shew mercy and compassions every man to his brother:—*Zech.* vii. 9.

...And let none of you imagine evil against his brother in your heart.—10.

GOD'S CARE FOR ANIMALS: BE KIND TO THEM.

And God created great whales, and every living creature that moveth,...after their kind, and every winged fowl after his kind: and God saw that it was good.—*Gen.* i. 21.

And God blessed them, saying, Be fruitful, and multiply...22.

...To every beast of the earth, and to every fowl of the air, and to every thing that creepeth upon the earth, wherein there is life, I have given every green herb for meat.—30.

...Of every living thing of all flesh...shalt thou bring into the ark, to keep them alive with thee...*Gen.* vi. 19.

And God remembered Noah, and every living thing, and all the cattle that was with him in the ark...*Gen.* viii. 1.

And when she (Rebekah) had done giving him drink, she said, I will draw water for thy camels also, until they have done drinking.—*Gen.* xxiv. 19.

And she hasted, and emptied her pitcher into the trough, and ran again unto the well to draw water, and drew for all his camels.—20.

And he (Jacob) said, the flocks and herds with young are with me: and if men should over drive them one day, all the flock will die.—*Gen.* xxxiii. 13.

...I will lead on softly, according as the cattle that goeth before me...be able to endure.—14.

Six years thou shalt sow thy land:...*Ex.* xxiii. 10.

But the seventh year thou shalt let it rest and lie still; that the poor of thy people may eat: and what they leave the beasts of the field shall eat.—11.

Six days thou shalt do thy work, and on the seventh day thou shalt rest: that thine ox and thine ass may rest...12.

And for thy cattle, and for the beast that are in thy land, shall all the increase thereof be meat.—*Lev.* xxv. 7.

...And Balaam smote the ass, to turn her into the way.—*Num.* xxii. 23.

And the angel of the Lord said unto him, Wherefore hast thou smitten thine ass these three times?...32.

...Unless she had turned from me, surely now I had slain thee, and saved her alive.—33.

Thou shalt not see thy brother's ox or his sheep go astray, and hide thyself from them: thou shalt in any case bring them again unto thy brother.—*Deut.* xxii. 1.

And if thy brother be not nigh unto thee, or if thou know him not, then thou shalt bring it unto thine own house, and it shall be with thee until thy brother seek after it...2.

Thou shalt not see thy brother's ass or his ox fall down by the way, and hide thyself from them: thou shalt surely help him to lift them up again.—*Deut.* xxii. 4.

If a bird's nest chance to be before thee in the way in any tree, or on the ground, whether they be young ones, or eggs, and the dam sitting upon the young, or upon the eggs, thou shalt not take the dam with the young.—6.

...That it may be well with thee, and that thou mayest prolong thy days.—7.

Who hath sent out the wild ass free? or who hath loosed the bands of the wild ass?—*Job* xxxix. 5.

He scorneth the multitude of the city, neither regardeth he the crying of the driver.—7.

The range of the mountains is his pasture, and he searcheth after every green thing.—8.

Gavest thou the goodly wings unto the peacocks? or wings and feathers unto the ostrich?—13.

Hast thou given the horse strength? hast thou clothed his neck with thunder?—19.

...The glory of his nostrils is terrible.—20.

He paweth in the valley, and rejoiceth in his strength: he goeth on to meet the armed men.—21.

Doth the hawk fly by thy wisdom, and stretch her wings toward the south?—26.

Doth the eagle mount up at thy command, and make her nest on high?—27.

...Her eyes behold afar off.—29.

BE KIND TO THEM.

Behold now behemoth, which I made with thee;... *Job* xl. 15.

Surely the mountains bring him forth food, where all the beasts of the field play.—-20.

He sendeth the springs into the valleys,...*Ps.* civ. 10.

They give drink to every beast of the field: the wild asses quench their thirst.—11.

By them shall the fowls of the heaven have their habitation, which sing among the branches.—12.

He causeth the grass to grow for the cattle :...14.

The trees of the Lord are full of sap ;...which he hath planted ;—16.

Where the birds make their nests: as for the stork, the fir trees are her house.—17.

The young lions roar after their prey, and seek their meat from God.—21.

He giveth to the beast his food, and to the young ravens which cry.—*Ps.* cxlvii. 9.

A righteous man regardeth the life of his beast... *Prov.* xii. 10.

THE BEAUTY OF HUMILITY AND MEEKNESS.

Behold now, I have taken upon me to speak unto the Lord, which am but dust and ashes.—*Gen.* xviii. 27.

I am not worthy of the least of all the mercies, and of all the truth, which thou hast shewed unto thy servant...*Gen.* xxxii. 10.

Now the man Moses was very meek, above all the men which were upon the face of the earth.—*Num.* xii. 3.

When thou wast little in thine own sight, wast thou not made the head of the tribes of Israel, and the Lord anointed thee king over Israel?— 1 *Sam.* xv. 17.

Then went king David in, and sat before the Lord, and he said, Who am I, O Lord God? and what is my house, that thou hast brought me hitherto?— 2 *Sam.* vii. 18.

And this was yet a small thing in thy sight, O Lord God; but thou hast spoken also of thy servant's house for a great while to come. And is this the manner of man, O Lord God?—19.

And what can David say more unto thee? for thou, Lord God, knowest thy servant.—2 *Sam.* vii. 20.

For thy word's sake, and according to thine own heart, hast thou done all these great things, to make thy servant know them.—21.

Seest thou how Ahab humbleth himself before me? because he humbleth himself before me, I will not bring the evil in his days...1 *Kings* xxi. 29.

But who am I, and what is my people, that we should be able to offer so willingly after this sort?... 1 *Ch.* xxix. 14.

Whereupon the princes of Israel and the king humbled themselves; and they said, The Lord is righteous.—2 *Ch.* xii. 6.

And when the Lord saw that they humbled themselves, the word of the Lord came to Shemaiah, saying, They have humbled themselves; therefore I will not destroy them, but I will grant them some deliverance...7.

Hezekiah humbled himself for the pride of his heart, both he and the inhabitants of Jerusalem, so that the wrath of the Lord came not upon them in the days of Hezekiah.—2 *Ch.* xxxii. 26.

And when he (Manasseh) was in affliction, he besought the Lord his God, and humbled himself greatly before the God of his fathers.—2 *Ch.* xxxiii. 12.

When men are cast down, then thou shalt say, There is lifting up; and he shall save the humble person.—*Job* xxii. 29.

The Lord...said, shall he that contendeth with the Almighty instruct him? he that reproveth God, let him answer it.—*Job* xl. 2.

Then Job answered the Lord, and said,—3.

Behold, I am vile; what shall I answer thee? I will lay mine hand upon my mouth.—4.

Once have I spoken; but I will not answer: yea, twice; but I will proceed no further.—5.

I have heard of thee by the hearing of the ear: but now mine eye seeth thee.—*Job* xlii. 5.

Wherefore I abhor myself, and repent in dust and ashes.—6.

...He forgetteth not the cry of the humble.—*Ps.* ix. 12.

Lord, thou hast heard the desire of the humble: thou wilt prepare their heart, thou wilt cause thine ear to hear.—*Ps.* x. 17.

The meek shall eat and be satisfied...*Ps.* xxii. 26.

The meek will he guide in judgment: and the meek will he teach his way.—*Ps.* xxv. 9.

...I humbled my soul with fasting; and my prayer returned into mine own bosom.—*Ps.* xxxv. 13.

The meek shall inherit the earth; and shall delight themselves in the abundance of peace.—Ps. xxxvii. 11.

The sacrifices of God are a broken spirit: a broken and a contrite heart, O God, thou wilt not despise. —*Ps.* li. 17.

...The earth feared, and was still,—*Ps.* lxxvi. 8.

When God arose to judgment, to save all the meek of the earth.—9.

Though the Lord be high, yet hath he respect unto the lowly...*Ps.* cxxxviii. 6.

The Lord lifteth up the meek.—*Ps.* cxlvii. 6.

For the Lord taketh pleasure in his people: he will beautify the meek with salvation.—*Ps.* cxlix. 4.

...He giveth grace unto the lowly.—*Prov.* iii. 34.

...With the lowly is wisdom.—*Prov.* xi. 2.

Before honour is humility.—*Prov.* xv. 33.

Better it is to be of an humble spirit with the lowly, than to divide the spoil with the proud.—*Prov.* xvi. 19.

By humility and the fear of the Lord are riches, and honour, and life.—*Prov.* xxii. 4.

...Honour shall uphold the humble in spirit.—xxix. 23.

If thou hast done foolishly in lifting up thyself, or if thou hast thought evil, lay thine hand upon thy mouth.—*Prov.* xxx. 32.

...The patient in spirit is better than the proud in spirit.—*Eccl.* vii. 8.

Thus saith the high and lofty One that inhabiteth eternity, whose name is Holy; I dwell in the high and holy place, with him also that is of a contrite and humble spirit, to revive the spirit of the humble, and to revive the heart of the contrite ones.—*Isa.* lvii. 15.

The Lord hath anointed me to preach good tidings unto the meek.—*Isa.* lxi. 1.

Thus saith the Lord,...*Isa.* lxvi. 1.

...To this man will I look, even to him that is poor and of a contrite spirit, and trembleth at my word.—2.

When Ephraim spake trembling, he exalted himself in Israel...*Hosea* xiii. 1.

He hath shewed thee, O man, what is good; and what doth the Lord require of thee, but to do justly, and to love mercy, and to walk humbly with thy God?—*Micah* vi. 8.

Seek ye the Lord, all ye meek of the earth, which have wrought his judgment; seek righteousness, seek meekness: it may be ye shall be hid in the day of the Lord's anger.—*Zeph.* ii. 3.

THE SIN OF PRIDE AND HAUGHTINESS.

Beware that thou forget not the Lord thy God,... *Deut.* viii. 11.

Lest when thou hast...built goodly houses, and dwelt therein;—12.

...And all that thou hast is multiplied;—13.

Then thine heart be lifted up, and thou forget the Lord thy God,...14.

And thou say in thine heart, My power and the might of mine hand hath gotten me this wealth.—17.

...That he (the king) may learn to fear the Lord his God,...*Deut.* xvii. 19.

That his heart be not lifted up above his brethren...20.

Talk no more so exceeding proudly; let not arrogancy come out of your mouth...1 *Sam.* ii. 3.

...Thine eyes are upon the haughty, that thou mayest bring them down.—2 *Sam.* xxii. 28.

When he (Uzziah) was strong, his heart was lifted up to his destruction: for he transgressed against the Lord his God.—2 *Ch.* xxvi. 16.

...His (Hezekiah's) heart was lifted up: therefore there was wrath upon him,...2 *Ch.* xxxii. 25.

Nothwithstanding Hezekiah humbled himself for the pride of his heart, both he and the inhabitants of Jerusalem, so that the wrath of the Lord came not upon them in the days of Hezekiah.—2 *Ch.* xxxii. 26.

If God will not withdraw his anger, the proud helpers do stoop under him.—*Job* ix. 13.

Trouble and anguish shall make him afraid ;... *Job* xv. 24.

For he stretcheth out his hand against God, and strengtheneth himself against the Almighty.—25.

Look on every one that is proud, and bring him low...*Job* xl. 12.

The wicked in his pride doth persecute the poor.— *Ps.* x. 2.

The wicked, through the pride of his countenance, will not seek after God : God is not in all his thoughts.—4.

He hath said in his heart, I shall not be moved: for I shall never be in adversity.—6.

The Lord shall cut off all flattering lips, and the tongue that speaketh proud things :—*Ps.* xii. 3.

Who have said, With our tongue will we prevail; our lips are our own : who is lord over us ?—4.

For thou wilt save the afflicted people ; but wilt bring down high looks.—*Ps.* xviii. 27.

...The Lord preserveth the faithful, and plentifully rewardeth the proud doer.—*Ps.* xxxi. 23.

Their inward thought is, that their houses shall continue for ever, and their dwelling places to all generations; they call their lands after their own names.—*Ps.* xlix. 11.

...Let not the rebellious exalt themselves.—*Ps.* lxvi. 7.

...Pride compasseth them about as a chain; violence covereth them as a garment.—*Ps.* lxxiii. 6.

...They have more than heart could wish...7.

They are corrupt, and speak wickedly concerning oppression: they speak loftily.—8.

They set their mouth against the heavens, and their tongue walketh through the earth.—9.

I said unto the fools, Deal not foolishly: and to the wicked, Lift not up the horn:—*Ps.* lxxv. 4.

Lift not up your horn on high: speak not with a stiff neck.—5.

...Him that hath an high look and a proud heart will not I suffer.—*Ps.* ci. 5.

Thou hast rebuked the proud that are cursed, which do err from thy commandments.—*Ps.* cxix. 21.

Lord, my heart is not haughty, nor mine eyes lofty: neither do I exercise myself in great matters, or in things too high for me.—*Ps.* cxxxi. 1.

Though the Lord be high, yet hath he respect unto the lowly: but the proud he knoweth afar off.—*Ps.* cxxxviii. 6.

...Pride, and arrogancy, and the evil way, and the froward mouth, do I hate.—*Prov.* viii. 13.

When pride cometh, then cometh shame...*Prov.* xi. 2.

Only by pride cometh contention...*Prov.* xiii. 10.

The Lord will destroy the house of the proud.—*Prov.* xv. 25.

Every one that is proud in heart is an abomination to the Lord: though hand join in hand, he shall not be unpunished.—*Prov.* xvi. 5.

Pride goeth before destruction, and an haughty spirit before a fall.—18.

Before destruction the heart of man is haughty.—*Prov.* xviii. 12.

An high look, and a proud heart,...is sin.—*Prov.* xxi. 4.

Proud and haughty scorner is his name, who dealeth in proud wrath.—24.

He that is of a proud heart stirreth up strife.—*Prov.* xxviii. 25.

A man's pride shall bring him low.—*Prov.* xxix. 23.

There is a generation, O how lofty are their eyes! and their eyelids are lifted up.—*Prov.* xxx. 13.

If thou hast done foolishly in lifting up thyself, or if thou hast thought evil, lay thine hand upon thy mouth.—32.

The lofty looks of man shall be humbled, and the haughtiness of men shall be bowed down, and the Lord alone shall be exalted...*Isa.* ii. 11.

For the day of the Lord of hosts, shall be upon every one that is proud and lofty, and upon every one that is lifted up; and he shall be brought low:—12.

And the mean man shall be brought down, and the mighty man shall be humbled, and the eyes of the lofty shall be humbled.—*Isa.* v. 15.

Shall the axe boast itself against him that heweth therewith?...*Isa.* x. 15.

Behold, the Lord, the Lord of hosts, shall lop the bough with terror : and the high ones of stature shall be hewn down, and the haughty shall be humbled.—33.

I will cause the arrogancy of the proud to cease, and will lay low the haughtiness of the terrible.—*Isa*. xiii. 11.

How art thou fallen from heaven, O Lucifer, son of the morning! how art thou cut down to the ground, which didst weaken the nations!—*Isa*. xiv. 12.

For thou hast said in thine heart, I will ascend into heaven, I will exalt my throne above the stars of God: I will sit also upon the mount of the congregation, in the sides of the north :—13.

I will ascend above the heights of the clouds; I will be like the most High.—14.

Yet thou shalt be brought down to hell, to the sides of the pit.—15.

They that see thee shall narrowly look upon thee, and consider thee, saying, Is this the man that made the earth to tremble, that did shake kingdoms ;—16.

That made the world as a wilderness, and destroyed the cities thereof; that opened not the house of his prisoners ?—17.

All the kings of the nations, even all of them, lie in glory, every one in his own house.—18.

But thou art cast out of thy grave like an abominable branch...19.

...The haughty people of the earth do languish.—*Isa*. xxiv. 4.

The crown of pride, the drunkards of Ephraim, shall be trodden under feet.—*Isa.* xxviii. 3.

Thus saith the Lord, Let not the wise man glory in his wisdom, neither let the mighty man glory in his might, let not the rich man glory in his riches. ...*Jer.* ix. 23.

Hear ye, and give ear; be not proud: for the Lord hath spoken.—*Jer.* xiii. 15.

But if ye will not hear it, my soul shall weep in secret places for your pride...17.

We have heard the pride of Moab, (he is exceeding proud) his loftiness, and his arrogancy, and his pride, and the haughtiness of his heart.—*Jer.* xlviii. 29.

Behold, I am against thee, O thou most proud, saith the Lord God of hosts: for thy day is come, the time that I will visit thee.—*Jer.* l. 31.

And the most proud shall stumble and fall, and none shall raise him up...32.

Thus saith the Lord God; Because thine heart is lifted up, and thou hast said, I am a God, I sit in the seat of God, in the midst of the seas; yet thou art a man, and not God, though thou set thine heart as the heart of God.—*Ezek.* xxviii. 2. ...But thou shalt be a man, and no God...9.

The king spake, and said, Is not this great Babylon, that I have built for the house of the kingdom by the might of my power, and for the honour of my majesty?—*Dan.* iv. 30.

While the word was in the king's mouth, there fell

a voice from heaven, saying, O king Nebuchadnezzar, to thee it is spoken; The kingdom is departed from thee.—*Dan.* iv. 31.

And they shall drive thee from men, and thy dwelling shall be with the beasts of the field:...seven times shall pass over thee, until thou know that the most High ruleth in the kingdom of men, and giveth it to whomsoever he will.—32.

...Those that walk in pride he is able to abase.—37.

When his heart was lifted up, and his mind hardened in pride, he was deposed from his kingly throne, and they took his glory from him.—*Dan.* v. 20.

And thou his son, O Belshazzar, hast not humbled thine heart, though thou knewest all this;—22.

But hast lifted up thyself against the Lord of heaven;...and the God in whose hand thy breath is, and whose are all thy ways, hast thou not glorified.—23.

The pride of thine heart hath deceived thee, thou that dwellest in the clefts of the rock, whose habitation is high; that saith in his heart, Who shall bring me down to the ground?—*Obad.* i. 3.

Though thou exalt thyself as the eagle, and though thou set thy nest among the stars, thence will I bring thee down, saith the Lord.—4.

Behold, his soul which is lifted up is not upright in him.—*Habak.* ii. 4.

For, behold, the day cometh, that shall burn as an oven; and all the proud, yea, and all that do wickedly, shall be stubble....*Mal.* iv. 1.

THE FOLLY OF CONCEIT.

He (God) respecteth not any that are wise of heart.—*Job* xxxvii. 24.

He flattereth himself in his own eyes, until his iniquity be found to be hateful.—*Ps.* xxxvi. 2.

Be not wise in thine own eyes...*Prov.* iii. 7.

The way of a fool is right in his own eyes: but he that hearkeneth unto counsel is wise.—*Prov.* xii. 15.

A wise man feareth, and departeth from evil: but the fool rageth and is confident.—*Prov.* xiv. 16.

All the ways of a man are clean in his own eyes; but the Lord weigheth the spirits.—*Prov.* xvi. 2.

Most men will proclaim every one his own goodness: but a faithful man who can find?—*Prov.* xx. 6.

Every way of a man is right in his own eyes: but the Lord pondereth the hearts.—*Prov.* xxi. 2.

...For men to search their own glory is not glory.—*Prov.* xxv. 27.

Answer a fool according to his folly, lest he be wise in his own conceit.—*Prov.* xxvi. 5.

Seest thou a man wise in his own conceit? there is more hope of a fool than of him.—12.

The sluggard is wiser in his own conceit than seven men that can render a reason.—*Prov.* xxvi. 16.

Let another man praise thee, and not thine own mouth; a stranger, and not thine own lips.—*Prov.* xxvii. 2.

The rich man is wise in his own conceit; but the poor that hath understanding searcheth him out.—*Prov.* xxviii. 11.

He that trusteth in his own heart is a fool.—26.

Woe unto them that are wise in their own eyes, and prudent in their own sight!—*Isa.* v. 21.

WE MUST CONTROL OUR ANGRY PASSIONS.

---o---

The Lord had respect unto Abel and to his offering:—*Gen.* iv. 4.

...And Cain was very wroth, and his countenance fell.—5.

And Cain talked with Abel his brother: and it came to pass, when they were in the field, that Cain rose up against Abel his brother, and slew him.—8.

And the Lord said unto Cain, Where is Abel thy brother? And he said, I know not: am I my brother's keeper?—9.

And he said, What hast thou done?...10.

Now art thou cursed from the earth, which hath opened her mouth to receive thy brother's blood from thy hand:—11.

When thou tillest the ground, it shall not henceforth yield unto thee her strength; a fugitive and a vagabond shalt thou be in the earth.—12.

Simeon and Levi are brethren; instruments of cruelty are in their habitations.—*Gen.* xlix. 5.

...Unto their assembly, mine honour, be not thou united: for in their anger they slew a man...6.

Cursed be their anger, for it was fierce; and their wrath, for it was cruel: I will divide them in Jacob, and scatter them in Israel.—7.

Then Saul's anger was kindled against Jonathan, and he said unto him,...do not I know that thou hast chosen the son of Jesse to thine own confusion?—1 *Sam.* xx. 30.

For as long as the son of Jesse liveth upon the ground, thou shalt not be established, nor thy kingdom. Wherefore now send and fetch him unto me, for he shall surely die.—31.

And Saul cast a javelin at him to smite him...33.

The word of the Lord came to Elijah...1 *Kings* xxi. 17.

Arise, go down to meet Ahab,...behold, he is in the vineyard of Naboth, whither he is gone down to possess it.—18.

And thou shalt speak unto him, saying, Thus saith the Lord, Hast thou killed, and also taken possession? ...In the place where dogs licked the blood of Naboth shall dogs lick thy blood, even thine.—19.

In those days, while Mordecai sat in the king's gate, two of the king's chamberlains, of those which kept the door, were wroth, and sought to lay hand on the king Ahasuerus.—*Est.* ii. 21.

And when inquisition was made of the matter, it was found out; therefore they were both hanged on a tree.—23.

Wrath killeth the foolish man...*Job.* v. 2.

Cease from anger, and forsake wrath :...*Ps.* xxxvii. 8.

For evildoers shall be cut off...9.

Give ear to my prayer, O God ;...*Ps.* lv. 1.

...Because of the oppression of the wicked : for they cast iniquity upon me, and in wrath they hate me.—3.

Evil shall hunt the violent man to overthrow him.—*Ps.* cxl. 11.

A fool's wrath is presently known...*Prov.* xii. 16.

He that is soon angry dealeth foolishly...*Prov.* xiv. 17.

He that is slow to wrath is of great understanding : but he that is hasty of spirit exalteth folly.—29.

A wrathful man stirreth up strife : but he that is slow to anger appeaseth strife.—*Prov.* xv. 18.

The wrath of a king is as messengers of death : but a wise man will pacify it.—*Prov.* xvi. 14.

He that is slow to anger is better than the mighty ; and he that ruleth his spirit than he that taketh a city.—32.

The discretion of a man deferreth his anger...*Prov.* xix. 11.

A man of great wrath shall suffer punishment...19.

He that soweth iniquity shall reap vanity: and the rod of his anger shall fail.—*Prov.* xxii. 8.

Make no friendship with an angry man ; and with a furious man thou shalt not go.—24.

He that hath no rule over his own spirit is like a city that is broken down, and without walls.—*Prov.* xxv. 28.

A stone is heavy, and the sand weighty; but a fool's wrath is heavier than them both.—*Prov.* xxvii. 3.

Wrath is cruel, and anger is outrageous...4.

Wise men turn away wrath.—*Prov.* xxix. 8.

An angry man stirreth up strife, and a furious man aboundeth in transgression.—22.

The forcing of wrath bringeth forth strife.—*Prov.* xxx. 33.

Be not hasty in thy spirit to be angry: for anger resteth in the bosom of fools.—*Eccl.* vii. 9.

And God said to Jonah, Doest thou well to be angry?....*Jonah* iv. 9.

GUARD THE TONGUE: AVOID STRIFE AND QUARRELS.

———o———

And Abram said unto Lot, Let there be no strife, I pray thee, between me and thee, and between my herdmen and thy herdmen; for we be brethren.—*Gen.* xiii. 8.

Is not the whole land before thee? separate thyself, I pray thee, from me: if thou wilt take the left hand, then I will go to the right; or if thou depart to the right hand, then I will go to the left.—9.

...He (Joseph) sent his brethren away, and they departed: and he said unto them, See that ye fall not out by the way.—*Gen.* xlv. 24.

Thou shalt not go up and down as a talebearer among thy people...*Lev.* xix. 16.

Thou shalt be hid from the scourge of the tongue. ...*Job.* v. 21.

Lord, who shall abide in thy tabernacle? Who shall dwell in thy holy hill?—*Ps.* xv. 1.

He that backbiteth not with his tongue, nor doeth evil to his neighbour, nor taketh up a reproach against his neighbour.—3.

Keep thy tongue from evil, and thy lips from speaking guile.—*Ps.* xxxiv. 13.

Seek peace, and pursue it.—14.

I said, I will take heed to my ways, that I sin not with my tongue : I will keep my mouth with a bridle. ...*Ps.* xxxix. 1.

Hide me from the secret counsel of the wicked;... *Ps.* lxiv. 2.

Who whet their tongue like a sword, and bend their bows to shoot their arrows, even bitter words:—3.

That they may shoot in secret at the perfect...4.

So they shall make their own tongue to fall upon themselves...8.

How long shall they utter and speak hard things ? —*Ps.* xciv. 4.

Whoso privily slandereth his neighbour, him will I cut off...*Ps.* ci. 5.

The mouth of the wicked and the mouth of the deceitful are opened against me : they have spoken against me with a lying tongue.—*Ps.* cix. 2.

Behold, how good and how pleasant it is for brethren to dwell together in unity!—*Ps.* cxxxiii. 1.

It is,...2.

As the dew of Hermon, and as the dew that descended upon the mountains of Zion...3.

Let not an evil speaker be established in the earth. ...*Ps.* cxl. 11.

Set a watch, O Lord, before my mouth; keep the door of my lips.—*Ps.* cxli. 3.

Strive not with a man without cause, if he have done thee no harm.—*Prov.* iii. 30.

He (a wicked man) deviseth mischief continually; he soweth discord.—*Prov.* vi. 14.

These...things doth the Lord hate :...16.

...A lying tongue,...17.

...Feet that be swift in running to mischief,—18.

...And he that soweth discord among brethren.—19.

Hatred stirreth up strifes: but love covereth all sins.—*Prov.* x. 12.

He that uttereth a slander, is a fool.—18.

In the multitude of words there wanteth not sin: but he that refraineth his lips is wise.—19.

The tongue of the just is as choice silver...20.

The lips of the righteous feed many...21.

He that is void of wisdom despiseth his neighbour: but a man of understanding holdeth his peace.—*Prov.* xi. 12.

A talebearer revealeth secrets: but he that is of a faithful spirit concealeth the matter.—13.

The wicked is snared by the transgression of his lips.—*Prov.* xii. 13.

There is that speaketh like the piercings of a sword: but the tongue of the wise is health.—18.

He that keepeth his mouth keepeth his life: but he that openeth wide his lips shall have destruction.—*Prov.* xiii. 3.

A soft answer turneth away wrath: but grievous words stir up anger.—*Prov.* xv. 1.

AVOID STRIFE AND QUARRELS.

The tongue of the wise useth knowledge aright: but the mouth of fools poureth out foolishness.—2.

A wholesome tongue is a tree of life...4.

The lips of the wise disperse knowledge...7.

A wrathful man stirreth up strife: but he that is slow to anger appeaseth strife.—18.

A man hath joy by the answer of his mouth: and a word spoken in due season, how good is it!—23.

The words of the pure are pleasant words.—26.

Righteous lips are the delight of kings; and they love him that speaketh right.—*Prov.* xvi. 13.

Pleasant words are as an honeycomb, sweet to the soul, and health to the bones.—24.

A froward man soweth strife: and a whisperer separateth chief friends.—28.

Better is a dry morsel, and quietness therewith, than an houseful of sacrifices with strife.—*Prov.* xvii. 1.

He that covereth a transgression seeketh love; but he that repeateth a matter separateth very friends.—9.

The beginning of strife is as when one letteth out water: therefore leave off contention, before it be meddled with.—14.

He loveth transgression that loveth strife...19.

He that hath a perverse tongue falleth into mischief.—20.

A fool's lips enter into contention, and his mouth calleth for strokes.—*Prov.* xviii. 6.

A fool's mouth is his destruction, and his lips are the snare of his soul.—7.

The words of a talebearer are as wounds, and they go down into the innermost parts.—*Prov.* xviii. 8.

A brother offended is harder to be won than a strong city: and their contentions are like the bars of a castle.—19.

Death and life are in the power of the tongue: and they that love it shall eat the fruit thereof.—21.

It is an honour for a man to cease from strife: but every fool will be meddling.—*Prov.* xx. 3.

He that goeth about as a talebearer revealeth secrets: therefore meddle not with him that flattereth with his lips.—19.

It is better to dwell in the wilderness, than with a contentious and an angry woman.—*Prov.* xxi. 19.

Whoso keepeth his mouth and his tongue keepeth his soul from troubles.—23.

Their (the evil men's) heart studieth destruction, and their lips talk of mischief.—*Prov.* xxiv. 2.

Go not forth hastily to strive, lest thou know not what to do in the end thereof, when thy neighbour hath put thee to shame.—*Prov.* xxv. 8.

Discover not a secret to another:—9.

Lest he that heareth it put thee to shame, and thine infamy turn not away.—10.

By long forbearing is a prince persuaded, and a soft tongue breaketh the bone.—15.

The north wind driveth away rain: so doth an angry countenance a backbiting tongue.—23.

He that passeth by, and meddleth with strife belonging not to him, is like one that taketh a dog by the ears.—*Prov.* xxvi. 17.

Where no wood is, there the fire goeth out: so where there is no talebearer, the strife ceaseth.—20.

As coals are to burning coals, and wood to fire; so is a contentious man to kindle strife.—21.

He that is of a proud heart stirreth up strife.—*Prov.* xxviii. 25.

...But wise men turn away wrath.—*Prov.* xxix. 8.

Seest thou a man that is hasty in his words? there is more hope of a fool than of him.—20.

An angry man stirreth up strife...22.

Be not rash with thy mouth, and let not thine heart be hasty to utter anything before God: for God is in heaven, and thou upon earth: therefore let thy words be few.—*Eccl.* v. 2.

Suffer not thy mouth to cause thy flesh to sin.—6.

BE NOT LED AWAY BY THE UNGODLY.

Thou shalt not follow a multitude to do evil;— *Ex.* xxiii. 2.

Thou shalt make no covenant with them, nor with their gods.—32.

They shall not dwell in thy land, lest they make thee sin against me: for if thou serve their gods, it will surely be a snare unto thee.—33.

After the doings of the land of Egypt, wherein ye dwelt, shall ye not do: and after the doings of the land of Canaan, whither I bring you, shall ye not do: neither shall ye walk in their ordinances.—*Lev.* xviii. 3.

And Moses rose up and went unto Dathan and Abiram;...*Num.* xvi. 25.

And he spake unto the congregation, saying, Depart, I pray you, from the tents of these wicked men, and touch nothing of their's, lest ye be consumed in all their sins.—26.

It came to pass when Solomon was old, that his wives turned away his heart after other gods: and his heart was not perfect with the Lord his God, as was the heart of David his father.—1 *Kings* xi. 4.

And the Lord was angry with Solomon, because his heart was turned from the Lord God of Israel.—9.

...Shouldest thou help the ungodly, and love them that hate the Lord? therefore is wrath upon thee from before the Lord.—2 *Ch.* xix. 2.

Should we again break thy commandments, and join in affinity with the people of these abominations? wouldest not thou be angry with us till thou hadst consumed us?—*Ezra* ix. 14.

Blessed is the man that walketh not in the counsel of the ungodly, nor standeth in the way of sinners, nor sitteth in the seat of the scornful.—*Ps.* i. 1.

Depart from me, all ye workers of iniquity...*Ps.* vi. 8.

Concerning the works of men, by the word of thy lips I have kept me from the paths of the destroyer.—*Ps.* xvii. 4.

I have not sat with vain persons, neither will I go in with dissemblers.—*Ps.* xxvi. 4.

I have hated the congregation of evil doers; and will not sit with the wicked.—5.

Draw me not away with the wicked, and with the workers of iniquity...*Ps.* xxviii. 3.

A froward heart shall depart from me: I will not know a wicked person.—*Ps.* ci. 4.

Whoso privily slandereth his neighbour, him will I cut off...5.

He that worketh deceit shall not dwell within my house: he that telleth lies shall not tarry in my sight.—7.

They did not destroy the nations, concerning whom the Lord commanded them:—*Ps.* cvi. 34.

But were mingled among the heathen, and learned their works.—35.

And they served their idols: which were a snare unto them.—36.

Therefore was the wrath of the Lord kindled against his people...40.

The bands of the wicked have robbed me: but I have not forgotten thy law.—*Ps.* cxix. 61.

Depart from me, ye evil doers: for I will keep the commandments of my God.—115.

Incline not my heart to any evil thing, to practise wicked works with men that work iniquity: and let me not eat of their dainties.—*Ps.* cxli. 4.

My son, if sinners entice thee, consent thou not.—*Prov.* i. 10.

If they say, Come with us,...11.

Cast in thy lot among us; let us all have one purse:—14.

My son, walk not thou in the way of them; refrain thy foot from their path.—15.

Discretion shall preserve thee, understanding shall keep thee:—*Prov.* ii. 11.

To deliver thee from the way of the evil man, from the man that speaketh froward things.—12.

Who leave the paths of uprightness, to walk in the ways of darkness;—13.

Who rejoice to do evil, and delight in the frowardness of the wicked;—14.

To deliver thee from the strange woman, even from the stranger which flattereth with her words ;—16.

Which forsaketh the guide of her youth, and forgetteth the covenant of her God.—17.

None that go unto her return again, neither take they hold of the paths of life.—19.

Enter not into the path of the wicked, and go not in the way of evil men.—*Prov.* iv. 14.

Avoid it, pass not by it, turn from it, and pass away.—15.

Remove thy way far from her, (the ungodly woman) and come not nigh the door of her house.—*Prov.* v. 8.

Forsake the foolish, and live ;—*Prov.* ix. 6.

He that followeth vain persons is void of understanding.—*Prov.* xii. 11.

The way of the wicked seduceth them.—26.

He that walketh with wise men shall be wise: but a companion of fools shall be destroyed.—*Prov.* xiii. 20.

Go from the presence of a foolish man, when thou perceivest not in him the lips of knowledge.—*Prov.* xiv. 7.

A violent man enticeth his neighbour, and leadeth him into the way that is not good.—*Prov.* xvi. 29.

Thorns and snares are in the way of the froward: he that doth keep his soul shall be far from them.—*Prov.* xxii. 5.

Cast out the scorner, and contention shall go out…10.

Make no friendship with an angry man ; and with a furious man thou shalt not go :—24.

Lest thou learn his ways, and get a snare to thy soul.—*Prov.* xxii. 25.

Be not among winebibbers; among riotous eaters of flesh.—*Prov.* xxiii. 20.

Be not thou envious against evil men, neither desire to be with them.—*Prov.* xxiv. 1.

Whoso keepeth the law is a wise son: but he that is a companion of riotous men shameth his father.—*Prov.* xxviii. 7.

He that followeth after vain persons shall have poverty enough.—19.

Whoso is partner with a thief hateth his own soul: he heareth cursing, and bewrayeth it not.—*Prov.* xxix. 24.

One sinner destroyeth much good.—*Eccl.* ix. 18.

I sat not in the assembly of the mockers, nor rejoiced; I sat alone because of thy hand.—*Jer.* xv. 17.

Flee out of the midst of Babylon, and deliver every man his soul: be not cut off in her iniquity.—*Jer.* li. 6.

Ephraim is joined to idols: let him alone.—*Hosea* iv. 17.

WORK AND INDUSTRY ENJOINED.
IDLENESS AND SLOTH A SHAME.

———o———

And the Lord God took the man, and put him into the garden of Eden to dress it and to keep it.—*Gen.* ii. 15.

In the sweat of thy face shalt thou eat bread, till thou return unto the ground...*Gen.* iii. 19.

Six days shalt thou labour, and do all thy work.—*Ex.* xx. 9.

And he (God) said unto me, Solomon thy son, he shall build my house and my courts...1 *Ch.* xxviii. 6.

And David said to Solomon, Be strong and of good courage, and do it: fear not, nor be dismayed: for the Lord God, even my God, will be with thee; he will not fail thee, nor forsake thee, until thou hast finished all the work for the service of the house of the Lord,--20.

Whatsoever is commanded by the God of heaven, let it be diligently done for the house of the God of heaven...*Ezra* vii. 23.

Establish thou the work of our hands upon us; yea, the work of our hands establish thou it.—*Ps.* xc. 17.

Man goeth forth unto his work and to his labour until the evening.—*Ps.* civ. 23.

Give not sleep to thine eyes, nor slumber to thine eyelids.—*Prov.* vi. 4.

Go to the ant, thou sluggard; consider her ways, and be wise:—6.

Which having no guide, overseer, or ruler,—7.

Provideth her meat in the summer, and gathereth her food in the harvest.—8.

How long wilt thou sleep, O sluggard? when wilt thou arise out of thy sleep?—9.

Yet a little sleep, a little slumber, a little folding of the hands to sleep:—10.

So shall thy poverty come as one that travelleth, and thy want as an armed man.—11.

He becometh poor that dealeth with a slack hand: but the hand of the diligent maketh rich.—*Prov.* x. 4.

He that gathereth in summer is a wise son: but he that sleepeth in harvest is a son that causeth shame.—5.

As vinegar to the teeth, and as smoke to the eyes, so is the sluggard to them that send him.—26.

He that tilleth his land shall be satisfied with bread...*Prov.* xii. 11.

The hand of the diligent shall bear rule: but the slothful shall be under tribute.—24.

The slothful man roasteth not that which he took in hunting: but the substance of a diligent man is precious.—27.

The soul of the sluggard desireth, and hath nothing: but the soul of the diligent shall be made fat.—*Prov.* xiii. 4.

...He that gathereth by labour shall increase.—11.

The way of the slothful man is as an hedge of thorns...*Prov.* xv. 19.

Slothfulness casteth into a deep sleep; and an idle soul shall suffer hunger.—*Prov.* xix. 15.

A slothful man hideth his hand in his bosom, and will not so much as bring it to his mouth again.—24.

The sluggard will not plow by reason of the cold; therefore shall he beg in harvest, and have nothing.—*Prov.* xx. 4.

Love not sleep, lest thou come to poverty; open thine eyes, and thou shalt be satisfied with bread.—13.

The thoughts of the diligent tend only to plenteousness; but of every one that is hasty only to want.—*Prov.* xxi. 5.

The desire of the slothful killeth him; for his hands refuse to labour.—25.

The slothful man saith, There is a lion without, I shall be slain in the streets.—*Prov.* xxii. 13.

Seest thou a man diligent in his business? he shall stand before kings; he shall not stand before mean men.—29.

Prepare thy work without, and make it fit for thyself in the field; and afterwards build thine house.—*Prov.* xxiv. 27.

I went by the field of the slothful, and by the vineyard of the man void of understanding;—30.

And, lo, it was all grown over with thorns, and nettles had covered the face thereof, and the stone wall thereof was broken down.—31.

Then I saw, and considered it well: I looked upon it, and received instruction.—*Prov.* xxiv. 32.

Yet a little sleep, a little slumber, a little folding of the hands to sleep:—33.

So shall thy poverty come as one that travelleth; and thy want as an armed man.—34.

The slothful man saith, There is a lion in the way; a lion is in the streets.—*Prov.* xxvi. 13.

As the door turneth upon his hinges, so doth the slothful upon his bed.—14.

The slothful hideth his hand in his bosom; it grieveth him to bring it again to his mouth.—15.

The sluggard is wiser in his own conceit than seven men that can render a reason.—16.

Be thou diligent to know the state of thy flocks, and look well to thy herds.—*Prov.* xxvii. 23.

The ants are a people not strong, yet they prepare their meat in the summer;—*Prov.* xxx. 25.

The conies are but a feeble folk, yet make they their houses in the rocks;—26.

The locusts have no king, yet go they forth all of them by bands;—27.

The spider taketh hold with her hands, and is in kings' palaces.—28.

She (a virtuous woman) seeketh wool, and flax, and worketh willingly with her hands.—*Prov.* xxxi. 13.

She riseth also while it is yet night, and giveth meat to her household…15.

She considereth a field, and buyeth it: with the fruit of her hands she planteth a vineyard.—16.

She girdeth her loins with strength, and strengtheneth her arms.—*Prov.* xxxi. 17.

She perceiveth that her merchandise is good: her candle goeth not out by night.—18.

She layeth her hands to the spindle, and her hands hold the distaff.—19.

She is not afraid of the snow for her household: for all her household are clothed with scarlet.—21.

She maketh herself coverings of tapestry...22.

She maketh fine linen, and selleth it...24.

She looketh well to the ways of her household, and eateth not the bread of idleness.—27.

Give her of the fruit of her hands; and let her own works praise her in the gates.—31.

The sleep of a labouring man is sweet...*Eccl.* v. 12.

...It is good and comely for one to eat and to drink, and to enjoy the good of all his labour that he taketh under the sun all the days of his life, which God giveth him: for it is his portion.—18.

Whatsoever thy hand findeth to do, do it with thy might...*Eccl.* ix. 10.

By much slothfulness the building decayeth; and through idleness of the hands the house droppeth through.—*Eccl.* x. 18.

A CONTENTED MIND.

———o———

And Esau said, I have enough, my brother; keep that thou hast unto thyself.—*Gen.* xxxiii. 9.

And Jacob said, Nay, I pray thee, if now I have found grace in thy sight, then receive my present at my hand...10.

Take, I pray thee, my blessing that is brought to thee; because God hath dealt graciously with me, and because I have enough...11.

...Behold, thou hast been careful for us with all this care; what is to be done for thee? wouldest thou be spoken for to the king, or to the captain of the host? And she answered, I dwell among mine own people.—2 *Kings* iv. 13.

And God said to Solomon, Because this was in thine heart, and thou hast not asked riches, wealth, or honour...but hast asked wisdom and knowledge for thyself,...2 *Ch.* i. 11.

Wisdom and knowledge is granted unto thee...12.

The Lord is the portion of mine inheritance and of my cup: thou maintainest my lot.—*Ps.* xvi. 5.

The lines are fallen unto me in pleasant places; yea, I have a goodly heritage.—6.

A CONTENTED MIND.

The Lord is my shepherd; I shall not want.—*Ps.* xxiii. 1.

Rest in the Lord, and wait patiently for him: fret not thyself because of him who prospereth in his way...*Ps.* xxxvii. 7.

A little that a righteous man hath is better than the riches of many wicked.—16.

A good man shall be satisfied from himself.—*Prov.* xiv. 14.

A sound heart is the life of the flesh: but envy the rottenness of the bones.—30.

He that is of a merry heart hath a continual feast.—*Prov.* xv. 15.

Better is little with the fear of the Lord than great treasure and trouble therewith.—16.

Better is a dinner of herbs where love is, than a stalled ox and hatred therewith.—17.

Better is little with righteousness than great revenues without right.—*Prov.* xvi. 8.

Better is a dry morsel, and quietness therewith, than an house full of sacrifices with strife.—*Prov.* xvii. 1.

A merry heart doeth good like a medicine...22.

Better is the poor that walketh in his integrity, than he that is perverse in his lips, and is a fool.—*Prov.* xix. 1.

Let not thine heart envy sinners: but be thou in the fear of the Lord all the day long.—*Prov.* xxiii. 17.

Fret not thyself because of evil men, neither be thou envious at the wicked.—*Prov.* xxiv. 19.

Hast thou found honey? eat so much as is sufficient for thee...*Prov.* xxv. 16.

Give me neither poverty nor riches; feed me with food convenient for me:—*Prov.* xxx. 8.

Lest I be full, and deny thee, and say, Who is the Lord? or lest I be poor, and steal, and take the name of my God in vain.—9.

Better is an handful with quietness, than both the hands full with travail and vexation of spirit.—*Eccl.* iv. 6.

Better is the sight of the eyes than the wandering of the desire.—*Eccl.* vi. 9.

...And the patient in spirit is better than the proud in spirit.—*Eccl.* vii. 8.

Say not thou, What is the cause that the former days were better than these? for thou dost not enquire wisely concerning this.—10.

Eat thy bread with joy, and drink thy wine with a merry heart; for God now accepteth thy works.—*Eccl.* ix. 7.

THE VALUE OF A GOOD NAME.

———o———

I will bless thee, and make thy name great.—*Gen.* xii. 2.

The Lord was with Joshua; and his fame was noised throughout all the country.—*Josh.* vi. 27.

Then she (Ruth) fell on her face, and bowed herself to the ground, and said unto him, (Boaz) Why have I found grace in thine eyes, that thou shouldest take knowledge of me, seeing I am a stranger?—*Ruth* ii. 10.

And Boaz answered and said unto her, It hath been fully shewed me, all that thou hast done unto thy mother in law since the death of thine husband: and how thou hast left thy father and thy mother, and the land of thy nativity, and art come unto a people which thou knewest not heretofore.—11.

And he said, Blessed be thou of the Lord, my daughter :...*Ruth* iii. 10.

...Fear not; I will do to thee all that thou requirest: for all the city of my people doth know that thou art a virtuous woman.—11.

And the women said unto Naomi, Blessed be the

THE VALUE OF A GOOD NAME.

Lord, which hath not left thee this day without a kinsman, that his name may be famous in Israel.—*Ruth* iv. 14.

Then the princes of the Philistines went forth: and it came to pass, after they went forth, that David behaved himself more wisely than all the servants of Saul; so that his name was much set by.—1 *Sam.* xviii. 30.

And when the queen of Sheba heard of the fame of Solomon concerning the name of the Lord, she came to prove him with hard questions.—1 *Kings* x. 1.

And she said to the king, it was a true report that I heard in mine own land of thy acts and of thy wisdom.—6.

And the fame of David went out into all lands; and the Lord brought the fear of him upon all nations.—1 *Ch.* xiv. 17.

And he (Uzziah) sought God:...and as long as he sought the Lord, God made him to prosper.—2 *Ch.* xxvi. 5.

And his name spread abroad even to the entering in of Egypt; for he strengthened himself exceedingly.—8.

His name spread far abroad; for he was marvellously helped, till he was strong.—15.

Mordecai was great in the king's house, and his fame went out throughout all the provinces: for this man Mordecai waxed greater and greater.—*Est.* ix. 4.

The righteous shall be in everlasting remembrance.—*Ps.* cxii. 6.

A good name is rather to be chosen than great riches, and loving favour rather than silver and gold.—*Prov.* xxii. 1.

A good name is better than precious ointment… *Eccl.* vii. 1.

Thus saith the Lord, Keep ye judgment, and do justice…*Isa.* lvi. 1.

Blessed is the man that doeth this,…that keepeth the sabbath from polluting it, and keepeth his hand from doing any evil.—2.

Unto them will I give in mine house and within my walls a place and a name better than of sons and of daughters: I will give them an everlasting name, that shall not be cut off.—5.

THE INFLUENCE OF GOOD PERSONS.

——o——

And the Lord said, If I find in Sodom fifty righteous within the city, then I will spare all the place for their sakes.—*Gen.* xviii. 26.

And Abraham answered and said,...27.

Peradventure there shall lack five of the fifty righteous: wilt thou destroy all the city for lack of five? And he said, If I find there forty and five, I will not destroy it.—28.

And he spake unto him yet again, and said, Peradventure there shall be forty found there. And he said, I will not do it for forty's sake.—29.

And he said, Behold now, I have taken upon me to speak unto the Lord: Peradventure there shall be twenty found there. And he said, I will not destroy it for twenty's sake.—31.

And he said, Oh let not the Lord be angry; and I will speak yet but this once: Peradventure ten shall be found there. And he said, I will not destroy it for ten's sake.—32.

And Laban said unto him, (Jacob) I pray thee, if

I have found favour in thine eyes, tarry: for I have learned by experience that the Lord hath blessed me for thy sake.—*Gen.* xxx. 27.

And it came to pass from the time that he had made him overseer in his house, and over all that he had, that the Lord blessed the Egyptian's house for Joseph's sake; and the blessing of the Lord was upon all that he had in the house, and in the field.—*Gen.* xxxix. 5.

For David's sake did the Lord his God give him (Jeroboam) a lamp in Jerusalem, to set up his son after him, and to establish Jerusalem:—1 *Kings* xv. 4.

Because David did that which was right in the eyes of the Lord.—5.

By the blessing of the upright the city is exalted.—*Prov.* xi. 11.

The evil bow before the good: and the wicked at the gates of the righteous.—*Prov.* xiv. 19.

When a man's ways please the Lord, he maketh even his enemies to be at peace with him.—*Prov.* xvi. 7.

RESPECT OLD AGE.

Thou shalt rise up before the hoary head, and honour the face of the old man, and fear thy God: I am the Lord.—*Lev.* xix. 32.

And he (Elisha) went up from thence unto Beth-el: and as he was going up by the way, there came forth little children out of the city, and mocked him, and said unto him, Go up, thou bald head; go up, thou bald head.—2 *Kings* ii. 23.

And there came forth two she bears out of the wood, and tare forty and two children of them.—24.

Thou shalt come to thy grave in a full age, like as a shock of corn cometh in in his season.—*Job* v. 26.

Now Elihu had waited till Job had spoken, because they (his friends) were elder than he.—*Job* xxxii. 4.

And Elihu...said, I am young, and ye are very old; wherefore I was afraid, and durst not shew you mine opinion.—6.

I said, Days should speak, and multitude of years should teach wisdom.—7.

The Lord blessed the latter end of Job more than his beginning....*Job* xlii. 12.

Cast me not off in the time of old age...*Ps.* lxxi. 9.

Now also when I am old and greyheaded, O God, forsake me not...*Ps.* lxxi. 18.

They (the righteous) shall still bring forth fruit in old age...*Ps.* xcii. 14.

Old men :...Let them praise the name of the Lord.—*Ps.* cxlviii. 12, 13.

The hoary head is a crown of glory, if it be found in the way of righteousness.—*Prov.* xvi. 31.

The beauty of old men is the grey head.—*Prov.* xx. 29.

Despise not thy mother when she is old.—*Prov.* xxiii. 22.

And even to your old age I am he; and even to hoar hairs will I carry you: I have made and I will bear; even I will carry, and will deliver you.—*Isa.* xlvi. 4.

The anger of the Lord hath divided them;...They respected not the persons of the priests, they favoured not the elders.—*Lam.* iv. 16.

...The faces of elders were not honoured.—*Lam.* v. 12.

HONOUR AND RESPECT DUE TO PARENTS.

Isaac digged again the wells of water, which they had digged in the days of Abraham his father; for the Philistines had stopped them after the death of Abraham: and he called their names after the names by which his father had called them.—*Gen.* xxvi. 18.

And Esau said unto his father, Hast thou but one blessing, my father? bless me, even me also, O my father...*Gen.* xxvii. 38.

When Esau saw that Isaac had blessed Jacob, and sent him away to Padan-aram, to take him a wife from thence;...*Gen.* xxviii. 6.

And that Jacob obeyed his father and his mother,...7.

And Esau seeing that the daughters of Canaan pleased not Isaac his father;—8.

Then went Esau unto Ishmael, and took unto the wives which he had Mahalath the daughter of Ishmael Abraham's son,...to be his wife.—9.

We have a father, an old man, and a child of his old age, a little one; and his brother is dead, and he alone is left of his mother, and his father loveth him.—*Gen.* xliv. 20.

And thy servant my father said unto us, Ye know that my wife bare me two sons:—*Gen.* xliv. 27.

And the one went out from me, and I said, Surely he is torn in pieces; and I saw him not since:—28.

And if ye take this also from me, and mischief befall him, ye shall bring down my grey hairs with sorrow to the grave.—29.

Now therefore, I pray thee, let thy servant abide instead of the lad a bondman to my lord; and let the lad go up with his brethren.—33.

For how shall I go up to my father, and the lad be not with me? lest peradventure I see the evil that shall come on my father.—34.

And Joseph said unto his brethren, I am Joseph; doth my father yet live?—*Gen.* xlv. 3.

Haste ye, go up to my father, and say unto him, Thus saith thy son Joseph, God hath made me lord of all Egypt: come down unto me, tarry not.—9.

And ye shall tell my father of all my glory in Egypt, and of all that ye have seen; and ye shall haste and bring down my father hither.—13.

And when Jacob made an end of commanding his sons, he...yielded up the ghost, and was gathered unto his people.—*Gen.* xlix. 33.

And Joseph fell upon his father's face, and wept upon him, and kissed him.—*Gen.* l. 1.

And Joseph commanded his servants the physicians to embalm his father...2.

My father made me swear, saying, Lo, I die: in

my grave which I have digged for me in the land of Canaan, there shalt thou bury me. Now therefore let me go up, I pray thee, and bury my father, and I will come again.—*Gen.* l. 5.

And Joseph went up to bury his father...7.

Honour thy father and thy mother: that thy days may be long upon the land which the Lord thy God giveth thee.—*Ex.* xx. 12.

He that smiteth his father, or his mother, shall be surely put to death.—*Ex.* xxi. 15.

And he that curseth his father, or his mother, shall surely be put to death.—17.

Ye shall fear every man his mother, and his father, ...I am the Lord your God.—*Lev.* xix. 3.

Cursed be he that setteth light by his father or his mother. And all the people shall say, Amen.—*Deut.* xxvii. 16.

And Samson's wife wept before him, and said, Thou dost but hate me, and lovest me not: thou hast put forth a riddle unto the children of my people, and hast not told it me. And he said unto her, Behold, I have not told it my father nor my mother, and shall I tell it thee?—*Judg.* xiv. 16.

And David went...to Mizpeh of Moab: and he said unto the king of Moab, Let my father and my mother, I pray thee, come forth, and be with you, till I know what God will do for me.—1 *Sam.* xxii. 3.

And Solomon loved the Lord, walking in the statutes of David his father...1 *Kings* iii. 3.

My son, hear the instruction of thy father, and forsake not the law of thy mother :—*Prov.* i. 8.

For they shall be an ornament of grace unto thy head, and chains about thy neck.—9.

Hear, ye children, the instruction of a father, and attend to know understanding.—*Prov.* iv. 1.

My son, keep thy father's commandment, and forsake not the law of thy mother :—*Prov.* vi. 20.

Bind them continually upon thine heart, and tie them about thy neck.—21.

A wise son maketh a glad father: but a foolish son is the heaviness of his mother.—*Prov.* x. 1.

A wise son heareth his father's instruction... *Prov.* xiii. 1.

A fool despiseth his father's instruction : but he that regardeth reproof is prudent.—*Prov.* xv. 5.

A foolish man despiseth his mother.—20.

...The glory of children are their fathers.—*Prov.* xvii. 6.

A foolish son is a grief to his father, and bitterness to her that bare him.—25.

A foolish son is the calamity of his father... *Prov.* xix. 13.

He that wasteth his father, and chaseth away his mother, is a son that causeth shame, and bringeth reproach.—26.

Whoso curseth his father or his mother, his lamp shall be put out in obscure darkness.—*Prov.* xx. 20.

Hearken unto thy father that begat thee, and despise not thy mother when she is old.—*Prov.* xxiii. 22.

The father of the righteous shall greatly rejoice: and he that begetteth a wise child shall have joy of him.—*Prov.* xxiii. 24.

Thy father and thy mother shall be glad, and she that bare thee shall rejoice.—25.

Thine own friend, and thy father's friend, forsake not...*Prov.* xxvii. 10.

Whoso robbeth his father or his mother, and saith, It is no transgression; the same is the companion of a destroyer.—*Prov.* xxviii. 24.

Whoso loveth wisdom rejoiceth his father...*Prov.* xxix. 3.

...Her children arise up, and call her blessed.—*Prov.* xxxi. 28.

A son honoureth his father...*Mal.* i. 6.

Behold, I will send you Elijah the prophet before the coming of the great and dreadful day of the Lord:—*Mal.* iv. 5.

And he shall turn the heart of the fathers to the children, and the heart of the children to their fathers, lest I come and smite the earth with a curse.—6.

THE SACRED TIE OF MARRIAGE.

And the Lord God said, It is not good that the man should be alone; I will make him an help meet for him.—*Gen.* ii. 18.

And the rib, which the Lord God had taken from man, made he a woman, and brought her unto the man.—22.

And Adam said, This is now bone of my bones, and flesh of my flesh: she shall be called Woman, because she was taken out of Man.—23.

Therefore shall a man leave his father and his mother, and shall cleave unto his wife: and they shall be one flesh.—24.

And Abraham said of Sarah his wife, She is my sister: and Abimelech king of Gerar sent, and took Sarah.—*Gen.* xx. 2.

But God came to Abimelech in a dream by night, and said to him, Behold, thou art but a dead man, for the woman which thou hast taken; for she is a man's wife.—3.

...I know that thou didst this in the integrity of thy heart; for I also withheld thee from sinning against me.—6.

...The thing proceedeth from the Lord:...*Gen.* xxiv. 50.

Behold, Rebekah is before thee, take her, and go, and let her be thy master's son's wife, as the Lord hath spoken.—51.

And Isaac brought her into his mother Sarah's tent, and took Rebekah, and she became his wife; and he loved her: and Isaac was comforted after his mother's death.—67.

Thou shalt not covet thy neighbour's wife... *Ex.* xx. 17.

Neither shalt thou take a wife to her sister, to vex her, beside the other in her life time.—*Lev.* xviii. 18.

When a man hath taken a new wife, he shall not go out to war, neither shall he be charged with any business: but he shall be free at home one year, and shall cheer up his wife which he hath taken.—*Deut.* xxiv. 5.

Blessed is every one that feareth the Lord;—*Ps.* cxxviii. 1.

Thy wife shall be as a fruitful vine by the sides of thine house: thy children like olive plants round about thy table.—3.

...Rejoice with the wife of thy youth.—*Prov.* v. 18.

Let her be as the loving hind and pleasant roe...19.

A virtuous woman is a crown to her husband: but she that maketh ashamed is as rottenness to his bones.—*Prov.* xii. 4.

Whoso findeth a wife findeth a good thing, and obtaineth favour of the' Lord.—*Prov.* xviii. 22.

A prudent wife is from the Lord.—*Prov.* xix. 14.

Who can find a virtuous woman? for her price is far above rubies.—*Prov.* xxxi. 10.

The heart of her husband doth safely trust in her...11.

Live joyfully with the wife whom thou lovest all the days of the life of thy vanity.—*Eccl.* ix. 9.

Take heed to your spirit, and let none deal treacherously against the wife of his youth.—*Mal.* ii. 15.

A GOOD MAN.

---o---

Enoch walked with God...*Gen.* v. 24.

Noah was a just man and perfect in his generations, and Noah walked with God.—*Gen.* vi. 9.

Thus did Noah; according to all that God commanded him, so did he.—22.

And the Lord said unto Noah,...thee have I seen righteous before me in this generation.—*Gen.* vii. 1.

And Pharaoh said unto Joseph,...there is none so discreet and wise as thou art.—*Gen.* xli. 39.

Behold now, there is in this city a man of God, and he is an honourable man...1 *Sam.* ix. 6.

And David behaved himself wisely in all his ways; and the Lord was with him.—1 *Sam.* xviii. 14.

Then Achish called David, and said unto him, Surely, as the Lord liveth, thou hast been upright, and thy going out and thy coming in with me in the host is good in my sight: for I have not found evil in thee since the day of thy coming unto me unto this day...1 *Sam.* xxix. 6.

I know thou art good in my sight as an angel of God...9.

And he (Hezekiah) did that which was right in the sight of the Lord...2 *Kings* xviii. 3.

He trusted in the Lord God of Israel; so that after him was none like him among all the kings of Judah, nor any that were before him.—5.

For he clave to the Lord, and departed not from following him, but kept his commandments...6.

And Asa did that which was good and right in the eyes of the Lord his God.—2 *Ch.* xiv. 2.

And his (Jehoshaphat's) heart was lifted up in the ways of the Lord...2 *Ch.* xvii. 6.

He (Hanani) was a faithful man, and feared God above many.—*Neh.* vii. 2.

There was a man in the land of Uz, whose name was Job; and that man was perfect and upright, and one that feared God, and eschewed evil.—*Job* i. 1.

When the ear heard me, then it blessed me; and when the eye saw me, it gave witness to me:— *Job* xxix. 11.

Because I delivered the poor that cried, and the fatherless, and him that had none to help him.—12.

The blessing of him that was ready to perish came upon me: and I caused the widow's heart to sing for joy.—13.

I was eyes to the blind, and feet was I to the lame.—15.

I was a father to the poor: and the cause which I knew not I searched out.—16.

The steps of a good man are ordered by the Lord: and he delighteth in his way.—*Ps.* xxxvii. 23.

The law of his God is in his heart; none of his steps shall slide.—31.

Mark the perfect man, and behold the upright: for the end of that man is peace.—37.

A good man sheweth favour, and lendeth: he will guide his affairs with discretion.—*Ps.* cxii. 5.

He shall not be afraid of evil tidings: his heart is fixed, trusting in the Lord.—7.

He hath dispersed, he hath given to the poor; his righteousness endureth for ever; his horn shall be exalted with honour.—9.

A good man obtaineth favour of the Lord... *Prov.* xii. 2.

A good man leaveth an inheritance to his children's children...*Prov.* xiii. 22.

A good man shall be satisfied from himself.— *Prov.* xiv. 14.

When a man's ways please the Lord, he maketh even his enemies to be at peace with him.—*Prov.* xvi. 7.

He that walketh righteously, and speaketh uprightly; he that despiseth the gain of oppressions, that shaketh his hands from holding of bribes, that stoppeth his ears from hearing of blood, and shutteth his eyes from seeing evil;—*Isa.* xxxiii. 15.

He shall dwell on high...16.

Daniel was preferred above the presidents and princes, because an excellent spirit was in him;... *Dan.* vi. 3.

A GOOD MAN.

Then the presidents and princes sought to find occasion against Daniel concerning the kingdom; but they could find none occasion nor fault; forasmuch as he was faithful, neither was there any error or fault found in him.—*Dan.* vi. 4.

Then said these men, We shall not find any occasion against this Daniel, except we find it against him concerning the law of his God.—5.

Then these men...found Daniel praying and making supplication before his God.—11.

...No manner of hurt was found upon him, because he believed in his God.—23.

A GOOD WOMAN.

And he (Boaz) said, Who art thou? And she answered, I am Ruth thine handmaid:—*Ruth* iii. 9.

And he said, Blessed be thou of the Lord,...10.

...All the city of my people doth know that thou art a virtuous woman.—11.

A gracious woman retaineth honour.—*Prov.* xi. 16.

Every wise woman buildeth her house...*Prov.* xiv. 1.

Who can find a virtuous woman? for her price is far above rubies.—*Prov.* xxxi. 10.

The heart of her husband doth safely trust in her, so that he shall have no need of spoil.—11.

She will do him good and not evil all the days of her life.—12.

She seeketh wool, and flax, and worketh willingly with her hands.—13.

She is like the merchants' ships; she bringeth her food from afar.—14.

She riseth also while it is yet night, and giveth meat to her household, and a portion to her maidens.—15.

She considereth a field, and buyeth it: with the fruit of her hands she planteth a vineyard.—16.

She girdeth her loins with strength, and strengtheneth her arms.—17.

She perceiveth that her merchandise is good: her candle goeth not out by night.—*Prov.* xxxi. 18.

She layeth her hands to the spindle, and her hands hold the distaff.—19.

She stretcheth out her hand to the poor; yea, she reacheth forth her hands to the needy.—20.

She is not afraid of the snow for her household: for all her household are clothed with scarlet.—21.

She maketh herself coverings of tapestry;...22.

Her husband is known in the gates, when he sitteth among the elders of the land.—23.

She maketh fine linen, and selleth it;—24.

Strength and honour are her clothing; and she shall rejoice in time to come.—25.

She openeth her mouth with wisdom; and in her tongue is the law of kindness.—26.

She looketh well to the ways of her household, and eateth not the bread of idleness.—27.

Her children arise up, and call her blessed; her husband also, and he praiseth her.—28.

Many daughters have done virtuously, but thou excellest them all.—29.

Favour is deceitful, and beauty is vain: but a woman that feareth the Lord she shall be praised.—30.

Give her of the fruit of her hands; and let her own works praise her in the gates.—31.

TRAIN UP CHILDREN IN THE WAY OF GOD.

———o———

I know him, (Abraham) that he will command his children,...and they shall keep the way of the Lord, to do justice and judgment...*Gen.* xviii. 19.

Ye shall observe this thing for an ordinance to thee and to thy sons for ever.—*Ex.* xii. 24.

...When your children shall say unto you, What mean ye by this service?—26.

That ye shall say, it is the sacrifice of the Lord's passover, who passed over the houses of the children of Israel in Eygpt, when he smote the Egyptians, and delivered our houses.—27.

Seven days thou shalt eat unleavened bread, and in the seventh day shall be a feast to the Lord.—*Ex.* xiii. 6.

And thou shalt shew thy son in that day, saying, This is done because of that which the Lord did unto me when I came forth out of Egypt.—8.

Only take heed to thyself,...lest thou forget the things which thine eyes have seen, and lest they depart from thy heart all the days of thy life: but teach them thy sons, and thy sons' sons.—*Deut.* iv. 9.

Thou shalt love the Lord thy God with all thine heart, and with all thy soul, and with all thy might.—*Deut.* vi. 5.

And these words, which I command thee this day, shall be in thine heart:—6.

And thou shalt teach them diligently unto thy children...7.

Gather the people together, men, women, and children,...that they may hear, and that they may learn, and fear the Lord your God, and observe to do all the words of this law:—*Deut.* xxxi. 12.

And that their children, which have not known any thing, may hear, and learn to fear the Lord your God...13.

For this child I prayed;...1 *Sam.* i. 27.

Therefore also I have lent him to the Lord; as long as he liveth he shall be lent to the Lord.—28. ...And the child did minister unto the Lord before Eli the priest.—1 *Sam.* ii. 11.

Now the sons of Eli were sons of Belial; they knew not the Lord.—12.

...And the child Samuel grew before the Lord.—21.

And the Lord said to Samuel,...1 *Sam.* iii. 11.

...I have told him (Eli) that I will judge his house for ever for the iniquity which he knoweth; because his sons made themselves vile, and he restrained them not.—13.

Now the days of David drew nigh that he should die; and he charged Solomon his son, saying,—1 Kings ii. 1.

I go the way of all the earth: be thou strong therefore, and shew thyself a man;—2.

And keep the charge of the Lord thy God, to walk in his ways, to keep his statutes, and his commandments, and his judgments, and his testimonies, as it is written in the law of Moses, that thou mayest prosper in all that thou doest, and whithersoever thou turnest thyself:—3.

That the Lord may continue his word which he spake concerning me, saying, If thy children take heed to their way, to walk before me in truth with all their heart and with all their soul, there shall not fail thee (said he) a man on the throne of Israel.—4.

And thou, Solomon my son, know thou the God of thy father, and serve him with a perfect heart and with a willing mind: for the Lord searcheth all hearts, and understandeth all the imaginations of the thoughts: if thou seek him, he will be found of thee; but if thou forsake him, he will cast thee off for ever.—1 Ch. xxviii. 9.

In the eighth year of his (Josiah's) reign, while he was yet young, he began to seek after the God of David his father...2 Ch. xxxiv. 3.

I (Obadiah) thy servant fear the Lord from my youth.—1 Kings xviii. 12.

Come, ye children, hearken unto me: I will teach you the fear of the Lord.—*Ps.* xxxiv. 11.

Thou art my hope, O Lord God: thou art my trust from my youth.—*Ps.* lxxi. 5.

O God, thou hast taught me from my youth: and hitherto have I declared thy wondrous works.—17.

I will open my mouth in a parable:—*Ps.* lxxviii. 2.

Which we have heard and known, and our fathers have told us.—3.

We will not hide them from their children, shewing to the generation to come the praises of the Lord, and his strength, and his wonderful works that he hath done.—4.

For he established a testimony in Jacob, and appointed a law in Israel, which he commanded our fathers, that they should make them known to their children:—5.

That the generation to come might know them, even the children which should be born; who should arise and declare them to their children:—6.

That they might set their hope in God, and not forget the works of God, but keep his commandments.—7.

Both young men, and maidens;...and children:—*Ps.* cxlviii. 12.

Let them praise the name of the Lord.—13.

My son, forget not my law; but let thine heart keep my commandments.—*Prov.* iii. 1.

I was my father's son, tender and only beloved in the sight of my mother.—*Prov.* iv. 3.

He taught me also, and said unto me, Let thine heart retain my words: keep my commandments, and live.—4.

He that spareth his rod hateth his son: but he that loveth him chasteneth him betimes.—*Prov.* xiii. 24.

Chasten thy son while there is hope, and let not thy soul spare for his crying.—*Prov.* xix. 18.

Even a child is known by his doings, whether his work be pure, and whether it be right.—*Prov.* xx. 11.

Train up a child in the way he should go: and when he is old, he will not depart from it.—*Prov.* xxii. 6.

Foolishness is bound in the heart of a child; but the rod of correction shall drive it far from him.—15.

Withhold not correction from the child: for if thou beatest him with the rod, he shall not die.—*Prov.* xxiii. 13.

Thou shalt beat him with the rod, and shalt deliver his soul from hell.—14.

My son, if thine heart be wise, my heart shall rejoice,—15.

The father of the righteous shall greatly rejoice: and he that begetteth a wise child shall have joy of him.—24.

Thy father and thy mother shall be glad, and she that bare thee shall rejoice.—25.

The rod and reproof give wisdom: but a child left to himself bringeth his mother to shame.—*Prov.* xxix. 15.

Correct thy son, and he shall give thee rest; yea, he shall give delight unto thy soul.—*Prov.* xxix. 17.

Remember now thy Creator in the days of thy youth.—*Eccl.* xii. 1.

The living, the living, he shall praise thee, as I do this day: the father to the children shall make known thy truth.—*Isa.* xxxviii. 19.

And all thy children shall be taught of the Lord; and great shall be the peace of thy children.—*Isa.* liv. 13.

TRUE FRIENDSHIP AND CONSTANCY.

And Naomi said unto her two daughters in law, Go, return each to her mother's house: the Lord deal kindly with you, as ye have dealt with the dead, and with me.—*Ruth* i. 8.

...And Orpah kissed her mother in law; but Ruth clave unto her.—14.

And she said, Behold, thy sister in law is gone back unto her people, and unto her gods: return thou after thy sister in law.—15.

And Ruth said, Intreat me not to leave thee, or to return from following after thee: for whither thou goest, I will go; and where thou lodgest, I will lodge: thy people shall be my people, and thy God my God:—16.

Where thou diest, will I die, and there will I be buried: the Lord do so to me, and more also, if ought but death part thee and me.—17.

And Naomi said unto her daughter in law, Blessed be he of the Lord, who hath not left off his kindness to the living and to the dead.—*Ruth* ii. 20.

And it came to pass, when he (David) had made an end of speaking unto Saul, that the soul of Jonathan was knit with the soul of David, and Jonathan loved him as his own soul.—1 Sam. xviii. 1.

Then Jonathan and David made a covenant, because he loved him as his own soul.—3.

And Jonathan stripped himself of the robe that was upon him, and gave it to David, and his garments, even to his sword, and to his bow, and to his girdle.—4.

And David fled from Naioth in Ramah, and came and said before Jonathan, What have I done? what is mine iniquity? and what is my sin before thy father, that he seeketh my life?—1 Sam. xx. 1.

And he said unto him, God forbid; thou shalt not die: behold, my father will do nothing either great or small, but that he will shew it me: and why should my father hide this thing from me? it is not so.—2.

Then said Jonathan unto David, Whatsoever thy soul desireth, I will even do it for thee.—4.

And Jonathan said, Far be it from thee: for if I knew certainly that evil were determined by my father to come upon thee, then would I not tell it thee?—9.

So Jonathan made a covenant with the house of David...16.

And Jonathan caused David to swear again, because he loved him:...17.

Then Saul's anger was kindled against Jonathan, and he said,...do not I know that thou hast chosen the son of Jesse to thine own confusion?...30.

For as long as the son of Jesse liveth upon the

ground, thou shalt not be established, nor thy kingdom. Wherefore now send and fetch him unto me, for he shall surely die.—1 *Sam.* xx. 31.

So Jonathan arose from the table in fierce anger, and did eat no meat:...for he was grieved for David, because his father had done him shame.—34.

And it came to pass in the morning, that Jonathan went out into the field at the time appointed with David...35.

...David arose...and fell on his face to the ground, and bowed himself three times: and they kissed one another, and wept one with another, until David exceeded.—41.

And Jonathan said to David, Go in peace, forasmuch as we have sworn both of us in the name of the Lord, saying, The Lord be between me and thee, and between my seed and thy seed for ever.—42.

Saul and Jonathan were lovely and pleasant in their lives, and in their death they were not divided. ...2 *Sam.* i. 23.

How are the mighty fallen in the midst of the battle! O Jonathan, thou wast slain in thine high places.—25.

I am distressed for thee, my brother Jonathan: very pleasant hast thou been unto me: thy love to me was wonderful, passing the love of women.—26.

And David said, Is there yet any that is left of the house of Saul, that I may shew him kindness for Jonathan's sake?—2 *Sam.* ix. 1.

...And Ziba said unto the king, Jonathan has yet a son, which is lame on his feet.—3.

TRUE FRIENDSHIP and CONSTANCY.

Now when Mephibosheth, the son of Jonathan... was come unto David,...2 *Sam.* ix. 6.

David said unto him, Fear not: for I will surely shew thee kindness for Jonathan thy father's sake, and will restore thee all the land of Saul thy father; and thou shalt eat bread at my table continually.—7.

Then said David, I will shew kindness unto Hanun the son of Nahash, as his father shewed kindness unto me. And David sent to comfort him by the hand of his servants for his father...2 *Sam.* x. 2.

And it came to pass when Hushai the Archite, David's friend, was come unto Absalom, that Hushai said unto Absalom, God save the king, God save the king.—2 *Sam.* xvi. 16.

And Absalom said to Hushai, Is this thy kindness to thy friend? why wentest thou not with thy friend?—17.

And Hiram king of Tyre sent his servants unto Solomon; for he had heard that they had anointed him king in the room of his father: for Hiram was ever a lover of David.—1 *Kings* v. 1.

Now when Job's three friends heard of all this evil that was come upon him, they came every one from his own place;...for they had made an appointment together to come to mourn with him and to comfort him.—*Job* ii. 11.

And when they lifted up their eyes afar off, and knew him not, they lifted up their voice, and wept;...12.

So they sat down with him upon the ground seven days and seven nights, and none spake a word unto him: for they saw that his grief was very great.—13.

TRUE FRIENDSHIP and CONSTANCY.

To him that is afflicted pity should be shewed from his friend.—*Job* vi. 14.

And the Lord turned the captivity of Job, when he prayed for his friends....*Job* xlii. 10.

Then came there unto him all his brethren, and all his sisters, and all they that had been of his acquaintance before, and did eat bread with him in his house: and they bemoaned him, and comforted him over all the evil that the Lord had brought upon him: every man also gave him a piece of money, and every one an earring of gold.—11.

As for me, when they were sick, my clothing was sackcloth :...*Ps.* xxxv. 13.

I behaved myself as though he had been my friend or brother: I bowed down heavily, as one that mourneth for his mother.—14.

A friend loveth at all times, and a brother is born for adversity.—*Prov.* xvii. 17.

A man that hath friends must shew himself friendly: and there is a friend that sticketh closer than a brother.—*Prov.* xviii. 24.

Faithful are the wounds of a friend...*Prov.* xxvii. 6.

Ointment and perfume rejoice the heart: so doth the sweetness of a man's friend by hearty counsel.—9.

Thine own friend, and thy father's friend, forsake not;...for better is a neighbour that is near than a brother far off.—10.

As in water face answereth to face, so the heart of man to man.—19.

THE RELIGIOUS USE OF MUSIC, AND ITS INFLUENCE.

———o———

He (Jubal) was the father of all such as handle the harp and organ.—*Gen.* iv. 21.

Thus the Lord saved Israel that day...*Ex.* xiv. 30.

Then sang Moses and the children of Israel this song unto the Lord, and spake, saying, I will sing unto the Lord, for he hath triumphed gloriously. ...*Ex.* xv. 1.

And Miriam the prophetess, the sister of Aaron, took a timbrel in her hand; and all the women went out after her with timbrels and with dances.—20.

And Miriam answered them, Sing ye to the Lord, for he hath triumphed gloriously; the horse and his rider hath he thrown into the sea.—21.

...It is not the voice of them that shout for mastery, neither is it the voice of them that cry for being overcome: but the noise of them that sing do I hear.—*Ex.* xxxii. 18.

Then Israel sang this song, Spring up, O well; sing ye unto it :—*Num.* xxi. 17.

Then sang Deborah and Barak,...*Judg.* v. 1.

Praise ye the Lord for the avenging of Israel,...2.

I, even I, will sing unto the Lord; I will sing praise to the Lord God of Israel.—*Judg.* v. 3.

And Saul's servants said unto him, Behold now, an evil spirit from God troubleth thee.—1 *Sam.* xvi. 15.

Let our lord now command thy servants,...to seek out a man, who is a cunning player on a harp: and it shall come to pass, when the evil spirit from God is upon thee, that he shall play with his hand, and thou shalt be well.—16.

And Saul said,...Provide me now a man that can play well, and bring him to me.—17.

Then answered one of the servants, and said, Behold, I have seen a son of Jesse the Bethlehemite, that is cunning in playing,...and the Lord is with him.—18.

And it came to pass, when the evil spirit from God was upon Saul, that David took a harp, and played with his hand: so Saul was refreshed, and was well,...23.

And it came to pass as they came, when David was returned from the slaughter of the Philistine, that the women came out of all cities of Israel, singing and dancing, to meet King Saul, with tabrets, with joy, and with instruments of musick.— 1 *Sam.* xviii. 6.

And the women answered one another as they played, and said, Saul hath slain his thousands, and David his ten thousands.—7.

And David arose, and went with all the people that

were with him from Baale of Judah, to bring up from thence the ark of God,...2 *Sam.* vi. 2.

And David and all the house of Israel played before the Lord on all manner of instruments made of fir wood, even on harps, and on psalteries, and on timbrels, and on cornets, and on cymbals.—5.

So David and all the house of Israel brought up the ark of the Lord with shouting, and with the sound of the trumpet.—15.

...And four thousand praised the Lord with the instruments which I made, said David, to praise therewith.—1 *Ch.* xxiii. 5.

David and the captains of the host separated to the service of the sons of Asaph, and of Heman, and of Jeduthun, who should prophesy with harps, with psalteries, and with cymbals...1 *Ch.* xxv. 1.

...Who prophesied with a harp, to give thanks and to praise the Lord.—3.

Thus all the work that Solomon made for the house of the Lord was finished:...2 *Ch.* v. 1.

...And the Levites took up the the ark.—4.

And the priests brought in the ark of the covenant of the Lord unto his place, to the oracle of the house, into the most holy place, even under the wings of the cherubims:—7.

It came even to pass, as the trumpeters and singers were as one, to make one sound to be heard in praising and thanking the Lord; and when they lifted up their voice with the trumpets and cymbals and instruments of musick, and praised the Lord, saying, For he is good; for his mercy endureth for ever: that then the house was filled with a cloud, even the house of the Lord.—2 *Ch.* v. 13.

And the priests waited on their offices: the Levites also with instruments of musick of the Lord, which David the king had made to praise the Lord, because his mercy endureth for ever, when David praised by their ministry; and the priests sounded trumpets before them...2 *Ch.* vii. 6.

And when he (Jehoshaphat) had consulted with the people, he appointed singers unto the Lord, and that should praise the beauty of holiness, as they went out before the army, and to say, Praise the Lord ; for his mercy endureth for ever.—2 *Ch.* xx. 21.

And the Levites stood with the instruments of David, and the priests with the trumpets.—2 *Ch.* xxix. 26.

And all the congregation worshipped, and the singers sang, and the trumpeters sounded...28.

Moreover Hezekiah the king and the princes commanded the Levites to sing praise unto the Lord with the words of David,...and they sang praises with gladness...30.

And the children of Israel that were present at Jerusalem kept the feast of unleavened bread seven days with great gladness: and the Levites and the priests praised the Lord day by day, singing with loud instruments unto the Lord.—2 *Ch.* xxx. 21.

And when the builders laid the foundation of the temple of the Lord, they set the priests in their apparel with trumpets, and the Levites the sons of Asaph with cymbals, to praise the Lord, after the ordinance of David king of Israel.—*Ezra* iii. 10.

And they sang together by course in praising and giving thanks unto the Lord.—11.

For in the days of David and Asaph of old there were chief of the singers, and songs of praise and thanksgiving unto God.—*Neh.* xii. 46.

I will sing unto the Lord, because he hath dealt bountifully with me.—*Ps.* xiii. 6.

...With my song will I praise him.—*Ps.* xxviii. 7.

Sing unto the Lord, O ye saints of his...*Ps.* xxx. 4.

Praise the Lord with harp: sing unto him with the psaltery and an instrument of ten strings.—*Ps.* xxxiii. 2.

Sing unto him a new song; play skilfully with a loud noise.—3.

...In the night his song shall be with me, and my prayer unto the God of my life.—*Ps.* xlii. 8.

...Upon the harp will I praise thee, O God my God.—*Ps.* xliii. 4.

I will sing of thy power; yea, I will sing aloud of thy mercy in the morning...*Ps.* lix. 16.

Sing forth the honour of his name.—*Ps.* lxvi. 2.

All the earth shall worship thee, and shall sing unto thee; they shall sing to thy name.—4.

I will praise thee with the psaltery, even thy truth,

O my God: unto thee will I sing with the harp, O thou Holy One of Israel.—*Ps.* lxxi. 22.

Take a psalm, and bring hither the timbrel, the pleasant harp with the psaltery.—*Ps.* lxxxi. 2.

Blow up the trumpet in the new moon, in the time appointed, on our solemn feast day.—3.

As well the singers as the players on instruments shall be there (Zion.)—*Ps.* lxxxvii. 7.

I will sing of the mercies of the Lord for ever.—*Ps.* lxxxix. 1.

It is a good thing to give thanks unto the Lord, and to sing praises unto thy name, O most High:—*Ps.* xcii. 1.

To shew forth thy lovingkindness in the morning, and thy faithfulness every night,—2.

Upon an instrument of ten strings, and upon the psaltery; upon the harp with a solemn sound.—3.

Sing unto the Lord with the harp; with the harp, and the voice of a psalm.—*Ps.* xcviii. 5.

With trumpets and sound of cornet make a joyful noise before the Lord, the King.—6.

I will sing unto the Lord as long as I live: I will sing praise to my God while I have my being.—*Ps.* civ. 33.

Awake, psaltery and harp: I myself will awake early.—*Ps.* cviii. 2.

By the rivers of Babylon, there we sat down, yea, we wept, when we remembered Zion.—*Ps.* cxxxvii. 1.

We hanged our harps upon the willows in the midst thereof.—2.

For there they that carried us away captive required of us a song...saying, Sing us one of the songs of Zion.—*Ps.* cxxxvii. 3.

How shall we sing the Lord's song in a strange land?—4.

Praise him with the sound of the trumpet: praise him with the psaltery and harp.—*Ps.* cl. 3.

Praise him with the timbrel and dance: praise him with stringed instruments and organs.—4.

Praise him upon the loud cymbals: praise him upon the high sounding cymbals.—5.

Ye shall have a song, as in the night when a holy solemnity is kept; and gladness of heart, as when one goeth with a pipe to come into the mountain of the Lord.—*Isa.* xxx. 29.

The Lord was ready to save me: therefore we will sing my songs to the stringed instruments all the days of our life in the house of the Lord.—*Isa.* xxxviii. 20.

THE FRAILTY OF LIFE.
PREPARATION FOR DEATH.

—o—

I know not the day of my death.—*Gen.* xxvii. 2.

O that they were wise, that they understood this, that they would consider their latter end!—*Deut.* xxxii. 29.

For we are strangers before thee, and sojourners, as were all our fathers: our days on the earth are as a shadow, and there is none abiding.—1 *Ch.* xxix. 15.

Is there not an appointed time to man upon earth? are not his days also like the days of an hireling?—*Job* vii. 1.

O remember that my life is wind...7.

For we are but of yesterday, and know nothing, because our days upon earth are a shadow:—*Job* viii. 9.

Are not my days few? cease then, and let me alone, that I may take comfort a little,—*Job* x. 20.

Before I go whence I shall not return...21.

Man that is born of a woman is of few days, and full of trouble.—*Job* xiv. 1.

He cometh forth as a flower, and is cut down: he fleeth also as a shadow, and continueth not.—2.

THE FRAILTY OF LIFE.

Seeing his days are determined, the number of his months are with thee, thou hast appointed his bounds that he cannot pass.—*Job* xiv. 5.

When a few years are come, then I shall go the way whence I shall not return.—*Job* xvi. 22.

One dieth in his full strength, being wholly at ease and quiet.—*Job* xxi. 23.

He draweth also the mighty with his power: he riseth up, and no man is sure of life.—*Job* xxiv. 22.

If he (God) set his heart upon man, if he gather unto himself his spirit and his breath;—*Job* xxxiv. 14.

All flesh shall perish together, and man shall turn again unto dust.—15.

In a moment shall they die, and the people shall be troubled at midnight, and pass away: and the mighty shall be taken away without hand.—20.

Lord, make me to know mine end, and the measure of my days, what it is; that I may know how frail I am.—*Ps.* xxxix. 4.

Behold, thou hast made my days as an handbreadth; and mine age is as nothing before thee: verily every man at his best state is altogether vanity.—5.

Surely every man walketh in a vain show: surely they are disquieted in vain: he heapeth up riches, and knoweth not who shall gather them.—6.

When thou with rebukes dost correct man for iniquity, thou makest his beauty to consume away like a moth: surely every man is vanity.—11.

O spare me, that I may recover strength, before I go hence, and be no more.—*Ps.* xxxix. 13.

Remember how short my time is...*Ps.* lxxxix. 47.

What man is he that liveth, and shall not see death?...48.

...We spend our years as a tale that is told.—*Ps.* xc. 9.

The days of our years are threescore years and ten; and if by reason of strength they be fourscore years, yet is their strength labour and sorrow; for it is soon cut off, and we fly away.—10.

So teach us to number our days, that we may apply our hearts unto wisdom.—12.

My days are like a shadow that declineth;... *Ps.* cii. 11.

The Lord pitieth them that fear him.—*Ps.* ciii. 13.

For he knoweth our frame; he remembereth that we are dust.—14.

As for man, his days are as grass: as a flower of the field, so he flourisheth.—15.

Thou takest away their breath, they die, and return to their dust.--*Ps.* civ. 29.

Lord, what is man, that thou takest knowledge of him! or the son of man, that thou makest account of him!—*Ps.* cxliv. 3.

Man is like to vanity: his days are as a shadow that passeth away.—4.

His breath goeth forth, he returneth to his earth... *Ps.* cxlvi. 4.

Boast not thyself of to morrow; for thou knowest not what a day may bring forth.—*Prov.* xxvii. 1.

For the living know that they shall die...*Eccl.* ix. 5. ...Man also knoweth not his time...12.

Set thine house in order: for thou shalt die, and not live...*Isa.* xxxviii. 1.

...All flesh is grass, and all the goodliness thereof is as the flower of the field:—*Isa.* xl. 6.

The grass withereth, the flower fadeth: because the spirit of the Lord bloweth upon it: surely the people is grass.—7.

...And we all do fade as a leaf...*Isa.* lxiv. 6.

Prepare to meet thy God...*Amos* iv. 12.

COMFORT AND SUPPORT IN THE HOUR OF DEATH.

———o———

Let me die the death of the righteous, and let my last end be like his!—*Num.* xxiii. 10.

If thou prepare thine heart, and stretch out thine hands toward him;—*Job* xi. 13.

If iniquity be in thine hand, put it far away,...14.

For then shalt thou lift up thy face without spot; yea, thou shalt be stedfast, and shalt not fear:—15.

Because thou shalt forget thy misery, and remember it as waters that pass away:—16.

And thine age shall be clearer than the noon day; thou shalt shine forth, thou shalt be as the morning.—17.

And thou shalt be secure, because there is hope; ...and thou shalt take thy rest in safety.—18.

Also thou shalt lie down, and none shall make thee afraid.—19.

Salvation belongeth unto the Lord...*Ps.* iii. 8.

He restoreth my soul:...*Ps.* xxiii. 3.

Yea, though I walk through the valley of the shadow of death, I will fear no evil: for thou art with me; thy rod and thy staff they comfort me.—4.

...And I will dwell in the house of the Lord for ever.—6.

O keep my soul, and deliver me...*Ps.* xxv. 20.

Into thine hand I commit my spirit: thou hast redeemed me, O Lord God of truth.—*Ps*. xxxi. 5.

For with thee is the fountain of life: in thy light shall we see light.—*Ps*. xxxvi. 9.

The Lord knoweth the days of the upright: and their inheritance shall be for ever.—*Ps*. xxxvii. 18.

Wait on the Lord, and he shall exalt thee to inherit the land.—34.

For this God is our God for ever and ever: he will be our guide even unto death.—*Ps*. xlviii. 14.

Restore unto me the joy of thy salvation; and uphold me with thy free spirit.—*Ps*. li. 12.

For thou hast delivered my soul from death: wilt not thou deliver my feet from falling, that I may walk before God in the light of the living?—*Ps*. lvi. 13.

My soul, wait thou only upon God; for my expectation is from him.—*Ps*. lxii. 5.

He that is our God is the God of our salvation; and unto God the Lord belong the issues from death.—*Ps*. lxviii. 20.

The sorrows of death compassed me,...*Ps*. cxvi. 3.

Then called I upon the name of the Lord; O Lord, I beseech thee deliver my soul.—4.

...I was brought low, and he helped me.—6.

Return unto thy rest, O my soul; for the Lord hath dealt bountifully with thee.—7.

For thou hast delivered my soul from death, mine eyes from tears, and my feet from falling.—8.

Precious in the sight of the Lord is the death of his saints.—15.

Open to me the gates of righteousness: I will go into them, and I will praise the Lord:—*Ps.* cxviii. 19.

This gate of the Lord, into which the righteous shall enter.—20.

The Lord is thy keeper :...*Ps.* cxxi. 5.

...He shall preserve thy soul.—7.

The Lord shall preserve thy going out and thy coming in from this time forth, and even for evermore.—8.

Bring my soul out of prison, that I may praise thy name...*Ps.* cxlii. 7.

He keepeth the paths of judgment, and preserveth the way of his saints.—*Prov.* ii. 8.

The fear of the Lord is a fountain of life, to depart from the snares of death.—*Prov.* xiv. 27.

The righteous hath hope in his death.—32.

For surely there is an end; and thine expectation shall not be cut off.—*Prov.* xxiii. 18.

The righteous perisheth, and no man layeth it to heart: and merciful men are taken away, none considering that the righteous is taken away from the evil to come.—*Isa.* lvii. 1.

He shall enter into peace : they shall rest in their beds, each one walking in his uprightness.—2.

...The king of Israel, even the Lord is in the midst of thee : thou shalt not see evil any more.—*Zeph.* iii. 15.

The Lord thy God in the midst of thee is mighty; he will save, he will rejoice over thee with joy; he will rest in his love, he will joy over thee with singing.—17.

LIFE AFTER DEATH.
FUTURE HAPPINESS.

——o——

Enoch walked with God: and he was not; for God took him.—*Gen.* v. 24.

Thou shalt go to thy fathers in peace.—*Gen.* xv. 15.

I have waited for thy salvation, O Lord.—*Gen.* xlix. 18.

See, I have set before thee this day life and good, and death and evil;—*Deut.* xxx. 15.

I have set before you life and death;...therefore choose life, that both thou and thy seed may live.—19.

See now that I, even I, am he, and there is no god with me: I kill, and I make alive.—*Deut.* xxxii. 39.

I rejoice in thy salvation.—1 *Sam.* ii. 1.

The Lord killeth, and maketh alive: he bringeth down to the grave, and bringeth up.—6.

He raiseth up the poor out of the dust,...to set them among princes, and to make them inherit the throne of glory.—8.

And he (David) said, While the child was yet alive, I fasted and wept: for I said, Who can tell whether God will be gracious to me, that the child may live?—2 *Sam.* xii. 22.

But now he is dead, wherefore should I fast? can I bring him back again? I shall go to him, but he shall not return to me.—2 *Sam.* xii. 23.

For I know that my redeemer liveth, and that he shall stand at the latter day upon the earth:—*Job* xix. 25.

...In my flesh shall I see God:—26.

Whom I shall see for myself, and mine eyes shall behold, and not another; though my reins be consumed within me.—27.

I have set the Lord always before me: because he is at my right hand, I shall not be moved.—*Ps.* xvi. 8.

Therefore my heart is glad, and my glory rejoiceth: my flesh also shall rest in hope.—9.

For thou wilt not leave my soul in hell; neither wilt thou suffer thine Holy One to see corruption.—10.

Thou wilt shew me the path of life: in thy presence is fulness of joy; at thy right hand there are pleasures for evermore.—11.

As for me, I will behold thy face in righteousness: I shall be satisfied, when I awake, with thy likeness.—*Ps.* xvii. 15.

He (the king) asked life of thee, and thou gavest him, even length of days for ever and ever.—*Ps.* xxi. 4.

His glory is great in thy salvation...5.

For thou hast made him most blessed for ever.—6.

He (the Lord) restoreth my soul...*Ps.* xxiii. 3.

Who shall ascend into the hill of the Lord, or who shall stand in his holy place?—*Ps.* xxiv. 3.

He that hath clean hands, and a pure heart,...4.

He shall receive the blessing from the Lord, and righteousness from the God of his salvation.—5.

O how great is thy goodness, which thou hast laid up for them that fear thee; which thou hast wrought for them that trust in thee before the sons of men!—*Ps.* xxxi 19.

For with thee is the fountain of life: in thy light shall we see light.—*Ps.* xxxvi. 9.

The Lord loveth judgment, and forsaketh not his saints; they are preserved for ever.—*Ps.* xxxvii. 28.

The righteous shall inherit the land, and dwell therein for ever.—29.

Mark the perfect man, and behold the upright: for the end of that man is peace.—37.

For the redemption of their soul is precious... *Ps.* xlix. 8.

That he should still live for ever, and not see corruption.—9.

But God will redeem my soul from the power of the grave: for he shall receive me.—15.

For thou hast delivered my soul from death: wilt not thou deliver my feet from falling, that I may walk before God in the light of the living?—*Ps.* lvi. 13.

My lips shall greatly rejoice when I sing unto thee; and my soul, which thou hast redeemed.—*Ps.* lxxi. 23.

Thou shalt guide me with thy counsel, and afterwards receive me to glory.—*Ps.* lxxiii. 24.

Surely his salvation is nigh them that fear him... *Ps.* lxxxv. 9.

There (the mountains of Zion) the Lord commanded the blessing, even life for evermore.—Ps. cxxxiii. 3.

...Lead me in the way everlasting.—Ps. cxxxix. 24.

The upright shall dwell in thy presence.—Ps. cxl. 13.

The wise shall inherit glory...Prov. iii. 35.

The path of the just is as the shining light, that shineth more and more unto the perfect day.—Prov. iv. 18.

The labour of the righteous tendeth to life.—Prov. x. 16.

In the way of righteousness is life; and in the pathway thereof there is no death.—Prov. xii. 28.

The way of life is above to the wise, that he may depart from hell beneath.—Prov. xv. 24.

Let not thine heart envy sinners: but be thou in the fear of the Lord all the day long.—Prov. xxiii. 17.

For surely there is an end; and thine expectation shall not be cut off.—18.

Who knoweth the spirit of man that goeth upward?... Eccl. iii. 21.

Then shall the dust return to the earth as it was: and the spirit shall return unto God who gave it.—Eccl. xii. 7.

Therefore with joy shall ye draw water out of the wells of salvation.—Isa. xii. 3.

He will swallow up death in victory; and the Lord God will wipe away tears from off all faces; and the rebuke of his people shall he take away from off all the earth: for the Lord hath spoken it.—Isa. xxv. 8.

And it shall be said in that day, Lo, this is our God; we have waited for him, and he will save us: this is the Lord; we have waited for him, we will be glad and rejoice in his salvation.—*Isa.* xxv. 9.

Thy dead men shall live, together with my dead body shall they arise. Awake and sing, ye that dwell in dust: for thy dew is as the dew of herbs, and the earth shall cast out the dead.—*Isa.* xxvi. 19.

And the work of righteousness shall be peace; and the effect of righteousness quietness and assurance for ever.—*Isa.* xxxii. 17.

And the ransomed of the Lord shall return, and come to Zion with songs and everlasting joy upon their heads: they shall obtain joy and gladness, and sorrow and sighing shall flee away.—*Isa.* xxxv. 10.

Israel shall be saved in the Lord with an everlasting salvation: ye shall not be ashamed nor confounded world without end.—*Isa.* xlv. 17.

Look unto me, and be ye saved, all the ends of the earth: for I am God, and there is none else.—22.

My righteousness is near; my salvation is gone forth, and mine arms shall judge the people,...*Isa.* li. 5.

Lift up your eyes to the heavens, and look upon the earth beneath: for the heavens shall vanish away like smoke, and the earth shall wax old like a garment...but my salvation shall be for ever, and my righteousness shall not be abolished.—6.

...With everlasting kindness will I have mercy on thee, saith the Lord thy Redeemer.—*Isa.* liv. 8.

Ho, every one that thirsteth, come ye to the waters,...*Isa.* lv. 1.

Incline your ear, and come unto me: hear, and your soul shall live...3.

...The Lord shall be unto thee an everlasting light, and thy God thy glory.—*Isa.* lx. 19.

Thy sun shall no more go down; neither shall thy moon withdraw itself: for the Lord shall be thine everlasting light, and the days of thy mourning shall be ended.—20.

Thy people also shall be all righteous: they shall inherit the land for ever...21.

For since the beginning of the world men have not heard, nor perceived by the ear, neither hath the eye seen, O God, beside thee, what he hath prepared for him that waiteth for him.—*Isa.* lxiv. 4.

And many of them that sleep in the dust of the earth shall awake, some to everlasting life, and some to shame and everlasting contempt.—*Dan.* xii. 2.

And they that be wise shall shine as the brightness of the firmament; and they that turn many to righteousness as the stars for ever and ever.—3.

Blessed is he that waiteth...12.

But go thou thy way till the end be: for thou shalt rest, and stand in thy lot at the end of the days.—13.

I will ransom them from the power of the grave; I will redeem them from death: O death, I will be thy plagues; O grave, I will be thy destruction.—*Hosea* xiii. 14.

Then they that feared the Lord spake often one to another: and the Lord hearkened, and heard it, and a book of remembrance was written before him for them that feared the Lord, and that thought upon his name.—*Mal.* iii. 16.

And they shall be mine, saith the Lord of hosts, in that day when I make up my jewels; and I will spare them, as a man spareth his own son that serveth him.—17.

Unto you that fear my name shall the Sun of righteousness arise with healing in his wings.— *Mal.* iv. 2.

CONCLUSION.

GOD WILL FULFIL HIS PROMISES.

———o———

And God said, This is the token of the covenant which I make between me and you and every living creature that is with you, for perpetual generations: —*Gen.* ix. 12.

I do set my bow in the cloud, and it shall be for a token of a covenant between me and the earth.—13.

And it shall come to pass, when I bring a cloud over the earth, that the bow shall be seen in the cloud:—14.

And I will remember my covenant, which is between me and you and every living creature of all flesh; and the waters shall no more become a flood to destroy all flesh.—15.

God is not a man, that he should lie; neither the son of man, that he should repent: hath he said, and shall he not do it? or hath he spoken, and shall he not make it good?—*Num.* xxiii. 19.

Know therefore that the Lord thy God, he is God, the faithful God, which keepeth covenant and mercy with them that love him and keep his commandments to a thousand generations.—*Deut.* vii. 9.

The Lord thy God blesseth thee, as he promised thee.—*Deut.* xv. 6.

Ye know in all your hearts and in all your souls, that not one thing hath failed of all the good things which the Lord your God spake concerning you; all are come to pass unto you, and not one thing hath failed thereof.—*Josh.* xxiii. 14.

The Lord hath performed his word that he spake.— 1 *Kings* viii. 20.

And he (Solomon) said, Lord God of Israel, there is no God like thee, in heaven above, or on earth beneath, who keepest covenant and mercy with thy servants that walk before thee with all their heart:—23.

Thou spakest also with thy mouth, and hast fulfilled it with thine hand.—24.

Know now that there shall fall unto the earth nothing of the word of the Lord, which the Lord spake...2 *Kings* x. 10.

The Lord hath performed his word that he hath spoken.—2 *Ch.* vi. 10.

For he spake, and it was done; he commanded, and it stood fast.—*Ps.* xxxiii. 9.

The counsel of the Lord standeth for ever.—11.

My mercy will I keep for him (David) for evermore, and my covenant shall stand fast with him.— *Ps.* lxxxix. 28.

414 GOD WILL FULFIL HIS PROMISES.

My covenant will I not break, nor alter the thing that is gone out of my lips.—*Ps.* lxxxix. 34.

Once have I sworn by my holiness, that I will not lie unto David.—35.

His seed shall endure for ever, and his throne as the sun before me.—36.

It shall be established for ever as the moon, and as a faithful witness in heaven.—37.

He hath remembered his covenant for ever, the word which he commanded to a thousand generations.—*Ps.* cv. 8.

He remembered his holy promise.—42.

For ever, O Lord, thy word is settled in heaven.—*Ps.* cxix. 89.

Thy word is true from the beginning: and every one of thy righteous judgments endureth for ever.—160.

Happy is he whose hope is in the Lord his God:—*Ps.* cxlvi. 5.

Which keepeth truth for ever.—6.

The Lord of hosts hath sworn, saying, Surely as I have thought, so shall it come to pass; and as I have purposed, so shall it stand.—*Isa.* xiv. 24.

The grass withereth, the flower fadeth: but the word of our God shall stand for ever.—*Isa.* xl. 8.

I have sworn by myself, the word is gone out of my mouth in righteousness, and shall not return, That unto me every knee shall bow, every tongue shall swear.—*Isa.* xlv. 23.

...I have spoken it, I will also bring it to pass; I have purposed it, I will also do it.—*Isa.* xlvi. 11.

For as the rain cometh down, and the snow from heaven, and returneth not thither, but watereth the earth, and maketh it bring forth and bud, that it may give seed to the sower, and bread to the eater:— *Isa.* lv. 10.

So shall my word be that goeth forth out of my mouth: it shall not return unto me void, but it shall accomplish that which I please, and it shall prosper in the thing whereto I sent it.—11.

And now therefore thus saith the Lord, the God of Israel,...*Jer.* xxxii. 36.

They shall be my people, and I will be their God:—38.

And I will make an everlasting covenant with them, that I will not turn away from them, to do them good...40.

Behold, the days come, saith the Lord, that I will perform that good thing which I have promised unto the house of Israel...*Jer.* xxxiii. 14.

Thus saith the Lord; If my covenant be not with day and night, and if I have not appointed the ordinances of heaven and earth;—25.

Then will I cast away the seed of Jacob, and David my servant...26.

I am the Lord: I will speak, and the word that I shall speak shall come to pass;...in your days,...will

I say the word, and will perform it, saith the Lord God.—*Ezek.* xii. 25.

I the Lord have spoken it: it shall come to pass, and I will do it;—*Ezek.* xxiv. 14.

They shall sit every man under his vine and under his fig tree; and none shall make them afraid: for the mouth of the Lord of hosts hath spoken it.— *Micah* iv. 4.

I AM THE LORD, I CHANGE NOT.—*Mal.* iii. 6.

THE END.